LIVE DIGITAL THEATRE

T0383388

Live Digital Theatre explores the experiences of Interdisciplinary Performing Arts practitioners working on digital performance and in particular live digital theatre.

Collaborating with world-leading practitioners – Kolectiv Theatre (UK), Teatro Os Satyros (Brazil), and The Red Curtain International (India) – this study investigates the ways to bring live digital performance into theatre training and performance making. The idea of Interdisciplinary Performative Pedagogies is placed within the context of the exploration of live digital theatre and is used to understand creative practices and how one can learn from these practices. The book presents a pedagogical approach to contemporary practices in digital performance; from interdisciplinary live performance using digital technology, to live Zoom theatre, YouTube, mixed media recorded and live performance. The book also combines a series of case studies and pedagogical practices on live digital performance and intermedial theatre.

This book will be of great interest to students and scholars in performing arts, digital arts, media, and gaming.

Aleksandar Sasha Dundjerović is a Full Professor of Performing Arts, a theatre director, an author, and an Associate Director of Research at the Royal Birmingham Conservatoire.

ROUTLEDGE ADVANCES IN THEATRE & PERFORMANCE STUDIES

This series is our home for cutting-edge, upper-level scholarly studies and edited collections. Considering theatre and performance alongside topics such as religion, politics, gender, race, ecology, and the avant-garde, titles are characterized by dynamic interventions into established subjects and innovative studies on emerging topics.

For more information about this series, please visit: https://www.routledge.com/ Routledge-Advances-in-Theatre–Performance-Studies/book-series/RATPS

LIVE DIGITAL THEATRE

Interdisciplinary Performative
Pedagogies

Aleksandar Sasha Dundjerović

Routledge
Taylor & Francis Group

LONDON AND NEW YORK

Cover image: Macbeth Projeto Cycle #6. Macbeth Live Digital Theatre.
Collaboration with Os Satyros. Directed by Aleksandar Dundjerović

First published 2023
by Routledge
4 Park Square, Milton Park, Abingdon, Oxon OX14 4RN

and by Routledge
605 Third Avenue, New York, NY 10158

Routledge is an imprint of the Taylor & Francis Group, an informa business

© 2023 Aleksandar Sasha Dundjerović

British Library Cataloguing-in-Publication Data
A catalogue record for this book is available from the British Library

Library of Congress Cataloging-in-Publication Data
Names: Dundjerović, Aleksandar Sasha, author.
Title: Live digital theatre : interdisciplinary performative pedagogies /
Aleksandar Sasha Dundjerović.
Description: Abingdon, Oxon ; New York : Routledge, 2023. |
Series: Routledge advances in theatre and performance studies | Includes
bibliographical references and index. |
Identifiers: LCCN 2022054626 (print) | LCCN 2022054627 (ebook) |
ISBN 9781032231334 (hardback) | ISBN 9781032231310 (paperback) |
ISBN 9781003275893 (ebook)
Subjects: LCSH: Theater--Production and direction. | Theater--Technological
innovations. | Performing arts--Technological innovations. | Digital media. |
Technology and the arts.
Classification: LCC PN2053 .D865 2023 (print) | LCC PN2053 (ebook) |
DDC 792.02/33--dc23/eng/20230119
LC record available at https://lccn.loc.gov/2022054626
LC ebook record available at https://lccn.loc.gov/2022054627

ISBN: 978-1-032-23133-4 (hbk)
ISBN: 978-1-032-23131-0 (pbk)
ISBN: 978-1-003-27589-3 (ebk)

DOI: 10.4324/9781003275893

Typeset in Bembo
by Taylor & Francis Books

For Maria and Mateo

CONTENTS

FIGURES

ACKNOWLEDGEMENTS

I want to thank the collaborators and colleagues who supported and contributed to the development, discussions and performance practices that made this material in creative performance practice and pedagogy possible. They accompanied me on this journey and provided insight represented in this book. Many theatre friends influenced my creative practice and teaching. I am incredibly thankful to Paddy Cronin, Maureen Brayan, Stephen Simms, Dan Horrigan Rodolpho Vasquez, Sumit La Roi, Maria Sanchez, Gwydion Colder, Rajinder Dudrah, Maja Vukušić Zorica, Svetlana Volic, and Ilva Bateman Navarro. My gratitude goes to all the students with whom I created theatre in the universities in Canada, the UK, Ireland, Brazil, Serbia and Russia. The students I taught over the years I equally learned from and so much of that exchange is part of this book.

I want to express my gratitude to the people who made this book possible, the wonderfully supportive and helpful team at Theatre and Performance, Routledge and my editors Laura Hussey and Swatti Hindwan; Research Directorate at Royal Birmingham Conservatoire and the Faculty of Arts, Design and Media, Associate Dean Tim Wall and Jamie Savon for providing support, funding and time for me to endeavour on this research project; research assistant Michael Fletcher for unique insights on the development of the manuscript, and Paul Sadot for his inspiration and discussion on live digital theatre. Special recognition goes to Maria J.M. Sanchez for her insightful comments and critical observations.

I thank my colleagues at the Centre for Interdisciplinary Performative Arts, Birmingham City University, and the working group Interdisciplinary Performative Pedagogies at the International Federation of Theatre Research (IFTR), who offered me invaluable support and influenced my thinking about digital theatre and interdisciplinary pedagogies. For visual sources provided I want to thank the

Canadian Centre for Architecture, Montreal and the University of Pennsylvania Stuart Weitzman School of Design, Architectural Archives, Philadelphia.

Finally, thank you to all production theatre venues that participated in developing live digital theatre inquiry. This book reflects on a process of co-creation in which everyone involved helped in their own way to shape the material presented for which I am very thankful.

INTRODUCTION

This book has its precedent in my exploratory creative practice and pedagogy over the last 20 years based on directing and devising multimedia performances and my study of interdisciplinary approaches in performing arts. My analysis of theatre and film practice of multidisciplinary visionary artist Robert Lepage and subsequently work on books on Brazilian Collaborative Theatre and Brazilian Performing Arts, founded on my Leverhulme Research Fellowship, provided years of investigation of the topic of the interdisciplinary creative process, both as a way of making aand also as teaching performance practice. The material in this book is approached from a performative media point of view as the investigation of the work of practitioners in theatre and performance art that included multimedia in their aesthetics and methodology. Since ancient times, the theatre has interconnected various artistic forms, always combining media arts – text, dance or physical expression of the body, music, space design and architectural structures, props and objects, costumes, and lights. With the development of digital computer technology, the creative process in theatre was connected to a plurality of media and arts that became technologically compatible and can now communicate with each other, making them even easier to be introduced within the medium of theatre. Digital and performance worlds are not adverse but very much two different realities that the audience embraces. Digital media makes content and delivery accessible to audiences creating new experiences and expectations. Through engagement with social networking and various digital platforms, the audience integrates digital media within communication processes. In exploring and adjusting performative pedagogies with theatre students, the changing nature of live arts within a contemporary creative cultural industry context had to be considered, particularly after the shock of lockdown due to the Covid-19 pandemic that banned physical interaction in the social space.

This book presents not only theoretical approaches to research about live digital theatre, as presented in part one, but also several pieces of practice that I have developed with students and professional actors over the last 10 years which relate to each chapter in part two of the book. The chapters focus on the mix of theory and performance practice by focusing on the author's training and teaching in various educational and cultural and national contexts (Canada, UK, Brazil, Colombia, Iran, Russia, Serbia and Romania), which he developed together with a group of co-creators and collaborators since 2000. The material's visual nature supports discussion in the chapters and through illustrations as examples of the type of live digital theatre explorations. The primary objectives of the book are the identification and representation of interdisciplinary performance practices and pedagogies within the live digital theatre through the investigation of modes of theoretical analysis and examples of practice. The outcome is a set of observations, analysis of systems and examples of exercises for creative practice and pedagogy of live digital theatre.

The essence of any theatre system is a performer, space and audience. As famously proclaimed by Peter Brook in a book published in 1968, *The Empty Space*, what is necessary for any theatre to take place is an empty space, "a man walks across this empty space whilst someone else is watching him, and this is all that is needed for an act of theatre to be engaged."[1] There is no theatre tradition as we know it without a performer to communicate to live spectators. In dramaturgy, the composition of text in theatre representation has its textual structures; literary storytelling has its structure so does live digital media performance, whose text consists of a combination of different arts and media. The relationship of traditional theatre elements (body, space and audience) needs to be recontextualised through new thinking on media and digital online performance as it takes place on the screen, taking into consideration computer technology that has significant influence on global culture, digital media and cinema.

Steve Dixon's *Digital Performance* (2007), Matthew Causey's *Theatre and Performance in Digital Culture* (2006), Gabriella Giannachi and Nick Kaye's *Performing Presence* (2011), Bill Black's *Theatre & The Digital* (2014) along with more recent work by Nadja Masura in *Digital Theatre* (2020) and the ongoing work of the IFTR working group Intermediality in Theatre & Performance (initially published in an edited collection of essays by Sarah Bay-Cheng et al. in *Mapping Intermediality in Performance*), are all important starting points as theoretical and practical background for this study of interdisciplinary performative pedagogies as applied to the practice of live digital theatre. The IFTR group has set up its aim to "examine the interrelationships of theatre with other media, the combinations of different media in performance and wider digital/postdigital culture through performance studies lens".[2] Looking at the changes that took place with the introduction of telepresence in performance though zoom live theatre from 2020 due to the pandemic lockdown, this book brings together performance practice and interdisciplinary performative pedagogies as a way to explore and understand creative methods in live digital theatre and live zoom theatre as a new live theatre platform.

FIGURE 0.1 Zoom Live Theatre *We'll meet again at Ricks*, 26th June 2020. Premiere on YouTube. Acting students on devising course, Royal Birmingham Conservatoire.

The central theme of this book – interdisciplinarity in performative pedagogies of live digital theatre charts the origins and application of a plurality of artistic forms and media in live theatre performance and how the methodologies of applied performance practice were arrived at in this form of digital theatre. It investigates multiple perspectives on histories, performance and visual art, cultural communities, performative practices, and the implications of live digital theatre as a creative practice and pedagogy that comes out and sits within the context of digital media performance as a relevant discourse. The complexity of the plurality of applied aesthetic, socio-cultural and political contexts in digital media performance will be shown in the book. Live digital theatre creatively utilises interdisciplinary approaches as hybrid performances, combining digital and physical space and action. The book traces live digital theatre origins from historical to contemporary experiments. The chapters examine performative pedagogies moving through forms of applied practice, examining performance models as central to contemporary digital networking and human communication.

Chapters are grouped into two parts, *Histories and Methodologies*, and *Pedagogic Praxis*. Explored in the book are concepts and contexts such as cultural archaeology of digital theatre, the intermediality of performance events that leads to the development of digital theatre, and dramaturgy exploring various theories pertinent to live digital theatre with digital media culture. In the second part, *Pedagogic Praxis*, there is an exploration of how creative practice and pedagogies of live digital theatre function through examples given in case studies.

The focus on participatory applied theatre methodology will be considered through the book as online agora notion of a global community, as multiple groups interrelate to co-create and co-exist in online productions. Live digital theatre facilitates the gathering of an international community that brings people together in the same sense as a local applied theatre. In the last section, I focus on the theories of live digital theatre, where cyberspace becomes the trans-topic location, providing the context in which people come together. The focus is on the dramaturgy of body space-time and liveness, helping us understand how certain elements are used in live digital theatre. Various practices and methodologies are explored to understand where live digital theatre sits within the digital media performance discourse. When discussing the creative process, it is essential to understand the methodologies behind it used in digital live digital theatre. It is necessary to understand that it is not about the technologies and tools by which live theatre is transmitted. It is about using technology as a creative resource. Digital technology is a way of making performance by applying different ways of existing in an online world in an online production. The second part of the book investigates case studies related to live digital theatre performances based on Teatro Os Satyros, The Red Courtin Theatre International and Kolectiv Theatre practices.

Chapter 1 presents contexts of live digital theatre and moves through various necessary points to establish the focus of the book on development of students learning performance practice and pedagogy within live digital theatre. Chapter 2, 'Cultural Archaeology', traces the historical origins and evolution of digital multimedia theatre and performance art culture, including precursors such as mixed media and radical performance art movements, multimedia and video art and use of computer technology. The selected historical periods of performance art practice present their impact through the inclusion of mixed media and multi-media within live productions. The focus is on innovation movements: Futurism, Dadaist, events at Cabaret Voltaire, Piscator's Cinematic Theatre and Soviet Avantgarde and performances of Surrealists, Bauhaus art, Happenings, Video Art, and in general 1960s and 1970s media performance and visual arts and practices using electronic media. The choice of what performance art movement to look at is informed by the inclusion of aestheticism of interdisciplinary pedagogy and practice and applied performance to society and culture.

Chapter 3, 'Intermediality' focuses on the pedagogy of performance art and theatre, on schools and art practices that have established intermedial, performative pedagogy by situating a performer's creative process within the centre of media interactivity. This chapter looks at the practitioners John Cage, Hélio Oiticica, Joanne Littlewood, Elisabeth La Compte and Robert Lepage who bring new media technologies into performance as creative pedagogies and personal methodology of making performance, which typically relies on bringing various arts and media together into one physical space shared with an audience.

This chapter will help situate the ontology and phenomenology of multimedia and digital theatre to give us an understanding of performance practice and pedagogy that come from interactions between different art media, and profoundly impact contemporary digital media performance and live digital theatre. Performative pedagogy is introduced within the examination of intermediality by looking at other schools of artistic creation that necessitate a variety of art methodologies in performance practice. I explore how pedagogies in multi-media performance modify electronic media: film, television, video art, and radio, once introduced into joint multiple connections existing within a space and body of a live theatre performance. The training and education of artists for intermedial performance is typically set up in an art studio practice where both students and young artists learn through engagement with multi-media performance and their own experience of making art from more senior artists (dancers, musicians, performers) who serve the function of a master teacher.

In Chapter 4, 'Dramaturgies', the focus is on systems that structure performance, such as the dramaturgy of live digital theatre. Theories that underpin creative systems for live digital theatre are contextualised. These theoretical analyses help us understand liveness, presence, body, image, space/time and audience participation. The focus is on the dramaturgical trajectory of actor – space – audience in live performance using digital media either as an element for production or a platform for representation of live digital theatre. To understand the plurality of contexts and fragmentary nature of live digital theatre, I introduce an addition to Philip Auslander's *liveness* and concept of *transtopia* emerging from Foucault's *heterotopia*, the terminology of Guy McAuley's *presence in space*, Henri Lefebvre's *lived space* and Deleuze's *the fold* and *crystals of time*, alongside valuable deliberation of Benjamin and Barthes's *photographic image*.

Chapter 5, 'Digital Agora' focuses on applied global performance as a meeting place in cyberspace for the international theatre community. It examines online works of applied theatre that bring together within the performance an international community of actors (amateurs, students and professionals) from different parts of the world. Focusing mainly on the development of pedagogy that formed the applied performance educational core, such as the work of Paolo Freire, Augusto Boal and John McGrath Schechner, we examine how pedagogy shaped the theatre practice and how this affected the performative pedagogy of applied digital theatre. Case studies are given as testimonials from applied theatre practitioners such as Rodolpho Vasquez (Brazil) and Sumit LeRoi (India). The chapter also looks at applied performance works in live digital theatre in a global community as a meeting place – digital agora. I also consider how this form of theatre responded to the physical restrictions of the Covid-19 pandemic and the transformation that allowed new global interactivity between different communities.

Part 2 begins with Chapter 6, 'Pedagogic Praxis' which explores a range of examples of how digital media is used in live performance practice. The key elements of theatre (live audience, space and performer) are established using elements that have been explained in Part 1, such as intermedial pedagogy, dramaturgy and applied global performance. Live digital theatre is explored, as created through the dislocation of space in online productions and conditions that mix cultural contexts, creative methodologies and digital technology in online live output. Given that Kolectiv Theatre has investigated the relationship between media, space, body, and audience participation since the year 2000, case studies from the company's practice, dealing with the use of digital media performance are included in this chapter. To study the use of digital media performance in live practice the focus is on three case studies, productions with various theatre venues, countries and languages, and working with performers whose experiences and levels range from experienced professionals to student actors. A live digital theatre using intermedial connections in the physical space that puts the performer's action at the centre of the creative process was at the core of all the projects directed and devised from 2008 to 2015. The productions were: *The Orchard Cycle* (2008–2011 Kolectiv Theatre, in the UK, Iran and Serbia), *The Club New World Order* (2009–2010), *Knajzevsko Srpski* (Royal Court Theatre, Serbia), and *Death of a Salesman* (2013, Everyman Theatre, Cork, Ireland and 2014 Belgrade Drama Theatre, Belgrade, Serbia).

Chapter 7 examines Interdisciplinary Performance Pedagogies using Shakespeare's *Macbeth* as a starting point for the exploratory process. The chapter presents documented experience of investigating interdisciplinary performance practice and pedagogies within live digital theatre using one core dramatic text. From 2017-2020, the case study *Macbeth Projeto #1–6* - a collaboration with students, staff from Royal Birmingham Conservatoire and Kolectiv Theatre- examined and applied interdisciplinary performative pedagogies through six cycles, creating different multimedia performances. The methodology is based on event scoring as developed in Lawrence and Anne Halprin's RSVP Cycles. The project was fully documented on the website www.macbethprojeto.co.uk as a case study of a research project that developed from April 2017 to December 2020 through different performance cycles exploring rehearsal methodologies of interdisciplinary performing practice and pedagogies from ritual and cinema theatre up to Zoom live theatre. The focus is on rehearsal strategies for interdisciplinary and international performances that create their narrative. The actual text is only a starting point, one of the resources in the creative process that uses different digital media technology.

Chapter 8, 'Live Theatre on Zoom', examines the students creative practice of performative pedagogies of live digital theatre and how multimedia performance functions within the scope of online productions by looking at productions of video art, choreography and Zoom live theatre. Both models of the live online shows were done as a course at Royal Birmingham Conservatoire as an online practice in 2020 and 2021. The productions were part of an ongoing research project exploring various web applications, video, film and live online telepresence forms to create performances and explore the actors' training and education. This chapter focuses on two case studies: *We'll meet at Rick's* Video art performance/choreography and *Amorphism: Zoom Wedding* and *When the Gods Come* live Zoom theatre. Based on these performances, the chapter explores creative practice methodologies. The pedagogy behind these methods is enabled through a simple technology linked to a computer working with an iPad tablet, smartphone or PC camera and screen. It can be live or video recorded, working on small image-driven scores by recording objects, space, voice, facial expression, or physical body movement.

Chapter 9, 'Conclusion: Performative Digital Futures' examines the implementation and limitation of live digital performance using both Zoom live online and physical theatre space with actors and audience, as an interactive cross between physical and digital in the form of phydital hybrid. The chapter looks at performative pedagogy and how it shapes the actor's and audience's experience. I return to the questions of interactivity in performance between liveness and presence, the interconnection between digital and physical performance elements and how they can complement each other in creating a narrative. By looking at the phygital performance of Kolectiv Theatre's *Andy's Factory in the Fun Palace* in September 2021and the works of Red Curtain Theatre International *Theatre Good Causes Festival* in April 2022, the conclusion emphasises the degree to which these performances are constructed through the use of digital media and the experience they provide for performers and audience. Finally, the book looks at the applicability of live digital theatre as a future model in Metaverse. What does the future hold for zoom live theatre and phygital performance being used as a pre-Virtual Theatre? It poses the question of the implementation and limitation of live digital theatre and its pedagogical role in creative practice and education of actors' performance makers within the polyvalent world of the theatre, where digital media performance has come to dominate how art is made, practised, and represented today.

The implications of this book are to open up various possibilities for further research into the field of live digital theatre, in an area of confluence between observing and participating, avatars and virtual bodies, interphase with machines and humans in computer gaming, YouTube influencing and TikTok home-made film shorts. The key terms *digital* and *media* are used by scholars in numerous different theatre and performing arts contexts. They indicate a plurality of media and their interconnection to computer technology and digital art. Moreover, the terms *performance practice* and *pedagogy* and their complex and multi-layered meanings – as used throughout the book – are studied within their academic disciplines and are at the core of our theoretical study. Because of this, we have to go into breadth and depth about the various implications of using these terms in an interdisciplinary context as well as being specific to what they imply within this material – setting up interdisciplinary performative pedagogies as relating to learning performance practice and theatre pedagogy, particularly in live digital theatre.

Notes

1 Brook, Peter, *The Empty Space* (Penguin Classic, 2008) p. 21
2 See website https://iftr.org/working-groups/intermediality-in-theatre-and-performance

PART 1

Histories and Methodologies

1
CONTEXTS OF LIVE DIGITAL THEATRE

We live in an image-driven world. Our life experience is increasingly digital – whether it involves social media or Artificial Intelligence (AI), or any visual content created through computer technology. Digital media culture dominates the 21st century; it is everywhere. It is the most advanced and fastest-growing form of expression for human communication and interaction with the world around us. Live digital theatre belongs to this world. What then is a live digital theatre in digital media culture? The answer is straightforward: it is what the title declares it to be. It occurs in a *live* interaction between the actors and the audience, in the context of *there and now*, in the same way that any theatre performance would have taken place in real-time in front of an audience. Live also refers to a rehearsal process involving live interaction among a creative team's members, such as actors, technicians, designers and a director. It is *digital* because it uses computer technology to create and present the production. Digital points to dual applicability: digital media introduced to a live theatre performance and a live theatre performance brought into digital media using telepresence, particularly on the Zoom platform. It is *theatre* taking place in the theatre discipline as a practice that brings the audience within a specified space where performers present their actions.

The most relevant reference is Steve Dixon's seminal book *Digital Performance*, which combines history, theory and practice examples.[1] The book encapsulates his experience since the 1990s with digital performance as a scholar, director and actor. Dixon positions digital performance in the context of performance art. He essentially situates digital performance within history, aesthetics and the artistic methodologies that underpin the creative processes of performance art. For Dixon, digital performance as an independent art form is the next stage in performance art, delivered through new digital technology, the computer, the

DOI: 10.4324/9781003275893-2

internet and visual media communication. In the first years of the 21st century, digital media had not wholly entered popular culture or become a necessity of everyday life. From the 2010s onwards, digital technology has enabled art to be interactive, allowing audience involvement and control over the artistic outcome. Live video communication on digital platforms, such as FaceTime, Skype, WhatsApp, Zoom and Teams, to name a few, has brought together people who are physically thousands of miles away from one another but can now meet and connect in cyberspace and in real-time as mediated reality. Because of the advancements in digital media technology, the focus is on theatre that can absorb a plurality of media and artistic expressions, including digital performance existing within performance art.

The art of theatre is a live experience for the audience. However, the compatibility of digital technologies within performance technology supports creative common grounds. With the latest advancements in computer programs for digital art creation and communication via digital media and fast internet connections that facilitate exchange and collaboration, live immersive digital space and physical space each constitute their virtual reality. The *real* in the digital world is not just an "impression" of the living environment; physical space in digital world is a "real" environment. Their qualities have socially and culturally equal presence and viability, but they represent opposites (physical and digital) that co-exist within live digital theatre.

Historically, theatre is a collective ritual, a set of social conditions agreed on by a community (be it a group, a city or a state), collaboratively telling a known story and sharing a common group identity. In the 5th century BC in the Acropolis in Athens, the Ancient Greek Theatre of Dionysus performed the first plays in front of the community members who were involved in the construction of the performance, where audience presence and interpretation gave meaning to the live performance. At the end of the 20th century, advancements in digital technology enabled video, films and images to be downloaded and manipulated on computers, providing creative freedom and allowing them to be brought into the dramaturgical structure of live theatre events. Digital theatre implies mediation, where a live show is recorded or transmitted to an audience, as in live theatre on television and film from a specific physical location. There is no immediacy or presence of an audience who observes on a screen. The performance event is occurring someplace else where the actors are, and the audience is located in another physical space. It is a transmission of a live theatre event. How then can live be at the same time digital? The same principles of live communication exchanges through digital platforms relate to the live digital theatre, where performers on screen, as a virtual stage space, communicate with the audience, seated not in rows in the auditorium, but at home. In online live productions, the audience engages with the performers through the computer screen, visual projection or television as they would in any live interaction on platforms, such as Zoom or Teams. The plurality of digital media in live theatre changes the nature of theatre interactions with space, performers, and audience that Auslander and Dixon have established.[2] Furthermore, the more recent use of live performance on digital platforms, such as live Zoom theatre, requires an approach that differs from that of previously established theatre practice and pedagogy.

Philip Auslander's concept of *Liveness*, established in 1999, before online theatre production, super fast internet and virtual reality, deepened the debate around duality of liveness, alluding to media culture where live underpins mediatised, and mediatised uses live to materialise itself.

Auslander observes, "Live performance now often incorporates mediatisation to the degree that the live event itself is a product of media technologies."[3] Auslander understands liveness as the binary opposition between live and mediatised only in a historical and cultural context, not aesthetic or creative, as mediatised had to be first live to provide a basis before it could become a mediatised experience. The division is the result of the commodification of the production of art and the cultural economy. However, in contemporary live performance, live and mediatised complement each other working from opposite ends of a spectrum, and their duality supports one another. Auslander's relation between live and mediatised performances, where the emphasis is not on the opposition but the relationship of mutual dependence, is a starting point in the establishing of connection between digital and physical worlds.

The digital performance exists within the matrix of different terminologies related to the connections between media and arts in theatre: multimedia (other disciplines distinguished as different cultural actions and practices), transmedia (used in art and communication referring to change in content and form from one medium to another), and intermedia (part of numerous discourses, seen as co-relations between different media that result in a redefinition of the media that are influencing each other).[4] Online and the internet raised liveness into the digital world where it can relate to two new forms: "online liveness" and "group liveness", as proposed by Nick Couldry.

> Online liveness: social co-presence on various scales from small groups in chat rooms to huge international audiences for breaking news on major Websites.
> Group liveness: the "liveness" of a mobile group of friends who are in continuous contact via their mobile phones through calls and texting.[5]

Dixon has a working definition of digital performance as the involvement of computer technology in creating live performing arts; Masura's identification of digital theatre is where the digital and theatre equally share common grounds essential to making the performance.[6] Live digital theatre and leading digital media performance share the same understanding that performance does not involve digital technology as a tool for creating and disseminating the production of theatre works. Digital technology is used as a creative art practice with specific aesthetic qualities and production elements that are born out of convergence and co-creation through various live and recorded media. *Digital Theatre*, as a generic name, refers to the use of digital technology used in making and representing live theatre, opera and dance. It is commonly used to describe the streaming of recorded live performances on film or for television for audience entertainment. However, Digital Theatre also plays a vital role in Theatre Education. The filmed theatre works are presented on now well-established web platforms such as Digital Theatre (www.digitaltheatre.com) and Digital Theatre Plus (www.digitaltheatreplus.com) or archived as new developments in interdisciplinary performance on Digital Performance Archive (http://ahds.ac.uk/performingarts/index.htm). Cinema presentations of filmed live theatre productions by the National Theatre Live, UK and Metropolitan Opera, US, is a recent development in the last twenty years, and they can be transmitted to audiences in distant locations. A significant result is the use of digital theatre platforms for education, bringing not only filmed performances as a finished product, but also the processes of making, such as workshops and rehearsal experiences, to students (as digital platform Digital Theatre +), thereby using digital technology to communicate live performance practice and pedagogy to users.

The pedagogy (as a method of learning and creating) of live digital theatre will be explored across all the chapters. This book charts the origins, development and methodology of creative practice of live digital theatre as a concept that relates to physical theatre and live online productions. It examines the coexistence of digital and live multimedia performance and pedagogy. It explores the presence of digital technology incorporated in live theatre with the audience sharing a physical space and the existence of live performance using new digital technology platforms, for example, Zoom Theatre. Live Theatre Performance using a digital platform to communicate with the audience employs a new technology as a methodology and a creative practice to facilitate online production.

Enter the Covid-19 Pandemic

From mid-March 2020, live theatre culture shifted online. In London, all theatres and almost 250 theatres across the UK faced closure. Over 15,000 performances were cancelled in the first three months of the Covid pandemic, and "the Covid pandemic reduced live performances by an average of 56.12% in venues across Italy, France, Germany, Spain, UK and USA".[7] It was a gradual unprecedented process. In the beginning, theatres closed the door and postponed the shows following the government's first recommendation on 23rd March as mandatory closure to stop the spread of the virus. Universities followed the government's protocol, introduced a lockdown and stay-at-home policy, and moved education online. The closure of theatres (in the creative industry and in the education sector) was a rupture with ordinary life and a new experience to understand and find a response to.[8] Soon after, the UK government recognised that during the coronavirus pandemic arts and entertainment had been one of the worst affected sectors, second only to the accommodation and service industry. Inventing and re-discovering new ways to live with the pandemic was essential. As early as July 2020, a multimedia theatre company, Border Crossings, presented its assessment to the government Department of Digital, Culture, Media and Sports (DCMS) Ministers.

> The current crisis does not make our cultural life something that should be held until things are "back to normal." We must recognise that we are undergoing a fundamental change in how we live—we have to imagine a different future. It will be from the cultural sector that essential new ideas emerge."[9]

"Going Digital" became a home for live theatre out of necessity to find "the new live".[10]

> Covid-19 took hold, and countries and cities worldwide entered lockdown with the closure of schools, cultural and sports venues and all non-essential businesses…Across the world, people were adapting to new social distancing guidelines….[11]

The Covid-19 virus descended on the world sometime after 2020, working its way across the globe starting from China. In late February, the virus spread through Italy, the first place in Europe to become affected. By spring, most of the countries were under strict government-imposed lockdown regulations. The pandemic led to a new reality, creating rupture in ordinary life. Live events were cancelled (all theatre had to stop), people were locked in their homes, no travel, masks and social distancing were imposed as norms. Transformation of global society commenced. Slavoj Žižek's concept of *rupture* is an event that can explain the transformation and break that takes place in a community under stress. For Žižek event "can be an occurrence that shatters ordinary life, a radical political rupture, or a transformation of reality, a religious belief, the rise of a new art form…".[12] With Covid-19, a point of rupture also introduced new concepts – "working from home on the online platform", "bubble", "furlough", "national lockdown", "vaccine passport", "mass movement of anti-vaxxers", "vaccine booster", "PCR tests", and "Passenger Locator Form". The social rupture was caused by the Covid-19 pandemic, where mass consumption of emotional responses and ambiguous political messages led to legal restrictions and breaking of live communication with family and friends. The fear of infection and death created a new reality, a transformation in which the answer to the closure of face-to-face communication and physical contact was to migrate into live online video communication and digital platforms and apps. An indoor existence became central to peoples' activities, from work to social engagements, online shopping and home food delivery.

We can see in theatre history that Throughout the 20th century, the incorporation of media technology into multimedia theatre could occur in any space, from traditional theatre buildings to urban spaces occupying any empty alternative location such as city squares, streets, factory warehouses and disused church halls and galleries. In any area, visual images and simple video recordings and projections allow different aesthetic experiences to be introduced into the dramaturgy of a performance. This can also be done through more elaborate computer-generated imagery, from green screen film projections to augmented and virtual reality environments, avatars and performers connected to the computer as human/machines. In the UK, funding cuts to the arts accompanied the emergence of the pandemic, further exacerbating the threat to live theatre. It has been generally noted that with the sudden appearance of Covid-19, the presence and exploration of digital technology within performance started to lose momentum. The impact of digital technology on live theatre was regarded mainly (by the mainstream theatre) as an *alternative* strand, allowing access to the live arts (theatre, opera, dance) distributed via digital technology or as an *accompaniment* to the multimedia performance aestheticism and dramaturgy taking place on stage with an audience present. In 2016,the Arts Council England, UK Theatre and Society of London Theatre commissioned a study about the impact on audiences "whether live attendances have declined or increased as a direct result of the availability of Live-to-Digital programming (…), survey responses indicate that theatregoers are neither more nor less likely to attend the live theatre if they experience it digitally".[13] These circumstances suddenly changed when lockdown measures thrust live digital theatre to the fore. The alternative *accompaniment* suddenly became the nexus for exploring and creating new pedagogical praxis. Consequently, a new space opened for expanding interdisciplinary approaches within the performing arts industry. In addition, the struggle of drama schools to find new methodologies to teach performance art in 2020–21 necessitated new ways of rethinking education, where live streaming online became part of practice base explorations of performance practice and the teaching curriculum.

In what follows, live digital theatre will be contextualised within various international and UK theatre practices. Examples are taken from companies I collaborated with in the USA, Canada, Brazil and India. The rise of live digital theatre in response to the global shutdown of live theatre and performing arts was instituted globally from the end of March 2020. The book focuses on the implications and different strategies theatres used to employ social media and digital technology for creative practice and new pedagogies as a response to lockdown: Zoom theatre production, Instagram, YouTube and Facebook live streaming; use of communication apps like WhatsApp, Twitter and Viber as rehearsal tools. How can this new use of digital media be built-in within the teaching and creative industry once we are out of this pandemic?

As John Bull points out, mainstream theatre is a central feature of the British cultural landscape; this does not merit a discussion as it is accepted as central to the culture. However, it is also deceptive "as its apparent transparency as a concept is…highly problematic and contentious".[14] Mainstream theatre in the UK refers to the centrality of a cultural industry sector that considerably impacts audiences. For example, "Theatres in London and across the UK attracted more than 34m visitors in 2018, generating ticket revenues of £1.28bn from 62,945 performances, according to figures from UK Theatre and the Society of London Theatre."[15]

Methodologies and Pedagogies of Interdisciplinary Performance

With a focus on interdisciplinary practice as pedagogy, the book is using Anne Halprin's RSVP Cycles, which influence process and outcomes.[16] Event scoring is the methodological process of making performance, where the phenomenological observation of performance in its corporal, participatory and experiential aspects is essential for learning and creating based on the individual or group environment. Therefore, a mixed research methodology is applied by bringing together theory, critical analysis, and case studies observations and experience using interdisciplinary practice research, observation and analysis of rehearsal processes and pedagogies to address performative pedagogies. The aim is to illustrate a creative processual framework, a system that offers an exciting practical approach to live digital theatre that will be helpful to theatre students and practitioners. This cross-disciplinary approach would provide new knowledge and understanding of live digital theatre, focusing on essential creative processes.

Digital media performance has a deep historical foundation in performance and visual art, using multiple media and computer technology and introducing them into a theatre. Another sub-theme of this book is the functionality of live digital media performance within a global, international community and applied theatre context that takes theatre out of the insularity of local and national power structures and dominant narratives, but still keeps the focus on what is relevant to a community. The performance practices of John Cage, Nam June Paik, Helio Oiticica, Laurie Anderson, Wooster Group, Robert Lepage, Teatro Os Satyros, to name but a few, are set in the context of 20th and 21st century inter-medial performance methodologies. The methodologies proposed in this book have a particular focus on applications of pedagogy and practice. The experience of digital media performance will be presented from the perspective of the practitioners as creative pedagogies – essentially, how to work with an inter-medial performer within the context of live digital theatre. The critical questions this research engages with are: what are the practices of performative pedagogies, necessary for a live digital theatre? What does the creative group process look like, and what are the elements of digital media performance technology used to build live digital media performance? What is the nature of liveness in live digital theatre, and how does it connect to other digital platforms for streaming recorded content already embedded in our daily lives?

Until now, no book has yet engaged with discourses of creative pedagogies within the performance practice of multimedia and live digital theatre. Considering the seismic change in performing arts that took place in 2020–21, a new form of online digital media performance has developed globally. When addressing the new phenomena of live digital online performance within the developed discourse on digital production, inter-media theatre and 20th century performance art, understanding performative pedagogies and practices becomes necessary. Regarding the established discourse on multimedia and digital theatre, critical attention has been devoted to the following books *Digital Performance* by Steve Dixon, *Theatre and Performance in Digital Culture* by Matthew Causey, *Performing Presence* by Gabriella Giannachi and Nick Kaye and most recently *Digital Theatre: The Making and Meaning of Live Mediated Performance* by Nadja Masura and *Live Visual: History, Theory and Practice* edited by Steve Gibson et al.[17] The original foundations of this book are rooted in my previous extensive and published research on the multidisciplinary work in the film, theatre and devising practices of Robert Lepage (Dundjerović, 2003, 2007, 2009).[18] However, no material has hitherto grappled with the practices and pedagogies needed for the creative process for digital media performance or with the new emerging media of live digital theatre.

The examples of performance practice as chosen case studies demonstrate a robust sense of how and why they have been selected. They represent the use of interdisciplinary pedagogies over several years across different models of digital media performance within the drama department and conservatories, shaping a teaching and learning practice that awarded the author Principal Fellowship of the Higher Education Academy and nomination as National Teaching Fellow in 2019. From the beginning of the lockdown, the author worked with Royal Birmingham Conservatoire acting students and staff on various levels of workshops and productions on live digital theatre in the experimental forum organised by the Centre for Interdisciplinary Performative Arts (CIPA). Research projects employed digital theatre as video choreography art using YouTube and Zoom online live theatre productions, and live stream performances without a live audience on Facebook and Instagram. For example, in post-show discussions with the audience (made of international audiences, academics, performing arts professionals and teachers), we discovered a great interest in live digital theatre and how to use it with students. Since the academic year 2021–22, drama schools have promoted courses in online production in addition to screen, theatre and television. New pedagogies have given rise to a new practice model relevant to media culture, replacing face-to-face communication with social media.

From April 2020 the author started examining the practice and pedagogy of live digital theatre at the Royal Birmingham Conservatoire (RBC), creating productions with students performed on public digital platforms. Since setting up Kolectiv Theatre, he was always intrigued by how performers can manipulate the performance space in the theatre building within the actual stage space, but also on how we can best use alternative spaces as performance environments to communicate with the audiences' ideas that emerge from a performance that we are making collectively. We started bringing different media languages into the performance space because it allowed us a versatile approach to dramaturgy and different ways of representing the material that they were communicating with the audience. We refused to work with complex technological tools in our creative process. We used the same media our audiences use in their everyday life which also made our rehearsals more manageable. So when the audience is watching the digital media projections in the theatre and interacting with live and mediated actions that are using the language of fragmented narrative structures, they are engaging with a familiarity of their experience of the image world they live in, multiple and fragmented narratives on their computers, the internet, social media, film and television.

The interdisciplinary approach of bringing together education, performance, digital media and visual art to examine practice is central to understanding creative practice and pedagogies. Live digital theatre organises collaborative digital methods and data collection within the context of research-led teaching. In this way, the implementation of live digital theatre is connected to practises of research-led teaching. The case studies used in this book were explored within the context of research-led teaching enquiry of experiential and action learning. How do we adapt our pedagogy to students involved in live digital theatre and explore creative approaches within performance practice? The book aims to present a variety of pedagogical approaches to theories and practices of live digital theatre with transformation from live physical into live digital space and hybrid physical and digital performance.

The author's personal experience since 2000 as theatre performance director and deviser with Kolectiv Theatre Productions (UK) and collaborations with world-leading practitioners Teatro Os Satyros (Brazil) and The Red Curtain International (India) to investigate ways to bring live digital media performance into theatre training and performance-making. The idea of Creative Performative Pedagogies is placed within the context of exploration of live digital theatre. It is used to understand creative practices and how one can learn from them. The book also combines a series of personal case studies and pedagogical practices on multimedia and live digital theatre.

The book looks beyond the relationship between live and mediated in the world of virtual reality where physical real and digital real are synonymised, conflated, and hybridised, to examine how practices and pedagogies are produced in multimedia integration in live performance and the presence of live performance within digital media. Although liveness is vital to performing arts (music, dance, opera, installation art), it is essential for theatre as its existence is in the interaction between spectator and performer, which creates the essence of the theatre art form. A theatre act without an audience does not exist as a theatre arts event. Reason and Lindelof established that "liveness is produced through processes of *audiencing* —as spectators bring qualities of (a)liveness into being through the nature of their attention – and processes of materialising in acts of performance, acts of making, acts of archiving and acts of remembering".[19] In the 20th century, the impact of media technology on performance as well as on the aestheticism of visual art was indispensable for the formation of an inter-disciplinary theatre language of the art in the way it was conceptualised and separated from physical space in the traditional proscenium theatre as a building with dedicated stage space and auditorium. So how does this interactivity between live media and the physical experience for the audience create reality in live digital theatre? What impact does interdisciplinary practice have on how performers make art, and what pedagogies can they refer to in an interdisciplinary performance context? For example, introducing film into theatre in Soviet avant-garde or video art in the process of making performances by Fluxus artists had a profound influence on art-making practice and the way performance events were received by the audience, the quality of the subjective experience, immersion into the material being presented, and the external reality brought into the space.

Historically, each critical performance practitioner or group of artists came out of a creative school. They developed a methodology and approach to pedagogy that produced a particular form of practice, be it theatre, dance, video art, film, music, poly-media, etc. For example, Russian theatre visionary Konstantin Stanislavski's method from the beginning of the 20th century was essential for developing the acting pedagogy that informed teaching and learning of acting and theatre practice for most Western drama schools and conservatoires. As with any theatre methodology that the centre uses to train the performers: Jerzy Grotowski, Eugenio Barba, Jacques Lecoq, Anna Halprin, Richard Schechner, and Anne Bogart, to name a few, perfor-mance practices are inseparable from performative pedagogy. They are interrelated, as the approach comes out of pedagogy and pedagogy frames the performing methods and technique. Therefore, throughout the book, the terms creative practice and per-formative pedagogies are referential to each other, intrinsically connected as both simultaneously influence one another. I will approach the interchangeability of prac-tice and pedagogy as a learning environment through surprising discoveries not pre-conceived and prepared in advance, a "duel" which Martin Buber, in writing about the philosophy of education, refers to as "in a real conversation...a real lesson, really embraced and not one of mere habit, a real duel and not a mere game."[20] It is too early to know if, following the experience of the pandemic, live digital theatre has resulted in a new theatre both live physical and digital creative methodology. Nevertheless, live digital theatre has shown its potential to establish performative pedagogies. There is a need to train actors to respond to the popularity of online productions and digital media in the creative industry.

Conclusion

The view of performative pedagogy used here requires learners and teachers to reflect on their practices and broader contexts, from the use of their body to references to space, media and other arts – somewhat similar to the established concept of performance pedagogy in teaching and learning. In performance pedagogy, students learn by relating to a real-life situation in a performance setting, where the teacher becomes a facilitator (director) who guides them through this experience. The emphasis is on the subjective position of the learners, to establish their ways of engaging with the outside world through self-creativity. It focuses on case studies that include exercises and innovative models that provide a reference for teaching and learning. The book emphasises skills-based and professional values combined with core knowledge through embodied learning and action research methodologies, referring to pedagogical approaches of collaborative, reflective and inquiry-based learning. I will bring these approaches to the understanding of live digital theatre pedagogy. In relation to performative pedagogies, the focus will be on interdisciplinary collective immersive experiences driven by subjective observation of reality as an ontological principle. My practice work, together with the creative practice of my collaborators, will be used to underpin the examination of live digital theatre.

Over the last 20 years, as a pedagogue, director and deviser with the multimedia performance group Kolectiv Theatre, I experimented in various productions, sociocultural, linguistic, and international contexts (Liverpool, Birmingham, Belgrade, Prijedor, Teheran, Cluj, Romania, and Prague). I explored digital theatre through interdisciplinary performance, mixing expressions of body, space, text, media, visual arts, music and audience participation. Typically, we would create locally and then go to smaller and more experimental European festivals. This pattern of creative practice resembles the working method of Ex Machina, Robert Lepage's Quebec City based performance company. In order to engage with my research about this kind of international festival theatre, I needed to develop a practice model to examine and understand it better. I discovered that this performative pedagogy worked well as a model for an educational environment. I employed experiments with multimedia and digital media performance as a critical language of theatre expression to advance students' learning of contemporary theatre within an interdisciplinary and international context. The work of Kolectiv Theatre, as the name suggests, was based on group interactivity, where I, with the help of group members, would facilitate an agenda for creative investigation. In performative pedagogy, no one centre would initiate creativity or dictate the narrative followed in the rehearsals. The group of performers was a mix of professionals and students. Most of them were students at university drama programmes that I was teaching; some were ex-students, and only a few would be acting in a professional capacity.

From the beginning, Kolectiv had a pedagogical educational aspect in which we collaborated with different artists – designers, musicians, choreographers and digital media artists. However, it was always based on students' work and experience. Organising the performance around the students' input, in response to the creative environment and audience involvement, was central to this pedagogy. Bringing different digital media into a performance language allowed us to communicate with the audience in a variety of geo-cultural locations and contexts. The audience was using the same media. They understood the media and were familiar with using social media platforms, video, computer games, digital apps and the language from fragmented structures, relevant to computer software and internet plurality of narratives. Incorporating digital media into performance practice in experience detailed here provided the performers (students) and the audience (usually younger experimental festival and fringe goers) a familiarity and ability to engage with material from other contexts, from "somewhere else" beyond what their language and culture would normally allow.

Notes

1 Dixon, Steve. *Digital Performance: A History of New Media in Theater, Dance, Performance Art, and Installation* (MIT Press, 2007).
2 Auslander, Philip. *Liveness: Performance in a Mediatized Culture* (Taylor & Francis Group, 2008); and Dixon. *Digital Performance.*
3 Auslander, 2008, p. 25.
4 See the terminology definition in Kattenbelt, Chiel, "Intermediality in Theatre and Performance: Definitions, Perceptions and Medial Relationships", in *Culture, Language and Representation*, Vol. VI (2008): pp. 19–29, p. 25.
5 Couldry, Nick. "Liveness, 'Reality' and the Mediated Habitus from Television to the Mobile Phone", *The Communication Review* 7 (2004), pp. 356–7.
6 See Masura, Nadja. *Digital Theatre: The Making and Meaning of Live Mediated Performance, US & UK 1990–2020* (Palgrave Macmillan, 2020).
7 Maria Chatzichristodoulou, Kevin Brown, Nick Hunt, Peter Kuling & Toni Sant (2022) "Covid-19: theatre goes digital – provocations", *International Journal of Performance Arts and Digital Media*, 18:1, p. 2
8 In London, the only other times theatres were closed over a long period was during the Blitz of German air raids in the Second World War, throughout the political upheaval of Puritanical rule in the mid-17th century, and during successive periods in the 16th century when epidemic of plague caused high mortality. The Society of London Theatre and UK Theatre estimated at the beginning of the Pandemic that 290,000 people working in the sector would be without any income.
9 UK Parliament website https://publications.parliament.uk/pa/cm5801/cmselect/cm cumeds/291/29106.htm
10 McCaleb, J.M. "Coronavirus: For Performers in Lockdown, Online is Becoming the New Live". *The Conversation* (March 20, 2020): https://theconversation.com/coronavirus-for-performers-in-lockdown-online-is-becoming-the-new-live-133961
11 UN Health. "The Virus That Shut Down the World: 2020, A Year Like No Other" (December 24, 2020): https://news.un.org/en/story/2020/12/1080702
12 Žižek's example is that on September 11, 2001, rupture attacks on New York set up a transformation of society, as he labels it, a "post-truth era". Garcia, Luz Paola, "Slavoj Žižek's Concept of Rupture—and Post-Truth", *Merion West* (April 29, 2019): https://merionwest.com/2019/04/29/slavoj-zizeks-concept-of-rupture-and-post-truth/. See also Žižek, Slavoj. *Event: A Philosophical Journey Through A Concept* (Melville House, 2014).
13 AEA Consulting. *From Live-To-Digital: Understanding of the Impact of Digital Developments in Theatre on Audiences, Production and Distribution*, October 2016: https://www.arts council.org.uk/sites/default/files/download-file/From_Live_to_Digital_OCT2016.pdf
14 Bull, John. "The Establishment of Mainstream Theatre, 1946–1979", *The Cambridge History of British Theatre* (Cambridge University Press, 2004).
15 Creative Industries Council. "Facts and Figures: Economic Contribution of UK Arts & Culture" (March 4, 2020): https://www.thecreativeindustries.co.uk/facts-figures/

industries-arts-culture-arts-culture-facts-and-figures-the-economic-contribution-of-the-arts
16 See Halprin, Lawrence. *The RSVP Creative Processes in the Human Environment* (New York: Georg .Braziller, 1970).
17 Dixon, Steve. *Digital Performance* (MIT, 2007); Causey, Matthew. *Theatre and Performance in Digital Culture* (Routledge, 2006); Giannachi, Gabriella and Nick Kaye. *Performing Presence: Between the Live and the Simulated* (Manchester University Press, 2011); and most recently Masura, Nadja. *Digital Theatre: The Making and Meaning of Live Mediated Performance, US &UK 1990-2020* (Palgrave, 2020); and edited book by Gibson, Steven, Stefan Arisona et al. *Live Visual: History, Theory and Practice* edited by Steve Gibson et al. (Routledge, 2023).
18 Dundjerović, Aleksandar. *The Cinema of Robert Lepage: The Poetics of Memory* (Wallflower Press, 2003); *The Theatricality of Robert Lepage* (McGill-Queen's University Press, 2007); *Robert Lepage: Routledge Performance Practitioners* (Routledge, 2009, 2nd ed. 2019).
19 Reason, Matthew and Anja Mølle Lindelof (eds) *Experiencing Liveness in Contemporary Performance: Interdisciplinary Perspectives* (Routledge, 2016), p. 1.
20 Buber, Martin. *Between Man and Man* (London: Routledge, 2002), p. 241.

2

CULTURAL ARCHAEOLOGY OF DIGITAL PERFORMANCE

The historical evolution and the ontology of digital media performance are rooted in mixed and multimedia theatre, the historical development of which spans from the early 20th century. Is there anything new that digital media performance brought to theatre apart from different technology and the use of computers as a tool that audiences can respond to, given their familiarity with the social media content and available digital platforms? Is live digital theatre the response to audiences who are driving change as digital media culture has become their way of communicating and part of the experience of everyday life? Matthew Causey dismissed the notion that the presence of digital in theatre generates something new and different, "nothing in cyberspace and the screened technologies of the virtual" is unique from what has been done before.[1] However, Causey's *nothing new* is an observation on content, informed by the technology available in 2007, but not on how the content has been re-mediated and reinterpreted to the audience, particularly with the development of video communication after 2020. The audience responds to the technology they connect to as part of their everyday life experience to perceive content mediated through digital platforms. Therefore, the chapter looks into past creative methodologies and performance pedagogies, particularly regarding the audience and their relationship with pre-digital and digital theatre.

The investigation of the origins of live digital theatre will not be situated within traditional theatre: space is not a conventional stage-auditorium building, the playwright's dramatic text is not served by theatre staging, the acting style does not use agencies of realistic characters, and audiences are not passive consumers following a textual narrative. The origins of live digital theatre come from another theatre tradition: performance art in a time where theatre history crosses new expressions and challenges the audience's perception, immersive space and

DOI: 10.4324/9781003275893-3

images that incorporate various art practices, and new media art theory and practice development. It comes from illusions of image media.[2] For Steve Dixon:

> Digital performance is an extension of a continuing history of the adoption and adaptation of technologies to increase performance and visual art's aesthetic effect and sense of spectacle, its emotional and sensorial impact, its play of meanings and symbolic associations, and its intellectual power.[3]

Theatre as a discipline has undergone significant changes due to influences from performance art and media that entered theatre-making in the 1960s. In theatre theory, a substantial shift from written dramatic text to the significance of live performance came at the beginning of the 21st century; in Lehmann's definitive book *Postdramatic Theatre*.[4] Lehmann argues that in post-dramatic theatre, or post-textual theatre, looking at theatre forms and aesthetics since the 1960s, the dramatic text is secondary to performative qualities. Lehman's post-dramatic theatre is referential not to dramatic text but "dramatic" as the representation of action, physical expression in space, ceremony, and mise-en-scene of a performance created on stage not serving a written text. Lehman recognises that the live presence of audiences in space-time becomes part of the dramatic content while performing is taking place *now*. The forms of performances are shaped through this relationship between the audience and action as a live organism that calls for spectators' participation. As Lehman points out, post-dramatic theatre is "not the transmission of signs and signals...but theatre becomes a moment of shared energies instead of transmitted signs".[5] Post-dramatic as new "dramatic" does not negate text; it builds new theatre on the old form of text. It can be seen as a textual transformation into performative qualities compatible with live digital theatre's dramaturgy. Another theatre theory that contextualises performance as events being at the core of theatre and not a dramatic text is Erika Fischer-Lichte's view of theatre and performance as playing with performance conditions and interrelated processes of transformation since the 1960s.[6] Performance as events explores the connection between events and the broader context of intellectual, political, and socio-cultural conditions. These two contemporary dramatic theories focus on performance art aesthetics and production methods as they enter modern theatre practice.

It has been established that computer technology is essential for digital art. Without computers, digital media performance does not exist. The archaeological "digging" of the culture of digital theatre will recommence by understanding what makes the culture of online live digital theatre, particularly its practices and pedagogies. This chapter is about the evolution of performance practices in live digital theatre. Where does live digital theatre come from? This is a critical question when bringing various visual and performing arts and media together. It overviews how digital media performance originated as performance practice methodology and creative pedagogy. It identifies some of the critical points in its development, mapping the past into a present-day live digital theatre. It analyses the environment and the socio-political conditions that have impacted the culture, including various media and technological discoveries as a new media language in theatre and performance arts. This chapter investigates breakthrough movements – Futurism, Dadaist, events at Cabaret Voltaire, Piscator's Cinematic Theatre, Soviet Avantgarde, mixed media performances of Surrealists, Bauhaus art, Happenings, Video Art, and multimedia performance in the 1960s and 1970s and practices of early cybernetic theatre and concept of Fun Palace that brought interdisciplinary digital media into a theatre performance.

Mixed Media and Radical Performance Art

As Dixon points out, early radical performance art, Dada and Surrealism, inspired digital performance and the "content and style of artistic expression". He continues: "Digital performance commonly explores representations of the subconscious, dreams, in fantasy worlds, as well as other central teams of early 20th-century surrealist art, film, and theatre".[7] The totality of performance art experiences and technological innovations in the 20th-century avant-garde contributed to multimedia and digital theatre development. Examining relevant art movements and theories configures digital media archaeology as they are present in live digital theatre. The past performance movements that come into the aesthetics and methodology of digital media performance are mapped.

The mixed media concept will be explored to understand the working mechanisms of digital performance. Mixed media is artwork made through various art materials from different disciplines, contrasting with multi-media, which integrates electronic media, particularly television, audio, and video. The Tate gallery website situates mixed media arts around 1912, contributing to the cubist collages and constructions of Pablo Picasso and George Braque, becoming open to various "attitudes to the media of art. Essentially art can be made of anything or any combination of things."[8] The tradition of mixing media aesthetics can be traced to the mid-19th-century opera composer and inventor Richard Wagner, who used the term *Gesamtkunstwerk* (total art or synthesis of art) as bringing different forms of art to create a coherent unit, which is relevant to the aesthetic idea of *total theatre* by Edward Gordon Craig that unifies all arts within the medium of theatre.[9] As theatre already consists of speech, song, space (scenography), movement, painting and light, it is an art form that can bring all other arts together in a room. Craig, developing further from Wagner at the beginning of the 20th century, revolutionised performance by mixing the actors' movement and masks (replacing actors with marionettes), abstract symbolical spaces (defined through screens, shapes and colour) and rhythm of music/sound. Craig's vision of total theatre replaced the actor with an Uber-marionette manipulated by the director, effectively creating the first digital performance avatar, as some kind of an ur-avatar of the human body, but present within physical performance space.[10]

Mixed arts adopted this artistic philosophy in the early interdisciplinary mixing of expression as in the Dada movement and Bauhaus school. The works of radical avant-garde in performance, similarly to digital revolution is breaking away from traditional art, delivered social and political messages by combining communication networks though acting, dance, poetry and music, painting, and sculpturing. These movements became part of performance art as an umbrella for various alternative theatrical expressions and social commentaries. Among the first were Futurists, in the first decade of the 20th century, whose soirées used different artistic disciplines and materials in mixed media performance events. Futurism aimed to synthesise art, connecting art with technology and the innovations of the day. We can see their many manifestos as a blueprint of a future digital theatre. Italian poet and playwright Filippo Tommaso Marinetti exuberantly declares that beauty in the world is the speed of "a roaring motor car which seems to run on machine-gun fire".[11] In Italy, Futurist painters became performance artists taking up performance events to express themselves. They set up the first mixed media art events, attacking society and culture of the past through image and sound poetry, abstract painting, graphic design and noise music. In 1909, the founding figure of Futurism, Marinetti, published the "Manifesto of Futurism", containing his vision of the movement, on the front pages of the Paris newspaper *Le Figaro*. The significant exposure of this publication gave the movement cross-European resonance. Futurism wanted to celebrate change by discrediting the art of the past. The keywords in the first manifesto were *revolt, courage, roaring motor car, the beauty of speed, revolution, energy, young and robust and violent assault of poetry*. These words promoted aggressive action (militarism, anarchism, glorification of war) and rejoiced in innovation, mechanisation and technology of the new century, welcoming the future.[12] Although Futurism was noted in art history for its con-tribution to visual art, most of the founding members focused their energy on thea-tre, giving it a central role in many Futurist manifestos. Theatre became the preferred art form for their expression due to its live interaction with audiences. Marinetti needed the live audience's interaction and response to engage in provocation and assault on the values of Italian society of the day. His first manifesto blasted the public; it called for destroying museums and libraries and rejecting tradition. Futurist soirées carried the same explosive energy as the manifestos.

Futurism was the first art movement to put the relationship between men and machines as central to their creative process, celebrating technological discoveries. The focus on integrating art and technology was essential for the futurist ideal of what culture and society could be made to look like in the future. For Futurists, machines and new technology were welcomed as a way the world would develop. Moreover, Futurists saw the convergence of different arts in theatre as the best way to organise the contemporary expression of self and society in a way that would relate to the world they were responding to. The short, fragmented theatre plays could be very well presented as performances in the live digital theatre. However, their real impact on the future were manifestos. The first manifesto rebelled against inert Italian culture. It was a subversion of the official and mainstream and an attack from the youthful generational movement that related to those, as they said, "not older than 30". Futurists proposed different approaches to making art, a burst of energy that moves society, and violent confrontation with established values, thus changing the perception of theatre performance events. Futurists were not doing text-based theatre; their performance was based on some sketches, but more than that, it was an event involving audience participation. They offered another way of making art and performance as their vehicle by setting up experiments. Mixed media performance brought on stage agitation through short, performed sketches, concise futurist poems, loud music as noise, and audience participation elicited through attack and provocation, deliberately creating a sense of danger and emergency.[13]

Futurists set up a context that would be followed by other performance art movements such as Dada and Happening, where interaction with the audience was participatory, intended to provoke involvement. As with live Zoom theatre many decades later, the audience was openly present and influenced the performance event. However, in a Futurist soirée, throwing insults at the audience and eliciting their response was part of an event. The audience accepted the game and set convention, and in an early example of participatory theatre, they responded by shouting back and hurling rotten vegetables and eggs. Performance as a recital was founded on noise, the sounds of machines and the street, and poetry built around one root word in repetition, which functioned more as a phoneme – a sound removed from the meaning behind the word. In Russia, Futurist artists, writers, musicians, and theatre-makers had a robust cultural presence underpinned by revolutionary political ideas allied with the 1917 Bolshevik revolution. Vladimir Mayakovsky, a key proponent of Russian Futurism and a leading poet, playwright, and actor, influenced revolutionary performance and art development in Soviet Russia. One of Mayakovsky's best-known plays, *Mystery-Bouffe*, written for the 1918 anniversary of the Revolution, is an attack on the Russian bourgeoisie, containing Futurist philosophy and a farcical agitprop re-working of a Christian mystery play. Russian theatre visionary Vsevolod Meyerhold directed the play as the first Soviet-style theatre production, marking a new era in society and culture. He took the Futurist conceptual basis of mechanisation and the symbiosis of art and technology to further develop his theatre constructivism through set and acting style, which later impacted his biomechanics.

Meyerhold embraced the aesthetic mechanisation of the performer and the new age ideology built on the idea that labour replaces creation, comparing able industrial workers to dancers in an ideal of creating a performer as a human robot. Meyerhold created non-human humans, a constructivist body that mechanically reproduced movements, an actor-avatar and a proto cyborg in a physical space. In *Mystery-Bouffe*, the actors' movements were repetitive and acrobatic, dressed in workers' uniforms on a set constructed of movable scaffolding as transformable units suggesting a factory machine. His bio-mechanics method is one of the precursors to the mechanical constructed body, with robotic precision movements.

This avatar sets up an almost mathematical model of sequences of physical etudes for actors' training, comparable to a computer's combinatory infrastructure. The plays of Revolutionary performance underline some of the previous themes and influences from Marinetti's Futurism. However, the Russian version of Futurism was rooted within Soviet state ideology and morphed as a tool for somewhat naive Communist political propaganda, using art to change the world. The Russian and Italian Futurist worldviews evolved from the angry attack, rage, and rejection of the past values of an old capitalist society in order to build a new world. Beyond presenting a caricature of the bourgeoisie, the embrace of the new world of technology and progress, led by artists, intellectuals, and the working class, pointed to a new world built in a new age out of the ruins of the old world through revolution and militant art.

However, it was Dada that became the avant-garde movement to take Futurist anger and the youthful, somewhat Utopian dream of a new perfect and much better society to a more advanced level of mockery and a rejection of the past, violently negating tradition and making deliberately non-sensical art. Dada was formed during the First World War as a reaction to it by artists and intellectuals who sought refuge in Zurich. It was a movement protesting, through performance art, the carnage of war that was ravaging European countries. Dada questioned every aspect of society through the satirical and non-sensical nature of their art events. Their grotesque refugee cabaret brought together a collage of various media, which responded to the dystopian cultural and social-political contexts of the time. The Dada movement confronted the crumbling values of old Europe with anti-war and anti-bourgeois rage and passion. In 1916, they used a nightclub setting to unleash Cabaret Voltaire performances that exploded in the space by mixing different media. The content was a collage of unconventionally staged poetry, reciting, music as silence and noises, performers with masks and cubist costumes, dance, manifestos, and theory reading.

Founded by the German poet Hugo Ball, the Dada movement attracted a group of artists from different countries who worked across different arts. They came from varied national backgrounds, including the French painter Marcel Duchamp, the painter and poet Francis Picabia, the Romanian-born French poet and performer Tristan Tzara, and the French-German sculptor, poet, and painter, Jean Arp, to name a few contributors. Through writing and mixed media performance events, Dada dismissed the canonical art established by the mainstream culture of the time and established authority. The context for their performance events was the dying socio-political order of old Europe during the First World War. Dada created a unique performance structure of fragmented events destabilising time and space unity. Their influence was enormous on performance art. After 1918, Dada spread internationally to Paris, Berlin and New York. Dada set the blueprint for interdisciplinary performance art, discord between time and space, dislocation of the human body, opening subconscious creativity, and a new way of deliberately engaging and challenging the audiences confronted with the performance. Dixon points out, "The destabilisation of time and space and, equally significantly, the visual fragmentation of the human body, unite the autistic trust of many surrealist and digital performance experiments."[14]

After the war, Dada morphed into the Surrealist movement through theoretical work, led by the French poet André Breton and his "Surrealist Manifesto" in 1924. Together with Louis Aragon and Philippe Soupault, Breton set the foundation of Surrealism in literature.

However, Surrealism extended its influence to film art in the works of Jean Renoir's "La Fille de l'eau" in 1924, Germain Dulac's "The Seashell and the Clergyman" in 1928 and the most influential, Luis Bunuel and Salvador Dali's "Un Chien Andalou" in 1929 and "L'Age d'Or" in 1930. Aesthetically, Surrealists used Dada collages and cut-ups as determinants of a visual style translated into digital media with editing capability, the cut-and-paste montage, making the computer a methodology for creating and manipulating images. They were participants in the arts events whose ideology they shared, as many belonged to the French Communist party. Aragon proclaimed that art has to serve social and political functions, announcing the end of the "art for art's sake approach", "apolitical works are militant works for the benefit of the bourgeoisie in power".[15] The view was that art has to be socially and politically engaged, in the same way as live digital theatre, for example, can empower communities to take an active social and political role by being internationally accessible online through live Zoom theatre (provided that there is access to electricity, computers and the internet).

Bauhaus, the avant-garde design movement, provided an educational archaeological background for the expansion of interdisciplinary creative performance pedagogy that prepared the background for pedagogies of live digital theatre. The artists of the Bauhaus school were pioneers in mixed media arts, shifting between fine arts and design and using artistic creativity to intermingle with technology and creative innovation. They provided a synthesis between art and technology, best evidenced in their architecture and buildings. The school's philosophy was demonstrated in the first Bauhaus exhibition in 1923 in Weimar, *Art and Technology – A New Unity*. The show was divided into two sections: Architecture and Art, and Design and Art, to underline their work based on how art examines the teaching of Architecture and, in turn, how architecture provides content for artistic design. Likewise, the section on Design and Art pointed to how everyday objects and their design were impacted by creative design. From 1923 to 1932, three Bauhaus directors, Walter Gropius (founder of Bauhaus, an educator, painter, sculptor, designer, and choreographer), Hannes Meyer and Ludwig Mies van der Rohe, provided different outlooks on the school and movement. However, as a point of departure, the critical importance of the 1923 exhibition is the robust artistic portfolio of artists coming together from different media.

In addition to architecture, the 1923 exhibition consisted of graphic design, painting, sculpting, choreography and poetry with Paul Klee, Wassily Kandinsky, and Gerhard Marcks. Oskar Schlemmer and Laszlo Moholy-Nagy had also taught in the Public Bauhaus Weimer Art School, founded by Walter Gropius in 1919. The school's central pedagogical philosophy positioned the principle of bringing together the art of design (architects, painters and sculptors) with industry to develop the artists as artisans able to work with objects and materials whilst joining arts, design and architecture. The idea of education through experiential learning as pedagogy was clearly outlined by Bauhaus and impacted future interdisciplinary pedagogies.

The approach to synthesising pedagogy and practice through the interconnectedness of multiple arts is exemplified in two leading Bauhaus creators whose works would have a future impact: Wassily Kandinsky and Oskar Schlemmer. Kandinsky's aspiration toward abstraction in conflating painting and poetry as a synthesis of words and colours in space is best seen in his sound poems with illustrations produced in his book *Sounds* in 1912.[16] He elaborated on the links between space, colour, lines and sounds. Schlemmer, a multidisciplinary artist – painter, choreographer and designer – gave an early idea of the virtual body. He created robotic costumes for Futurist dance, "The Triadic Ballet" (1922), transforming performers in costumes into the geometrical figure as robot bodies where human presence is absent.[17] His pioneering vision of intelligent robots as artificial figures, *Kunstfiguren*, remotely controlled and even self-propelled, suggests an ideal for an avatar. It provides an excellent example of a live performer representing a current virtual body through the synthesis of dance with technology. In 1923 Schlemmer started working on a pedagogical model for a modern multi-art conservatorium in the Bauhaus school. In the theatre workshop, Schlemmer developed the practice pedagogy and theory of Bauhaus theatre. As with architecture and design, experimenting with fundamental elements of form, such as shape, colour, and material, but without any particular goal, became primary in foundational training. As a performance that is anti-narrative and anti-mimetic, Schlemmer refers to his theatre plays not as drama texts but as dance, having a prior interest in articulating space where the human body converts into an object and geometrical figure. The mathematical interaction between body and space is what one faces in a live digital theatre where the performance is on a 2D screen, and the performer is self-filming, arranging the body's position and objects within space on the screen. Bauhaus pedagogy focuses on the students' understanding of the dynamics of motion and change, bringing together performance space and movement. The Bauhaus school was closed by the Nazis. Some artists and teachers then emigrated to the US, joining a new educational direction to establish multidisciplinary arts education at Black Mountain College.

Cinematic Theatre

The relevance of cinematic theatre is in establishing a new creative process by hybridising two distinct art forms. The new theatre of the Soviet Revolution provided the cinematic language for the new art form – cinema. Bringing into cinematic practices a *language* of theatre-making through the treatment of space/image in the film, montages, and cameras is essential for the interdisciplinary practice of live digital theatre, where film and theatre methods interphase. Bringing film within live theatre reconceptualised the perception of the proscenium stage as an approach to transforming space through a visual image. It was central to the works of Happenings and the Fluxus group. Advancements in digital technology allowed the theatre to join live and filmed pieces and to use performers and dancers who moved through space in an environment created through multiple film projections on different surfaces such as walls, ceilings, objects, and even the actors' costumes. In 1965, Robert Whitman, in the Happening *Prune Flat*, "a double image of one of the performers was achieved by projecting a film of only her onto the live figure, in exact scale".[18] He was exploring blending real and superimposed projections in visual installation. By projecting a film of a naked woman taking a shower on a plastic curtain onto which water was sprayed, a full-scale film image created the effect of the simultaneous coexistence of different media. In contemporary theatre, Robert Lepage mixes film and video projections with live images, companies such as Blast Theory project virtual reality onto diverse surfaces, and Punchdrunk creates hybridised spaces through site-specific, immersion, and video/film images.

Crossing two artistic disciplines, theatre and film, was initially institutionalised as part of the cultural policy of the new regime in a new approach to proletarian art that was, in its essence, interdisciplinary. The use of cinema in theatre came from ideological conditions prompted by the Soviet Revolution. In Soviet Russia, after the revolution of 1917, the state-supported development of new art aimed to create anti-bourgeois art for the new man, the proletarian class, who needed to be enlightened and educated in the new revolutionary proletarian ideology. Using theatre performance and film was essential in educating due to the high level of illiteracy. "At the time of the revolution, most Russians were peasants toiling under the yoke of big landowners and eking out a meagre existence. More than 60 per cent of the population was illiterate."[19] The Soviet avant-garde spread with the Soviet Revolution across society and culture, making new art for a new century. This was the starting energy and belief of the Russian Revolution in October 1917. Propaganda was a process of education that required a relatively sophisticated, informed audience. Conversely, agitation motivated the audience to action by appealing to their emotions with short, stark stories. Definitions from the first edition of *The Great Soviet Encyclopaedia* link propaganda with education and agitation with organization/mobilization.[20]

After 1918, cinema became the new art form of the Revolution. It was a new and popular medium that communicated understandable short film images to the masses, something like today's Instagram or TikTok. The critical influence on Russian mixed media expression came from the constructivist movement. It started in Russia in 1915 and was founded by architect, painter and stage designer Vladimir Tatlin. Tatlin was under the influence of Italian Futurism and poet

Marinetti's manifestos. Constructivism had a significant impact on Russian revolutionary art, particularly on theatre and film development. Russian constructivist
art, became an official art form in Soviet Russia. It responded to the need to align
art to society's socialist (communist) ideology. Constructivism was the product of
industrial institutions, engineering principles, and the organisation of material
properties, not a style with specific aesthetic qualities. The constructivist credo
was that artistic activities must achieve societal functionality; art on its own has no
value but is a model that demonstrates present-day conditions in an industry-
driven society with workers at the helm. Art is not there to represent reality but
function; the abstract functionality of a piece of artwork is above cultural
specificities.

After the First World War and in the interwar years, dissatisfaction with society
and the economy provided performance art with new agency. It showed the way
towards a new world and a romantic view of a future society that eventually gave
rise to Nazism in Germany and Fascism in Italy. Exploring mixed arts and using
the latest technology, primarily in film, as a communication tool that could relate
to the masses expressed art's new social function and ideology. In France, con-
juring movies into live theatre started with pioneering experiments in the 1920s
as part of popular entertainment in fragmented music halls and cabaret performances, refining illusion and effects. In the early 1920s, in Berlin, architect,
sculptor, and painter Fredrick Kiesler, who worked across a mixture of media,
believed that art should provide the collective experience of life. His theatrical
expression was made through abstractions that brought the high tech of his time
into moving kinetic space, consisting of elements such as film projection, rolling
screens, large circular film screens, water, mirrors and flashlights. Kiesler explored
the perspective and illusion of one physical environment with film projections
that included the actors' live action on the stage within the visual projection.
Media and live images in the space worked together as one mediated expression.
The influence of Italian Futurism and Marinetti on the Russian avant-garde was
substantial. They propagated the destruction of traditional harmony and rejected
the old world in favour of a new world where revolutionary art responded to the
expectations of the age of technological advancement and social and political
changes. This was the ideal philosophical and aesthetic position for revolution in
Russia.

In addition to having film projections included in the performances, revolutionary theatre found its purpose as the art to move the masses through a methodology consisting of a fragmented event-driven eclectic mix of new forms such
as red cabaret, variety shows, agitki (short plays as agitational propaganda), street
performances and large site-specific spectacles. Live digital theatre incorporates
visual narratives of mass media production. It integrates virtual, and augmented
reality with the visual language used in social media. – TikTok, Facebook/
Metaverse, WhatsApp, Viber and Instagram, and video communication platforms
such as Zoom. In 1922, The Factory of the Eccentric Actor (FEKS) published

their pamphlet "The Eccentric Manifesto", promoting technology, electrification and anti-Stanislavski acting realism pedagogy. However, their production of Gogol's *Wedding*, integrating film projections within a theatre production, came to a disappointing conclusion after the audience and critics rejected it. Ideologically, the film used in theatre as a new medium gave a novel revolutionary aesthetic. A new politically revolutionary age needed a new theatre. The mainly new medium of film was seen by Vladimir Ilych Lenin as a favourite art to address the masses in Russia and convey communist messages. Aligning Soviet film montages with dialectical principles became important for educating people about revolutionary ideas. Marxist philosophy through dialectical materialism, as an official Soviet communist ideological position, is represented in the foundations of Lev Kulishev, Sergei Eisenstein and Dziga Vetrov's theory and practice of film montage. Dialectical materialism, through montage, communicates thoughts and feelings by juxtapositioning sequences of images using poetics of visual images in silent films to evoke revolutionary experiences in the audience.

The new political reality of the Soviet era required the communication of emotions and political messages primarily to the uneducated and illiterate masses that quickly needed to cultivate a new political worldview. Lenin saw propaganda as a process of education that needed an audience knowledgeable to a certain extent. On the other hand, agitation had to motivate the audience to participate in the revolution, to mobilise. So, agitprop, an essential tool in educating and mobilising the masses for the revolution, necessitated new practices from film and theatre, a new way of making art that could enlighten people about their new function in the Soviet state. With visionary filmmaker and theorist Sergei Eisenstein, who pioneered film montage theory and practice, the film became an art form that substantially impacted audiences. Eisenstein's ground-breaking ideas on montage were formulated in his seminal 1925 film, *Battleship Potemkin*, which depicted a 1905 mutiny aboard a Royal Navy ship, underpinning the Soviet ideology of workers, farmers and soldiers taking power. Eisenstein's experiments with montage started from another medium and mixed two different methodologies – theatre and cinema. While attending the theatre studio of Vsevolod Meyerhold and scenography practices in the avant-garde group FEKS, Eisenstein learned the functionality of media and constructivist arts practice. He started to work as Meyerhold's assistant in 1921 in the production of *A Doll's House*, transforming the realistic stage space into a constructivist art abstraction. The new practice required a new approach to acting, staging, scenography and textual adaptation, as well as new pedagogy. The new performance practice of responding and applying theatre to social and cultural conditions initiated the creation of a new pedagogy where creative results required the director to be a pedagogue. After 1918, the training of student actors at the Moscow Art Theatre Studio was built on various realistic and non-realistic performance practices. The director was also a teacher, a master to follow and learn the craft from. "The director's first task was, therefore, intensive training of actors, the aim of which was to work out purely physical means of expression. The basic subject of the training, apart from boxing, fencing, acrobatics, jumping into the water, and riding horses, was biomechanics and its principles…"[21]

In Meyerhold's studio, pedagogy was interdisciplinary relevant both to theatre and cinema and based on biomechanics and eurhythmics, crossing theatre and cinema, with actors-training devised to help actors achieve physical and group expressivity through body and movement. In Meyerhold's pedagogy, the actor's body was a machine and learning how to control that mechanism was essential. The actor's art was equated to work, a means of industrial production. Meyerhold borrowed Fredrick Taylor's Scientific Management philosophy of breaking down the workers' factory activities into separate actions. Taylor observed workers, timed and recorded their activities, determining the tasks needed to complete the job and the most economical movements to get those tasks done. Meyerhold transformed this thinking into theatre and the efficacy of actors' physical activity through actions done at exact times, with rules of movement, purpose, and economy to achieve a specific expression and desired effect. Meyerhold's bio-mechanics sees performers as human machines in a space that resembles a factory. As in a factory, a theatre set includes treadmills, turning wheels, cubes, trapeze multiple levels, and machines. The main purpose was not to stage a text but to present the political and ideological concept of workers' power and to use theatrical exploration to discover a new revolutionary stage language. Above all, the theatre was engaging as Soviet political propaganda.

As a young theatre director, Eisenstein adopted Meyerhold's constructivist approach, combining art and technology, extending it to what he was more interested in – performativity, authorship, visuality, and physicality of expression. Like Meyerhold, Eisenstein did not make theatre support the verbal text and actors' vocal interpretation. It was an art with aesthetic consideration and a whole stage spectacle with a political message, which offered the director–author concept. In 1922, Eisenstein included different practices of circus acts, agitprop, songs, and the projection of his film, *Glamov's Diary*, in live theatre. He brought Meyerhold's influence back to his group of actors, a group of amateur artists typical of the Soviet avant-garde workers' arts state organisation *Proletkult*. His directing of Ostrowski's *The Wise Man*, a Russian realistic comedy text, in 1923, was cut to 25% of its original. Inspiration for theatricality was found in a circus as the most important form of entertainment for the Russian people's revolution. Learning from Meyerhold's theatre constructivism, seeing the stage as a machine, Eisenstein wanted theatre to produce an overall effect on the spectatorship, "an attraction is the fundamental unit of the theatrical effect…Attractions as units of the stage-audience interaction enter mutual relations; to denote them, Eisenstein introduces the term 'montage.'"[22] The staging of *The Wise Man* is considered one of the most significant theatre works, where Eisenstein applies his concept of "montage of attraction", which he would fully conceptualise once he moved into cinema into his theory of film montage. "Montage of attraction", the idea behind film montage, comes from another media – theatre – as a cross-over of one art form into another, and political awakening of the audience by distancing from aesthetic involvement to embrace the functionality and historical necessity. And with the introduction of video art into theatre performance, for example in the work of The Wooster Group, the montage would come back into multimedia performance. Synergy of theatre and cinema became essential in short films created on smartphones camera edited on apps and than shared by WhatsApp in rehearsals for Zoom live digital theatre.

By reflecting modern industrial world Constructivist art entered Soviet cinema through montage as a film's essential narrative and structural element. Dziga Vetrov established Soviet documentaries, newsreels, and cinema realism as an industry through the effective use of montage and camera. Vetrov is most known for his 1929 accomplishment, a documentary film, *Man with a Movie Camera*, where Vetrov used a camera as an eye. He set up a theory based on the camera as a human eye; the camera is an instrument capturing actual real life, developing Eisenstein's poetics into a documentary film and newsreel. Vetrov used Constructivism to produce Soviet films as a tool for the narrative of social change and gained international influence on the development of other practitioners. More importantly, Vetrov took the movie into the outside environment making it part of the human experience of the world. He created a cinematic documentary language as a unique artistic expression, thus making the film an independent medium, free from theatrical references and the studio setting.

In 1920s Germany, suffering from economic poverty, Berlin was the centre of artistic and ideological battles. The left was gaining strength, and the theatre was a significant driver of political and cultural influence. Theatre director Erwin Piscator took Eisenstein's ideas further to affect the spectatorship with the totality of epic theatre expression. Piscator started exploring successfully projected films on stage, connecting them with theatre plays. Wildly considered a multimedia theatre pioneer and cinematic theatre creator, Piscator used documentary footage to accentuate political issues, bringing edited newsreels into the performance space. Piscator was influenced by the destructions of the First World War and his experiences running a variety of theatres for soldiers on the Belgium front. He wanted to bring outside political affairs into the theatre; for him, every aspect of contemporary existence (early 20th century) was articulated by political events, "to give theatre a social function by making it capable of portraying and communicating on the political realities of the age".[23] After the First World War, Piscator started making engaged and politically relevant film/theatre productions relating to Germany's political situation at the time. The Weimar Republic, the state left of broken Germany, sustained heavy losses in the war, was very poor, and had high unemployment. Piscator's montage of theatre and film directly results from dialectical principles. He wanted the stage to represent the human stories of love, death, punishment, and betrayal, and then extend this to the outside world to point to historical necessities and dialectical processes. He needed cinema screens to project referent film material.

Piscator's political activism in theatre brought him into contact with anti-establishment and anti-war Dadaism, which had spread across Europe after the

Great war. One of Dada's artistic devices was photomontage, which juxtaposes separate images to make subjective and fragmented segments superimposed on prints. Photomontage became an essential principle in Piscator's theatre. Under Soviet revolutionary theatre, Piscator's political theatre allied to the Weimar proletariat's struggle for power. Piscator set up an agitprop group, the Proletarian Theatre; here, in a short period (about six months), he staged seven plays for working-class proletarian audiences, promoting revolution as a way to resolve social problems. In 1925, Piscator devised the documentary production *In Spite of Everything*. He adapted text and created dramaturgy for devised performance by inserting film news, political texts and direct quotations from known public figures, making an interplay of documentary narrative. Adopting the Marxist philosophy of dialectical materialism, Piscator developed theatre dialectics through the conflict of social forces, political use of opposite principles and juxtaposition of a series of present and historical events. He arrived at the truth through systematic contradictions of material conditions that produce ideas, as conflicting forces with contradictions are seen as a determining factor for continued interactivity.

The ability to make an engaged theatre comment on the totality of political situations necessitated a theatrical apparatus that could allow adequate production. A new type of production and communication with the audience that could provide a political viewpoint had to focus on the theatre machinery rather than on the play script. Piscator's documentary theatre used film projections, treadmills, and platforms, allowing simultaneous acting areas to structure the play in the space. In 1927, Piscator's seminal production embodied cinematic theatre and political dialectic performance in the adaptation of Ernst Toller's *Hoppala Wir Lebene*! Following Piscator's belief, theatre acted as a political tribunal in this performance. However, underneath the party politics and propaganda, what is significant in this production is an expression of a protagonist's destiny, an individual captured by historical forces. Moreover, this production is essential as an example of a creative methodology for multimedia theatre, and in addition, as Dixon observes, "one of the most historical precursors to the digital theatre".[24] Piscator documentary theatre used different media film projections, radio broadcast, sculptural–architectural monumental space, all physical properties of the stage as a machine, scaffolding and mobile transparent screen.

Using visual projections instead of a traditional stage set made of realistic physical material allows for transforming space and changing performers' environments without using theatre stage technology and doing any physical set change. The development of digital technology-mediated visual environments provides three-dimensional locations for performers. In *Hoppala, Wir Lebene* a performance narrative was devised that integrated visual and spatial properties with the episodic structure of self-contained events. For Dixon, Piscator made "self-contained episodes, in much the same way that hypermedia fictions and other online experiences including web-surfing do".[25]

1960s: Development of Video Art Performance

Video art in performance comes out of performance arts responding to social and cultural revolt; it is not only about technological gadgetry but, more importantly, about a way of seeing the world and interpreting it through an art form that interconnects with media. The 1960s to the mid-1970s were impacted by numerous political and social changes and movements relating to anti-establishment sentiment in youth culture. The height of the Cold War, the growing sense of instability over possible nuclear war with the Soviet Union, and the spread of global communication through television made the world more aware of geopolitical circumstances. Paris's famous 1968 student revolt epitomised dissatisfaction with the stalemate establishment and corrupt bourgeois values across the Western world. The movement was labelled counterculture. Counterculture in the USA provoked social and cultural transitions that reflected civil rights and new freedoms for human sexuality and women's rights, new age spirituality, the sexual revolution, and crucial anti-Vietnam war activism. Performance, visual art, and music responded to these influences and it was artistic voice that answered and embodied the ideas of these movements. Performance art in this period provided a powerful applied political tool for promoting change. Performance responded to new political circumstances by presenting the views of a group of artists organised around these counterculture movements, from where they were driving and contributing ideas. New technologies were included in the devising process, and space for performance migrated outside of mainstream theatre venues that the establishment controlled. In the 1960s, performance art started to share qualities of Process Art or Action Art prominent in arts (Jason Pollack's process of painting as an art form in itself), where making art is central and more important for the artistic endeavour than a final product. The creative process is not hidden; reframing the boundaries between different components of performance practice remains open and the dominant aspect of the work.

As a pedagogical practice, the beginnings of video art performance are connected to the small creative art community in Black Mountain College, North Carolina. Founded by John A. Rice in 1933, learning creative arts practice brought together the Bauhaus school's inventiveness and a combination of multidisciplinary characteristics. The educational model in performing arts was a laboratory for the interchange between arts and science expended in the Bauhaus school. The visual concepts for performance were absorbed in post-Dada and Surrealist influences referring to open form improvisations, chance, and accidental actions. In the summer school of 1952, artists, dancers and musicians' teachers at Black Mountain College – John Cage, Robert Rauschenberg, and Marce Cunningham created a seminal interdisciplinary performance called symbolically *Untitled Event* that pioneered something in an open and flexible form, live art events and set up a model that would be followed in the the 1950s as a Happening. Live art became the natural next step in the visual representation of the multilayers approach to paintings in space with natural objects. With experimental music, John Cage, music theorist, composer and artist, pioneered chance and incidental composition and taught classes in the late 1950s at the New School for Social Research in New York City. Cage's pedagogy was based on the invention of their notations for music, the interpreter's free choice, and the ability of performers to decide how to use their instrument. Pioneer of electroacoustic music and indeterminacy in music, he was also essential for other arts, particularly the development of modern dance through his collaboration with his partner, choreographer Merce Cunningham. The students-artists who met in Cage's classes, formed the first Fluxus Avant-Garde art movement in 1959, which was essential for the future development of audio and visual multimedia practice.

In 1959, Allan Kaprow, a student of John Cage at the college, created the live art event *18 Happenings in 6 Parts*, presented in a gallery in New York. Kaprow invited the audience to experience and be part of the event as something that happens spontaneously, using blending of all-around-the-wall film, slide projections, and wall-sized mirrors. At the beginning of the event, the performers gave the audience three cards with instructions relating to six parts of the event, each containing three Happenings coinciding in time with each other. A bell signalled the beginning and the end of each event. The audience could move between the events following the care instructions, making their connections out of those fragments. The success of this live event resulted in a new visual participatory installation called Happening, which became a popular art form in 1960s New York, spreading to other cultural centres. The absence of meaning and overall narrative in Happenings allowed each artist to develop their visual imagery for objects in action in the space. This event-driven, audience interactive approach related to multidisciplinary artists who were good at working in-between different arts disciplines, typically poets, painters, designers, musicians and actors. Happenings then spread to Europe, with Yves Klein and Jean-Jacques Lebel in France and Adrian Henri and Jeff Nuttall in England creating Happenings. The way in which Happenings relate to the audience and space, the use of multiple media, and how the performer addresses the audience, influenced the formation of live digital theatre aestheticism.

With more advancements in technology, the invention of the Video Tape Recorder (VTR) was the beginning of another phase of creativity in setting up a context for multimedia performance. In 1951, and with the discovery of the magnetic head that could provide a better-quality picture in 1953, the recording of television programmes was possible. By 1965, VTR was made for home use by Sony.

Some of the technological developments of the 1960s that were influential on multimedia art include the creation of video and integrated circuits in computer electronic components, giving birth to microelectronics. This period saw the advancement of video technology and the introduction of portable cameras. For artists, the technological simplicity of a videotape recording (VTR) machine permitted easier access. The inexpensiveness of screen and video monitors allowed many groups to integrate media within performance space, bringing film and video into theatre performances. Since the 1970s, video technology has become accessible on the market for home use and a valuable tool for visual and performance artists. In 1965, the introduction of the Sony Portupak portable electronic camera changed the art scene. Developed as part of the new VTR technology, Portupak had a transformative effect on the artistic approach to visuality, performance space and own creative practice. Market available electronic technology, video, camera and mixers became tools for recording, documenting and creating, integrating the technology of the new medium into performance practices, allowing individuals to add their own approach to how tech is utilised to articulate illusion and reality.

From the early 1970s, VCR and video cameras became more widespread for home use. As VCR technology became more financially affordable and available to independent theatre groups, becoming part of the new technology for making performances. As an economical and cheaper option than building a wood or metal set, the video became a visual setting as scenography.

The mobile camera Portapak was mainly popular with artists to record outside life, and their own performances, and reach wider audiences inspired by television communication. By bringing mediated visuality into the space, video (and film previously) allowed non-theatre spaces to become performance locations. Any site – galleries, warehouses, community halls, garages, old fire stations, etc. – could be transformed through video into a performance space. Video also allowed multiple locations to converge within the theatrical space. Video technology captures visual images and the performers' actions as a combination of living, recorded and multimedia ways of communicating with audiences. Actors could be part of a video image or carry portable projectors; their bodies could be a projection surface, and stage events could be filmed with a camera and shown live on a television screen or projected on stage. Now there were multiple possibilities for video and audio interaction with live performance, where multimedia technology broke down the barriers of theatrical practice into different production elements, blurring the lines between actor, camera and screen.

Andy Warhol, a visual and pop artist and maker of Happenings, started using Sony cameras in 1971 in London to explore the medium of video to create experimental films in his iconic work. He made videotape recordings voyeuristic observations and filming life as art, creating screen-printed art, and setting up a cable channel to communicate with his followers/subscribers, famously proclaiming that he was making art in that way because "I want to be a machine." In many ways, Warhol, with his iconic media personality, was a precursor to digital communication and art, including internet platforms that have followers and likes, influencers and cult personas operating within the totality of visual and narrative presence. In this period, multimedia's impact on art came from several diverse artistic references and cross-disciplinary exchanges: Fluxus, Performance art, Pop Art, experimental film, avant-garde music, and contemporary dance and theatre. In the following decades, key practitioners such as Bob Wilson, Elisabeth LeCompte, Robert Lepage, Meredith Monk, Yvonne Rainer and Trisha Brown, to name just a few, explored multimedia in theatres.

Video art performance reflected an alternative approach to the creative process and highlighted ideological differences that groups of artists and movements held as counterculture. In addition to having a spatial presence, in the late 1960s, live performance video projection corresponded to intense political conditions and cultural changes. Using television sets and videos of found footage material was made more accessible to artists who were previously creating their own film material. Video became a symbol of protest, a response to the hegemonic influence of television, of what was in the mid-1960s the beginning of television culture that dominated everyday life in the USA. The collective performance reflected community spirit and beliefs. They shared common values prompted by anti-Vietnam war sentiment and deeply held desire for significant social and cultural change. Most Western theatre and performance artists were on the political left of the capitalist structures and mainstream theatre. That social consciousness was visible in the choice of venue, performance aestheticism and the combination of preferred art forms most suitable for their expression. Multimedia performance art events were about activism and anger, fused with a response to everyday life and political action.

In 1962, the Judson Dance Theatre company based in the Judson Memorial Church in New York created its multimedia practice based on the pedagogical environment of Merce Cunningham's studio, where the company members studied. Cunningham's arts pedagogy looked at dance as an experience of movements shared by all of us as physical actions, "you can see what it is to break these actions up in different ways, to allow passion, and it is passion, to appear..."[26] The company studied with Robert and Judith Dunn, who, in turn, were students of John Cage's experimental music, introducing the indeterminacy of exploring the boundaries of what can be considered dance. The Judson Dance Theatre brought together filmmakers, dancers, visual artists and composers, all of whom functioned outside the conventional use of a form of representation. The performance practice created was nourished in artistic and cultural conditions influenced by Pop Art, installations, and performance art Happenings in the 1960s. They made a space where a professional dancer could collaborate with non-dancers to devise multimedia dance performances.

There was no formal choreography or virtuosity of a technique but a series of actions, such as games, rules and tasks, with improvisation as the primary approach to creativity. Conditions were created where "any movements that arose within those boundary conditions became a dramatic action".[27] Due to the interconnectivity approach to practice, boundaries between dance and theatre became blurred. Pina Bausch comments that it is "a simple question of when it is dance, when is it not. Where does it start? When do we call it to dance? It is related to bodily consciousness and how we form things."[28] The emphasis on the body as the embodied presence became the central preoccupation of multimedia within live theatre. In the 1970s, the space for media performance transformed with video technology from "me and my body in space" into "me and my body on the screen in space". Mediating presence in live and recorded reality became an essential aspect of performance and visual arts. This progresses with the digital version, where physical body presence translates into digitalisation as a cyber body, bringing together live and virtual.

The response with a new practice and pedagogic methodology for collaboration in devised performance came from The Dancers Workshop Studio in San Francisco. In 1964, the creative method RSVP Cycles was created by Anna Halprin and her husband, landscape architect, Lawrence Halprin. The focus of this method was on the physical body and spatial environment. It became a performance lab bringing together explorations with the body – physical expressivity and creativity, and relationship to space, involving innovators in cross-disciplinary collaboration – dancers, designers, performance and visual artists, musicians, poets and writers of the time. Anna's workshops and studio drew on cult artists such as Meredith Monk, Yvonne Rainer, Trisha Brown, John Cage, Terry Riley, Alan Kaprow of the Environmental Happenings movement, and Merce Cunningham. Anna Halprin was a pedagogue and her approach was based on simple body movements focused on the self within the body in relation to space. The couple had studied Bauhaus at Harvard and were interested in developing community participation in the design process, connecting art with nature in urban living. Together they created the RSVP Cycles, using communication ideas (in French, the request for a response), arranged in the convenient order RSVP as an

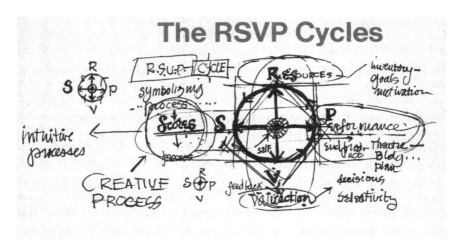

FIGURE 2.1 RSVP Cycles Diagram (Book Cover) Cover. Lawrence Halprin drawings from Lawrence Halprin Collection, The Architectural Archives, University of Pennsylvania

invitation to the audience to respond and encourage participation. The initials indicating Resource, Score, Valuation, and Performance are an innovative methodology in creative dance and design processes that could also be applied to different disciplines from dance to landscape design.[29] A critical aspect of the RSVP Cycles is their ability to adapt to any human creative process and their flexibility to transform and evolve. The RSVP Cycles provide freedom to creative practitioners to engage, through playing, with the environment and resources during the various stages of the creative process. This working process provided a learning environment for devising performance using a fundamentally multimedia approach. The Cycles were the perfect synergy of body and space, an essential element of group performativity, and the origin of devised theatre pedagogy, providing performers with multi-vision and a strategic outline from which to work.

Cybernetic Theatre

Alongside the political and cultural evolutionary changes in society of the 1960s (birth of pop art and culture, women's liberation and civil rights movements, Anti-Vietnam war civil unrest in the USA, the development of international youth counterculture and the global protests of 1968), came the development of computer technology, which brought revolutionary change and provided the impetus for the digital multimedia performance creative process. As in the period of the First World War, which politicised art in Europe, in the USA, the politics of the anti-establishment and social turmoil of the 1960s had a strong impact on performance, which embodied and directly reflected these changes. It has been established that digital performance began with the use of computers in the creative process of theatre-making. Computer technology allowed performance artists, directors-authors and collaborative creative groups to experiment with multiple media and arts in their productions because they all used the same language of digital computer technology: sound and light design, music and visual images, film and video with Computer Generated Imagery (CGI) and digitally mastered Visual Effects (VFX). Mass media communication via television was an essential inclusion into performance art during that period in the same way the internet provided a global communication connection in the 1990s.

Today's computers came out of a *thinking machine* as an accidental discovery while trying to find a mechanism to unlock the encryptions used by Enigma, the German Navy secret code machine in the Second World War. The British mathematician Alan Turing invented the device to decode Enigma. Turing's thinking machine, also known as a universal Turing machine, captured principles of computer science and provided a foundation for developing computer technology.[30] By the 1950s, businesses in the USA saw the advantage of using computer technology. Computers became essential to business and led to the birth of a new industrial age known as the digital revolution that would change people's lives and society. In the 1960s, computer technology was in its infancy.

Computers were very bulky and cumbersome. Due to substantial economic costs, the early computers in the USA were only available to either university or military institutions. Inthe beginning experiments with computer arts and films resulted from the people who had access to a computer, namely scientists/and industrialists. In 1965, a pioneering computer-generated art and film exhibition was held in New York in Howard Wise Gallery, by a wealthy industrialist interested in integrating art and technology. The artists' use of those first analogue computers was the precursor to early digital art pioneers. Computer-created imagery became a distinctive artistic expression; editing analogue and digital gave new optimism to visual artists.

In the 1970s, computers were compared to the human brain, entering popular imagination through sci-fi. Electronic brains became commercially popular and part of a new generation's wish to benefit from their personal computers.[31] In England, the progress of computer technology in visual arts and music was strongly represented. In 1968, London's Institute of Contemporary Arts created a large public exhibition, *The Cybernetic Serendipity – The Computers and the Arts*, bringing together 325 artists and engineers; with computer graphics, film animation, and computer-played music centralised on cybernetic machines.[32] In the 1960s, Cybernetic Theatre was the artistic philosophy that amalgamated interdisciplinary connections between theatre performance, architecture design and computer science to create a new methodology for the artistic, creative process. As a performance practice, it was in a very direct way a precursor of live digital theatre: computer, space and performer engaged in an interactive duality of physical and digital space, immersive images and sensorial audience participation, performers, and spectator computer-controlled relations.

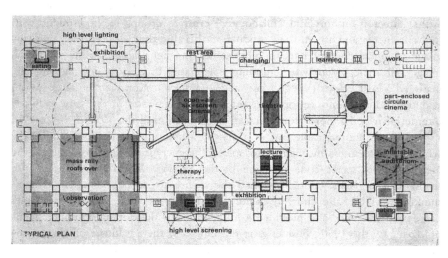

FIGURE 2.2 Typical plan of Fun Palace complex ca. 1964
Cedric Price fonds Canadian Centre for Architecture @CCA

In 1965, Gordon Pask, cybernetician and mathematician, developed the manifesto "Proposals for a Cybernetic Theatre" for the project performance–architectural interactive creative learning environment *Fun Palace*. The idea for *Fun Palace* was initiated as an extension of theatre practitioner Joan Littlewood's Theatre Workshop's innovative method through improvisation and audience participation and visionary architect and educator Cedric Price, education theorist and innovator. As a community arts amusement venue, Fun Palace was supposed to be a transformative art space for the educational and cultural activities of the ordinary people in the community who may not have had access to education in Britain in the 1960s. It was a proposal for hybridisation as the first interdisciplinary and interactive venue bringing together theatre, architecture and computer technology. Pask's cybernetics is based on the conception that everything is a communication system. He applies those communication systems to the design of a space and to a series of performance actions that will be taking part in it.[33] As a closed system, a matrix of space and time, and a mesh of live connections between audience, space and actors, Cybernetic Theatre is "a world of overlapping and crossing semiotics and reference frames that would process feedback from the audience to the actors on stage – through a carefully designed computer program – to create new knowledge and epistemological networks".[34]

The method of Cybernetic Theatre practice correlated to Halprin's RSVP Cycles. The Cycles have been connected as a practice methodology relevant to Second-order Cybernetics, known as the new Cybernetics, developed between 1968 and the mid-1970s.[35] Ranulph Glanville, cybernetician and design theorist and professor of architecture, came up with the new cybernetic notion of design developed following the nature of feedback and communication, transformation and process that invites spontaneous creativity (which is the essence of the RSVP Cycle). Tim Scholte positions " Glanville's second-order cybernetic formulation of the design process within the categorical boundaries of Halprin's RSVP Cycles", pointing out that the RSVP Cycles reinforce Glanville's claim that "the cybernetic conception of design, and its procedural, ethical and aesthetic entailments, reflect...the 'mechanism' at the heart of its most successful extant practises".[36] Cybernetics' examination of the relation between theory and practice is not in the applicability of one to another, but in its circularity by building on each other in the communication process. This communicational idea central to the RSVP method is relevant to the cybernetic theatre (and later on to live digital theatre). In that sense, when analysing a system such as the RSVP Cycles, the system itself can incorporate those systems of communication; predicted questions and answers that will have an outcome – a performance, landscape design, or any other creative artefact – that will change depending on the system. There is a lack of control from the point of view of the designer/deviser, as it is all based on methods of communication. To respond to the enquiry, the system must adapt and predict all the possible answers. Through the four phases, RSVP Cycles allow the practitioners to deal with simultaneous multiple queries that have, as an outcome, an open-ended creation.

Conclusion

The cultural archeology and origins of digital performance are in performance art political art activism as a social theatre of change responding to local community topics and themes. As they responded to world events, most of the Dada artists were from international backgrounds; manifestoes proclaimed their radical and big picture of the world. Manifestoes were produced to set up ideological and artistic principles as a cultural and political revolution declaring a programmatic set of objectives behind the art movement. Performance art practices' approach to making art transgressed and even directly rejected established bourgeois art and traditional theatre, often text-based literary theatre. As a weapon against social and artistic conventions, they attacked the past by proposing radical social and political programmes and contexts to which a generation of young artists responded. They wanted to be anti-art, subverting norms and celebrating protest, rejecting established values of the academic fine art tradition and society, seeking to influence man and change the world through art.

Direct communication and connection in the early avant-garde, as in contemporary digital media and social networks, provided the necessary connection with the audience to relate to content without an intermediary (in opposition to the practice in traditional theatre that would have structured narrative provided by playwrights and concept by the director, with actors representing these themes and ideas on stage). New digital media, as before television and video, found their presence in performance events; in the same way, digital technology shaped the way contemporary theatre is experienced by audience. However, outside of technological developments, multimedia theatre in the 20th century had a limited understanding of what digital technology could do to educate actors and use interdisciplinary performative practice pedagogies to make a live performance. Undoubtedly, the actor/performer's body, either real or virtual, is at the centre of theatre performance and sits at the crossing point of different media. Multimedia in live theatre necessitates that the actor enters a collaborative partnership with other media as they are another performance element, a group member, or an environment in a dramatic scene. This leads us to performance practitioners who operated within what has been established as an academic concept of Intermediality, which will be examined in the next chapter.

Notes

1 Causey, Matthew. *Theatre and Performance in Digital Culture* (Routledge, 2007).
2 See the analysis of the historical development of visual image as an explanation for new media creations in virtual art in Oliver Grau, *Virtual Art* (The MIT Press, 2003).
3 Dixon, Steve. *Digital Performance: A History of New Media in Theater, Dance, Performance Art, and Installation* (MIT Press, 2007), p. 40.
4 Lehmann, Hans-Theis, *Postdramatic Theatre*, trans. Karen Jurs-Munby (Routledge, 2006).
5 Lehmann, 2006, p. 150.

6   See Fischer-Lichte, Erika, *The Transformative Power of Performance* (Routledge, 2008).
7   Dixon, 2007, p. 67.
8   Tate, "Art Term: Mixed Media". https://www.tate.org.uk/art/art-terms/m/mixed-media
9   See Walton, Michael ed. *Craig on Theatre* (Methuen Drama, 1983).
10 Avatar is a computer-generated electronic image of the human body that can be controlled by a computer user (as in a computer/video game).
11 Marinetti, "The Futurist Manifesto", *Le Figaro* (20 February, 1909), p. 1.
12 See https://www.societyforasianart.org/sites/default/files/manifesto_futurista.pdf
13 See Image https://collections.library.yale.edu/catalog/2009459
14 Dixon, 2007, p. 68
15 Quoted in Lewis Helena, "Surrealists, Stalinists, and Trotskyists: Theories of Art and Revolution in France between the Wars", *Art Journal*, vol. 52, no. 1, 1993, pp. 61–68, p. 61.
16 Kandinsky, Wassily. *Sounds* (Yale University Press, 1981).
17 See O. Schlemmer's *Das Triadische Ballet* https://www.youtube.com/watch?v=AxD1OXpCLLk
18 Dixon, 2007, p. 91.
19 Behrent, Megan "Education, Literacy, and the Russian Revolution", *Culture Matters* (November 3, 2017) seen on https://www.culturematters.org.uk/index.php/k2-users/item/2651-education-literacy-and-the-russian-revolution
20 MacKay, John. "Built on a Lie: Propaganda, Pedagogy, and the Origins of the Kuleshov Effect", in Jonathan Auerbach & Russ Castronovo (eds). *The Oxford Handbook of Propaganda Studies* (OUP, 2014), pp. 219–236.
21 Szczepański, Tadeusz. "The Wise Man Reconsidered Some Notes on the Performance", in Lars Kleberg and Hakan Lovgren *Eisenstein Revisited* (Stockholm: Almqvist & Wiksell International) p. 12.
22 Szczepański, 1987, p. 22.
23 Innes, Christopher. *Erwin Piscator's Political Theatre: The Development of Modern German Drama* (Cambridge University Press, 1972), p. 194.
24 Dixon, 2007, p. 78.
25 Ibid.
26 Cunningham, Merce, "You Have to Love Dancing to Stick to it", in Michael Huxley and Noel Witts (eds). *20th Century Performance Reader* (Routledge, 1996), p. 153.
27 Martinez Sanchez, Maria Jose. *Dynamic Cartography: Body, Architecture and Performative Spaces* (Routledge, 2020), p. 54.
28 Servos, Norbert. Pina Bausch-Wuppertal Dance Theater, or, The art of Training a Goldfish: Excursions into Dance (Ballett-Buhmen-Verlag Publication, 1984), p. 230.
29 See Halprin, Lawrence. *Motation*; Lawrence Halprin — Halprin Landscape Conservancy (halprinconservancy.org)
30 Turing's theoretical (1936 paper on Computable numbers) and practical (machine decoder for Enigma) research became the foundation of computer science, and today influences every aspect of contemporary computer technology and the development of Artificial Intelligence.
31 See Hally, Mike. *Electronic Brains: Stories from the Dawn of the Computer Age* (Joseph Henry Press, 2005).
32 Reichardt, Jasia (ed.). *Cybernetics, Arts and Ideas* (London: Studio Vista, 1971), p. 11.
33 Pask, Gordon. *Proposals for a Cybernetic Theatre* (1964), typed manuscript is available digitally on https://pangaro.com/pask/ProposalCyberneticTheatrePask1964r.pdf
34 Pask, 1964.
35 See Scholte, Tom. "Design Cybernetics Enacted: The RSVP Cycles and Devised Theatre", in Thomas Fischer & Christiane M. Herr (eds). *Design Cybernetics: Navigating the New* (Springer Verlag, 2019).
36 Scholte, 2019, p. 3.

3
INTERMEDIALITY

Theatre, from ancient times, interconnects, various artistic forms – storytelling, dance or physical expression of the body, music, space design and architectural structures, props and objects, costumes, and lights. As shown in the previous chapter, historically, performance art is the form from which live digital theatre developed. Dixon's "digital performance" concept is rooted in the strong tradition of performance art that further developed with computer technology.[1] Performance art aesthetically and pedagogically was always functioning as a multimedia form, establishing multidisciplinary connections. Introducing site-specific location, audience immersive experience, visual and audio images, and electric and digital media, theatre and performance art quickly accepted developments in new technology and included them in performative aesthetics. Advancements in digital technology allowed the integration of visual, audio, light design, and computer-generated images as they became compatible in terms of their use and extended to the multimodality of theatre performance; practitioners collaborate and explore their practice by bringing other media into their work.

The term intermediality is distinctive to digital performance and multimedia culture. However, it is also inherent to a live theatre pointing to pre-digital and radical avant-garde. It draws on many different artistic systems of creating meanings and forms of expression that can be introduced into performance practice. Discussing the work of multimedia theatre by Robert Lepage, Christopher Blum, observes that the aesthetics paradigm can be seen as "a formal-aesthetic approach to the theatre which, broadly understood, sees the stage, not in terms of its splendid medial isolation but as a space or even hypermedium where various media can be incorporated".[2] This impact on pedagogies creates new ways of understanding performance practice approaches. One of the IFTR Working Groups, *Intermediality in Theatre and Performance*, investigates the interrelation

DOI: 10.4324/9781003275893-4

between theatre and other media and the interconnectivity of different media in performance. Their aim is: "Locating theatre and performance as the focal point from which we survey, receive and re-engage with the media of film, television and the digital technologies foregrounds the performance process as integral to the intermedial exchange".[3] Crossing the boundaries of digital and other media introduced within the space and temporality of live performance creates new representation methods as acting now functions in the multimodality of theatre. The question for this chapter is to look for the pedagogies of creative practice from which we draw innovative practice methods within the intermediality of performance.

This chapter investigates schools of practice and methods and focuses on intermediality as the critical aspect of their pedagogies that will impact live digital theatre. We are starting from the visual and design art practice in the teaching of Bauhaus through the educational experience of Black Mountain College that incorporated the experiential pedagogy of John Cage and Fluxus, to Hélio Oiticica Tropicalism, interdisciplinarity of cyber theatre and understanding of performers' collaborative practice and a montage of mediated and live in the Wooster Group to improvisations with media in Robert Lepage transformative performativity. They all work outside the established pedagogies that are founded on a single art discipline (theatre, music, art, media, dance etc.), rejecting influences from the other art forms. The main reason for intermediality in theatre of these artists and companies is fluidity in the use of several different arts, and they best communicate by bringing one artistic expression within another. Often, in-between connections produce a new way of creating performance expression. Also, their approach to creative practice is outside of teaching and learning by mainstream institutions that support the dominant cultural and political narratives. We will examine the confluence of media, arts, and disciplines as the foundation of performative pedagogy and practice in live digital theatre.

The Black Mountain College and John Cage

Intermediality in theatre is about relations between different media within live performances. If we extend this understanding of media as text to Julia Kristeva's concept of "intertextuality", we can situate intermediality in a matrix of connections to the world of media references. Kristeva's inter-textuality points to relationships within individual texts as a matrix of other texts, where one literary text is made of relations to arts, social and cultural and subjective psychoanalytical influences through citation, repetition and transformation of content and conventions. The intertextuality rejects the understanding of the text as a self-contained entity viewing it as meanings taken from other texts or discourses. Kristeva points out that "Intertextuality is perhaps the most global concept possible for signifying the modern experience of writing".[4] Similarly, as intertextuality relates to one text referencing another, as a site of several different texts, intermediality in theatre points to the relationships between two or more media within the performance event, and with digital media culture, intermediality in theatre became a method for performers' creative practice and pedagogy.

The school that radically changed the approach to education for artists, that wanted "to be a school like no other", was set up in North Carolina, in the United States.[5] It was called the Black Mountain College. In 1933, John Andrew Rice, a significant figure in the development of liberal education, established a pedagogical approach of teaching art as a collaborative experience through integrating visual arts, music and theatre equally with other disciplines. Similarly to Bauhaus, as pointed out in Chapter 2, an innovative multidisciplinary school of arts, architecture, and design, Rice wanted to create a new generation of educated artists through a plurality of connections between artistic disciplines. Around the same time in Germany, the Bauhaus School was closed when the political mass movement of Nazis in 1933 took over the government, and before the start of the Second World War, most of its leading artists and teachers emigrated to the USA. With them came their arts practice and pedagogical methods. The student–teacher relationship was based on the artistic colony ethos of those who lived together in a community and collaborated. The teacher was a master, and students were apprentices learning by observing and helping the master at work and making their approach to creativity in the teacher's group and studio.

The Black Mountain College's arts education philosophy balanced humanities and arts with a democratic and communal society, educating a whole person. Some of the critical points of Rice's innovations in pedagogy were: "(1) the centrality of artistic experience to support learning in any discipline; (2) the value of experiential learning; (3) the practice of democratic governance shared among faculty and students; (4) the contribution of social and cultural endeavours outside the classroom".[6] The small community attracted artists from multiple disciplinary approaches, such as painters, poets and playwrights, dancers, performers, and musicians. The influence of Bauhaus's teaching was introduced and further developed by Joseph and Annie Alberts, who were among the first teachers in Black Mountain College, creating a method for teaching practice and effective pedagogy that became emblematic. With interdisciplinary strategy and experimentation in arts, the college produced over the next 25 years a new generation of artists who made a significant impact on American avant-garde. Black Mountain College closed in 1953; however, it provided an educational environment where American artists have drawn, producing a generation of influential students in the latter part of the 20th century educated within intermedial pedagogy.

In the summer school of 1952, teachers of Black Mountain College – musician John Cage, design artist Robert Rauschenberg, and dancer-choreographer Merce Cunningham participated in a groundbreaking intermedial performance referred to as an untitled event, or simply as *Theatre Piece No.1*. The event pioneered interdisciplinary performative pedagogies and set up a creative practice and pedagogy model that would be followed as an example in the 1950s. Working with freedom, exploring the relationship between art, technology, and body came together at the final rehearsal; the untitled event explored the fusion of design, dance and music made as equal and independent elements. These experiments pointed to live art as it became the natural next step in the visual representation of the multilayers approach to action and paintings in space with real objects, referring to action art, happenings and developments in performance art in the 1960s. In this period, media in performance proliferated, exploring the synergy between different disciplines. Technological development such as the video camera and recorder had transformative effects on media performances' mediateness, visuality, and locality. As with the inclusion of video in a theatre, media in arts required a new approach to the pedagogy of practice.

In experimental music, John Cage (music theorist, compositor and visual artist) pioneered inter-determinacy, chance and incidental creativity in music composition, believing in duration over harmony, with a more comprehensive interdisciplinary method that was developed from working in other disciplines of art (visual art [paintings and prints], prose writings, poetry, performance events and installation art). Cage's creative practice and pedagogy were influential across different arts – his thinking about the time, silence, process, and chance operation in his composition. Cage brought together the visibility of mechanistic intervention and technological manufacture of a musical instrument as an object and part of a composition, referring to his early works as "inventions".[7] His famous production in the 1940 work of prepared piano as an improvisation on the physicality of piano (borrowing from expressionist and absurd painting) used the piano as an art installation object in space, combining organic – wood and mechanical – metal structure. The sound was also altered; Jones explains that

> By inserting nuts, bolts, screws, and other mechanical (Frankenstein?) bits under the strings, Cage changed their timber and emphasised their percussive capabilities. He also rendered them unsuitable as vehicles for the vocal and instrumental traditions of Western harmony, putting listeners in mind the Balinese gamelan.[8]

While teaching from 1957 to 1959 at the New School for Social Research in New York City, Cage developed a pedagogy based on his approach to practice allowing students to invent their notations for music, to have interpreters' free choice in approaching composition, and to develop their ability as performers to decide how to use instruments, altering their visual objects and sound properties. His writing from the 1960s points out that his ideas about creative practice are not only limited to music but "extend these originally musical concepts…into the realm of poetry and creative writing in general".[9] Cage notation is showing a process of "un-connectedness" between elements that are in relational proximity in composition; it is a score as in dance or cartography, annotation with flexible open structure, indicating repetitions and durations, and combination of various timings of sounds, his "determinations and variations of other".[10] This way of scoring, in addition to music composition, can be very useful to the composition and structuring of performance events, dance, and theatre, particularly in simultaneous, immersive, and promenade site-specific circumstances. Cage's creative approach to music compositions and his visual arts was based on the chance of using the *I Ching*, the Chinese "Book of Changes", as a generator of random chance; he "tosses coins to free sounds" allowing "sounds to be themselves".[11] For Cage, structure in the composition is not about harmony but the temporal division of sounds and silences. As a pioneer of electroacoustic and indeterminacy in music composition, Cage was essential in bringing his practice into other arts, particularly the development of modern dance, through his collaboration with his partner, choreographer Merce Cunningham. The group of students formed from his experimental and creative practices using open structure, chance, non-traditional instruments, and indeterminacy in music created their community. The students – artists who met in Cage's classes, formed the first Fluxus Avant-Garde art movement in 1959, which is essential for the future development of audio and visual multimedia practice.

The artists involved in the international and interdisciplinary Fluxus, a diverse community of artists in the mid-1960s and 1970s, such as founding members and group coordinator architect and designer George Maciunas, performance artist and activist Yoko Ono, painter and initiator of art concept "happenings" Allan Kaprow, George Brecht, artist and music composer and Nam June Paik, pioneer of video art, among other members, held a common belief that creative process is more important than the finished product. John Cage was considered a "father" of the movement. Fluxus was very open to various creative methods, and different pedagogical aims, the guiding influences that came from Cage were the use of everyday objects and involving chance as an innovative material in arts. His teaching of composition as the temporal structure was essential for forming artists who attended his classes and came together to set up the New York Audio Visual Group, based in New York City, that later became Fluxus. The first Fluxus called proto-Fluxus events were staged in a gallery, AG Gallery in New York, in 1961, as a reading of a poem with similar events happening in the gallery, and later provided scenes for experimental and performance art in alternative venues to traditional theatre.

Fluxus and Nam June Paik

Fluxus' creative practice was based on the pedagogy of intermediality in performance and visual events. The group's approach to visual arts – space design, writing and performing – was to merge art and life and use technology at that time to break boundaries between disciplines, fusing them into one non-distinguishable unity. Although Fluxus was very open to various methods and different aims, the guiding influences that came from Cage were the use of everyday objects and involving chance as a creative material in arts. The space for performance for Fluxus events had to be located outside of theatre buildings and gallery systems, deliberately not as part of a mainstream venue on the banlieu of recognised, legitimate cultural locations for arts. Fluxus' approach to arts – space design, writing and performing, was to merge art and life. Fluxus would include audience participation in their performance as part of the process. As part of a discussion about Fluxus performance pedagogy, Marija Grinuik developed the term 'Hyper-performer' that refers to the participatory performance focused on the active involvement of audience participation where audience members were part of the performance and intermediality of the Fluxus network as "the space between media, focused on the sensorial experience of the participants".[12] Their inspiration came from the past movements of Futurism and Dadaism, and their direct impact came from two dominant artistic figures: Marcel Duchamp and John Cage. Cage was considered a 'father' of the movement as it was formed based on his teaching of creative practices. In their manifesto, they proclaim a call to action for an ideology against the prevailing elitism of high art and, in the spirit of Dada, cried out, "purge the world from bourgeois sickness...dead art, imitation, artificial art...purge the world of 'Europeanism'!"[13]

As one of the members in the early phases of Fluxus, Nam June Paik marked the 1960s with his remarkably influential artwork. Paik, who was Korean American, made video art integrating it within performance space, pioneering installation art. Paik's initial training was in classical music. Inspired by John Cage's teaching and creative practice, Paik, in his early career, wanted to combine music with the sounds from real life, exploring intermedial connections in bringing together audio, visual, dance and electronic media elements with historical and religious contexts relevant to his society at the time. In the early 1960s, Paik was experimenting with social and cultural critique in the form of video images existing in the physical space installation to address audiences with what he saw, social self-obsession with new television media and electronic technologies.

Through his manipulation of the electronic video image in establishing a relation to the performer's body, Nam June Paik created a media performance that engaged with the audience's interpretative experience. In "Cybernated Art", his brief one-page manifesto from 1966, Paik relates cybernetics to a network of relational processes, stating that "cybernetics, the science of pure relations, or the relationship itself, has its origin in karma...As the Happening is the fusion of various arts, so cybernetics is the exploration of boundary regions between and across various science."[14] In using television as an art object, a sculpture with physical extensions, Paik would place powerful magnets on a TV set to rework electronic video images. Paik invented video sculptures and technical devices such as demagnetisers and video-synthesizers. He combined signals into synthetic and natural images; Paik sculpted video/television images connecting them to clothing, garden architecture, creating aesthetics based on object and image. Paik's video art was a perfect creative ground for collaboration with performance artists extending video art into live performance space. In 1975, Paik worked with

Merce Cunningham in *Marce by Marce by Paik*. This collaboration resulted in the first experimental dance video as a "dance film" using video-synthesizers to create multi-layer effects juxtaposing physical movement and visual images. The visual background uses a television screen with video images (a range of landscapes and abstract environments) and interaction with dancers' physicality, edited with soundscape based on manipulation of external real-life sounds, TV, dogs barking, and the voice of two men in a telephone conversation.

For example, Paik was the first to use a television set as an art object juxtaposing it to the statue of Buddha in a 1974 installation of *TV Buddhas*, creating video dances and integrating video with live performances. His practice methodology impacted the development of new media arts and future decades of multimedia performance artists. He was the first in 1974 to point in the future direction in which technology would provide connectivity for boundary-free communication between people globally, coining the phrase "electro superhighway".[15] This term is the first pointer toward what will eventually become a digital connection and broadband communication, the internet. In 1995 Paik created one of his most influential video installations *Electronic Superhighway: Continental U.S., Alaska, Hawaii*, 51 connected television screen video channels with neon lights that outline monitors and sounds.

Hélio Oiticica's Tropicalism

Another important way of thinking about the intermediality of theatre as a creative practice and pedagogy is hybridisation. Hybridity is one of the central philosophical concepts in the 20th century, and writers such as Homi Bhabha use hybridity for the construction of transcultural forms of identity within postcolonial conditions.[16] Hybridity is a concept that has many forms, applications and loose interpretations. Still, it generally refers to mixing local and foreign references (ideas and beliefs) or cultures, languages and races. In performance arts, hybridity refers to a mixture of various performative traditions in creating something new or, as in live digital theatre, a combination of physical and digital creative expression that makes a hybrid form of physical-digital live performance. Performance artist Guillermo Gómez-Peña sees hybridity as an outcome of "border culture" or a site of mutual penetration that is either physical or psychological.[17] For Gómez-Peña, hybridity in Latin American art is a process expressed from colonial times. The method of cross-mixing hybridisation, where various interactions between cultures, people, skills, and traditions occur, had a resurgence in Brazil in the 1960s with the Tropicalia movement.

Brazilian Tropicalism had the most significant impact on global music, as a cross between electronic and Brazilian traditional music, through the composers Caetano Veloso and Gilberto Gil. From a fusion of traditions and contemporary influences in music, the other arts – film, theatre, and poetry mix artistic influences primarily between Europe and Latin America (Brazil). The movement was central in Brazilian arts activism, protest, and visual/live experience of restrictive military dictatorship government politics. It is also a site for communication, power struggle, negotiations, and collisions. As a mixture of outside Western and local Brazilian art, it was a political protest as a response to militant nationalism and pressures of Catholic religion instituted by the military dictatorship regime that, in a military coup, took power with the help of the US CIA-funded cover insurgency in 1964 (lasting for 21 years).

In live and visual arts, the concept of hybridity in the Tropicalia movement was established in the work of Hélio Oiticica's artist from Rio de Janeiro. The movement Tropicalism (*Tropicália*) came out of Oiticica's 1967 visual art installation *Tropicália*. Although created for a museum-enclosed space, the installation *Tropicália* brought into the indoor space a tropical favela architecture recreating the outdoors environment, complete with a hut, lots of light, sandpit, live tropical plants – palm trees together with parrots, accompanied by recorded atmospheric sounds, and a TV set. Hélio Oiticica materialises the idea of the sensorial experience "inviting this spectacle to enter the atmosphere, and he creates that providing the visitors with immersive experience."[18] Moreover, audience participation in the process of experiencing was essential for the performance event to occur. Their interaction completed the materiality of the artistic concept. They were asked to walk barefoot in the sandpit and experience the environment of tropical plants and birds, becoming participants in the installation. They become co-creators in the performative event by interacting with the space and objects.

Oiticica's work is essential for understanding the practice of a fusion of intermediality that is coming from different sources and entering into a mix within his process of making art. The philosophical foundations of *Tropicalism* have their precedent in cultural anthropophagy. As an original Brazilian art movement, in the 1920s, the poets in Sao Paulo started their avant-garde modernist revolt, led by playwright and poet Oswald de Andrade. He lived in Paris during the Primitivism, Futurist and Dada arts revolution and fashioned the Anthropophagic movement as the Brazilian model of arts interventions in society. He rooted the anthropophagic utopia in the Brazilian cannibal native tribe Tupi. Oswald de Andrade made the fictional national past into an artistic model for a future national culture, placing the idea of anthropophagi – cannibalisation as a way of creating something new by devouring, cannibalising, in a postcolonial context – eating white man culture and art and making its own. This response to the colonial culture of Europe was a model for Brazilian national arts. In 1922, the Semana de Arte Moderna presented a new modernist school of artists working in art studios in different disciplines: performance, paintings, poetry, sculpture and lectures about the avant-garde. In addition, the Anthropophagic Manifesto from 1928 was published in Sao Paulo, proclaiming new Brazilian primitive art made of the best parts of old European art traditions, in short, verbose, and punt-like proclamations, similarly to Futurist later date manifestos. Oswald De Andrade "subverted the ideology of European cultural conquest, transmuting it together

FIGURE 3.1 Hélio Oiticica, *Tropicália*, 1967, Tate Modern
Photo by Maria Jose Martinez Sanchez

with African and native Brazilian influences, and making out of these elements a new understanding of arts and culture that was nationally relevant for Brazil".[19] Out of the encounters between native, African and European traditions came the idea of devouring other arts and cultures. The anthropophagic performance is simultaneously a process of community immersion and experience and collaborative creation involving the audience in a ritual-like passage between different worlds clashing or *asynthesising* each other, for example, the structure of Candomblé rituals and a Catholic religious service. The modernist movement was the most significant departure, placing Brazil on an international stage and setting up a new pedagogy that would significantly influence the Tropicalism and artists of the 1960s.

Oiticica's first art school was associated with the Brazilian Neo-Concrete movement, where he developed visual arts based on geometry and colour. As a

break-away movement from 1950s Concrete art inspired by theories of cybernetics, the Neo-Concrete manifesto from 1959 promoted a subjective and
expressive approach away from rational, scientific and mechanical visual arts.
However, Oiticica's painting of wood that was hanging brought structural three-
dimensional space establishing the space as a significant creative trigger, transitioning from visual to performance art. Effective for the development of Tropicalism in Oiticica's practice is his initial contact with people living in favela
Morro da Mangueira in Rio de Janeiro. Getting Brazilian references from favela
into Neo-Concrete art of expressive and subjective visual/performance art laid a
foundation for the Oiticica *Tropicália* installation. Incorporating the audience into
a hybrid experience of the *Tropicália* environment, as in the anthropophagic process of getting the human body to a ritual, shifted "practices from visual arts to
the context of collaborative and participatory performing arts".[20] Hybridisation
was an essential aspect of mixing in *Tropicália* that is also expressed through
mixed-media experimental performance. Using a mixture of music, space,
objects, texture, fixed-film images moving in the space and still projections in an
installation that allowed for participatory audience involvement came out of
Brazilian visual and performance art.

In 1971 Oiticica escaped to New York from the Brazilian military regime and
oppressive conservative clerical nationalist dictatorship. Oiticica's exposure to the
New York visual and performance art scene centralised the intermediality of
experiences with immersion and audiences' sensory embodiment and presence.
Audience participation in real-time interactivity with large-scale installations
depends on the design of a space. Oiticica's site-specific installations explore
environments that could be perceived by the audience using all senses. He called
this approach *Delirium ambulatorium*. The creative process is triggered through the
subjective experience of the site as an experienced location which translates into
the art piece. The method is based on the discovery of space by walking around
the city or designated area without a fixed destination exposing yourself to different experiences and stimuli from the surrounding enticement. These stimuli
are taken back into the workshop and built into installation materials. The act of
wondering brings impressions from an authentic space remediated in artistic
imagination into visual and audio images. Martinez Sanchez points out that
"Delirium Ambulatorium brings the experience of the labyrinthine space of the
favela to Oiticica's work, clearly materialised in Parangolés and Tropicalia and
also visible in the Cosmococas."[21]

Oiticica's seminal work, *Block-Experiments in Cosmococa—Program in Progress*
(1973–1974), was developed through a collaborative process with avant-garde
Brazilian filmmaker Neville D'Almeida. *Cosmococa* was conceived in New York,
influenced by mixed-media installations, underground arts, Andy Warhol practice, and Brazilian avant-garde cinema. However, the live event was not documented, and there is no record of performative installation. The event applies the
Oiticica concept of 'super-sensorial', involving all senses in arts experience,

engaging the audience to enter the world of installation interrelating with it exploring areas of personal freedom in response to military repression in Brazil.

Cosmococa, made of nine 'super-sensorial' environments, embodied Oiticica's idea of 'quasi-cinemas', where he wanted to merge art and individual life experience. Each environment had instructions for the audience and consisted of the fixed film images moving in the space, slide projections, soundtrack, and cocaine powder drawings. The boundaries between visual arts and cinema became part of the integrated experience for the audience. Audience behaviour was central to the development of the installation. They were lying down in space in different ways, surrounded by visual projections, and "films were split into images or captures projected in the space".[22] It was not limited by time and had no actual beginning as an open program in progress. Playing with temporality was achieved through fragmented time and different durations with projected slides and still images. Oiticica's supratentorial approach as a creation of an immersive environment in New York's *Cosmococa* created a precedent for the audience's experience of Augmented and Virtual reality. It is rooted in the digital performance practice of mixed reality within live performance. We can see that Oiticica emphasises audience participation and immersion within the installation, and his 'super-sensorial' experience accords with the central notion of mixed reality VR and AR digital performance, viewed by a group of people living in a space as an event offering communal engagement.

From the 1970s, hybridity in combining recorded media and live performance through multimedia became globally widespread as a practice and teaching of performance art and theatre. The dialogue between stage and screen entered the performance space, where the screen introduced another level of reality into the performative experience. It became a traditional aestheticism and communicational device to include television monitors on set and video projections in a live performance. Technology was cheaper to use and to introduce into theatre and dance performances. The main characteristic of the experimental theatre was the focus on visual elements. Visuals became equal, if not more important, to the verbal and performance practitioners included in their work use of film and video.

The Cybernetic proposal developed by Gordon Pask on the architectural design idea of Fun Palace by Cedric Price in 1964 was a response to an interdisciplinary collaborative creative process founded on theatre actions and workshop pedagogy of Joanne Littlewood. The uniqueness of Fun Palace was in its new way of educating the community through what Littlewood called the university of the streets, "a laboratory of pleasure providing room for many kinds of action".[23] It was a joint venture and a utopian idea of an adaptable interactive space for people to engage in arts and culture as an interdisciplinary pedagogy envisioned by theatre artists, architects, and cyberneticians. Fun Palace reflected Joanne Littlewood's company Theatre Workshop's vision of training performers to interact with a variety of media and audiences, creating a model of education based on people's palace and culture houses following the Soviet Union Model of the education and arts venues for the working-class, bringing community and culture together in participatory performance around issues that matter to the community. Joan Littlewood played a significant role in initiating the Cybernetic Theatre through her workshop approach that emphasises an improvisational development of the parts of the performance. She brought together architecture (Price) as a performative interactive space and cybernetics (Pask) as a way to measure audience responses to arts events. For Cedric Price, *Fun Palace* was the vision of transformative architecture that builds on Littlewood's performance space for architectural space as a transformative event. Bringing cybernetics and space design had to measure the human behaviour in an environment as a relation of the body to space and also to predict human behaviour and invented narratives as they can come out of an interaction between performers, audience, media and space. The *Fun Palace* proposed an analogue spatial learning system, as part of which Paskian machines provided the first steps into architecture driven by a human–machine relationship. The projects outlined above drew from the notion of feedback, causality, recursiveness, and human participation and can be regarded as essential ingredients for (design) cybernetics. The visionary project *Fun Palace* was a utopian concept that never materialised. Still, it was an inspirational vision for the time to come, an idea that envisaged a culturally complex community, empowering people to be creators and consumers of art, where the audience can engage interactively and educationally, bringing together theatre, dance, film projections, video art, installation and sound/music.

Elisabeth LeCompte and The Wooster Group

Establishing performance practice and pedagogy within performance studies is connected to the group's creative methodology of Environmental Theatre. It came from experimentation with a body in space, in its environment. In 1967, Richard Schechner founded The Performance Group, the basis for developing environmental performance practice. The Garage was a name for a building, a former metal-stamping factory, and a run-down space in Soho. Soho was a natural part of New York, underdeveloped and full of empty warehouses, and therefore cheap to rent and accessible to performance artists. The Garage was converted into a black box theatre where the experimental theatre work was developed and produced by Schechner. Artists found cheap areas to reinhabit by renting or buying ex-industrial properties that could be turned into their art studios and performance venues. The main change came from the relation between performer and space and a unique location where both performers and audience are together, removing the formal physical barriers of the 'fourth wall' or having a proper theatre stage. In the tradition of Futurist, Dada and Happening, acknowledgement and confrontation with an audience as the first cases of immersive experience outside of the convention of the 'fourth wall' was also an essential aspect of Schechner's relation to the participatory role of the audience of the 1960s. Inter-relations between different media systems of communication – the physicality of live performers' bodies; the same space shared with the audience, become an environment defined by these systems within which the performance exists. The now iconic production of *Dionysius in 69* (D69), devised over a year-long period with Schechner and the group, displayed all the elements of experimental theatre: workshop improvisation drove rehearsals, openly showing the creative process to the audiences, interactivity between performer and audience, environmental theatre design – eliminating the separation between audiences and actors' space, group performances that continue to change over time, where actors rotate in different roles. *D69* was the first performance of The Performance Group that opened in 1968, emerging from Schechner's workshop, which started to develop in conjunction with his teaching at New York University that began shortly before.

After 1980, the Performance Group was succeeded in Garage by the Wooster Group, which is still active today. In 1980, out of his extended practice, Schechner established an educational program by setting up Performance Studies at Tisch School of Arts, New York University. His pedagogical approach was to apply performance to a broad spectrum of ideas, starting from the premise that performing is to act in life the same way as one would on stage or screen. Schechner created performance studies as an academic discipline related to various human activities. As he says, "anything and everything can be studied 'as' performance."[24] These performance activities correlate to everyday life: playing, sports games, entertainment, ritual, politics, and mass media, and could be extended so that performance can relate to the construction of ideas around race, gender, and identity. Performance studies legitimise a discipline of performing arts that could be studied and trained, such as collaborative group theatre, devising performance, applied performance, multimedia performance, digital performance art, and dance and physical theatre.

In the 1980s, the Wooster Group inherited the environmental performance methodology of Richard Schechner. It continued working in the Garage as a flexible multiple-use space developing its aestheticism in the direction of inter-mediality of theatre through exploration of elements of performance and visual art. The founders of the Wooster Group in 1975 were director Elizabeth LeCompte and her partner at the time, actor and writer Spalding Gray. It was set up in 1980 as a company continuing from Schechner's Performance Group, adding as core members Kate Valk, Jim Clayburgh, Willem Dafoe (latter Elizabeth's partner) and Peyton Smith. One of the main characteristics was that the group kept the performance ethos of a collective community creative as a theatre family and maintained a core membership with a full-time ensemble and evolving artistic associates. The Wooster Group created an iconic aesthetic and radically experimental performance that forged intermedial connections between group devising and the use of famous electronic media. Intermediality in the Wooster

Groop became internationally recognised for opening the boundaries of what can be used in theatre-making, using the experience of performance and visual arts, incorporating media, video, audio, and film, using a collage of texts, reinterpreting classical theatre and devising autobiographical material, exploring physical movement, and space design. As David Gordon points out, they were

> combining a highly sophisticated, rarefied aesthetic sense and a rigorously intellectual critical practice with an intense, often subversive energy. They became notorious for reenacting videos of themselves tripping on acid while also working with dedication to refine their craft and achieve their unique theatrical effects, built on virtuoso performance and flawless timing. Deconstructing text by combining multiple sources of material, splintering representation, and pioneering the use of cutting-edge video in sound technologies kept the group constantly at the forefront of theatre.[25]

One of the trademarks of the Wooster Group collaboration is the deconstruction of the textual material from an existing classical modernist drama, using it to create a new performance founded on fragments that become a starting source for a performance multimedia experience. Elisabeth LeCompte's performance deconstruction, as Arnold Arson observes in 1985, writing about the Wooster Group's *LSD* manifesto, is not applying Derrida's deconstructionist theories; "LeCompte says she is aware of the critical movement but has not read any of the sources – the Group's recent work provides virtually the only example of deconstructionist ideas put into practice in the American theatre".[26] The path to deconstruction was not through Derrida but by fragmentation of events and creating a new experience involving performer, audience, space and media. The expertise of Fluxus and methodology developed by the New York live visual arts scene was something the Wooster Group would be familiar with as a shared cultural context. On a production level, the Wooster Group ran the Garage as a shareholder within the Grand Street Artists Co-op, established in the 1960s under the Fluxus movement. The Wooster Group's practice and pedagogy in a collective unconscious way of passing ways of making art inherited from Fluxus, which are the contexts of chance and open ending, and understanding that the process of creating is more important than the finished product.

Wooster Group is an approach to referencing texts' internal and external relations as with Kristeva's intertextuality; however, including within interconnections the scope for other media, in particular, film and video, referencing popular culture and mass media. We can also see a direct relation to the creative film process. The practice method was based on a montage of attractions, the Eisenstein technique, used for a montage of different media with live action. Intermediality in Wooster Group theatre engaged with texts, visual images and audio content, stage design, physical movement, and an expressionistic acting style closer to performance art. LeCompte performance space has different visual layers created through scores reminiscent of Eisenstein film storyboards, using a montage of scenes as a video montage program inspired by visuals and aural images. By montage of multiple forms of expressions taken from different media as aesthetic references, notably the video presented on screen and TV monitors, they merged live performance with mediated content either recorded or shown live while happening in another part of a performance space.

In the 1980s, as a starting resource for their intermedial performances, The Wooster Group used dramaturgy of established American classics such as the controversial production of *Rout 1&9*, adapted from the play *Our Town* by Thornton Wilder and the now canonical *LSD* (*… Just the High Points…*), rewriting of *The Crucible* by Arthur Miller. Using as a source for collaborative creation fragmented scenes and themes as raw material they would further develop performance through the intermedial multireference using video art. LeCompte claims that she never read Miller's text and that group performance practice "evolved out of happenstance and accident".[27] Gordon points out from the rehearsal's observation that performers "are often speaking lines they are hearing via earpieces, then stepping out of character to discuss the lines, then incorporating the recording and transcription of these same conversations"[28]. The Wooster pedagogy involves experiential actors' performance creativity and group authorship combining live and media within collaborative creation. In addition, characters, dialogues, and scenes came from blending classics with other popular culture and social materials ideas, as echoes and quotations were taken from contemporary life and events as a response and reference point. In both performances, the video was another active member of the group, a performer in the space, part of an action that was interconnected with live performance and audience presence that was deliberately acknowledged. Continuing from a creative methodology based on Schechner's actors' group creative process, the Wooster Group extended into intermediality by creating performances as if montage film. The process was about transformation and not working towards a final product that allowed the group to make changes to performance within a perpetual rehearsal process developing out of performer, audience, space, and media interactivity. The rehearsal process provided an environment for the actors and involvement in the performance making; they were learning LeCompte's methodology by doing it in a performance. As an experience of making is essential and not the finished product, the emphasis is on improvisation as an exploration and playing with sources. An interdisciplinary pedagogical environment is founded on an experimental way of practice. The actor learns how to present new material without knowing what to expect at the end, not focusing on an expert delivery but discovering new material that may or may not be part of the performance, but is part of development.

In an adaptation of *Our Town*, the performance starts from a gallery outside before it moves to a black box space in the Garage, where above the stage are four TV monitors showing the action of a play stylised as television soap opera in contrast to a group acting of the live play. Particularly with the critically acclaimed production of the landmark *LSD*, which was also known to the public because of a court case that Arthur Muller wanted to bring against the Group due to infringement of copyrights. The production use of video and technology was very sophisticated in applying performance content through TV monitors. Applying film methodology – close-ups, point-of-view-shot, fast forward, and a montage of sequences – on multiple monitors was content used to drive part of a storytelling that incorporates various media and live performance in one 'hyper-media'. The Wooster Group brought experiences of performance and visual arts into a theatre; it was a theatre based on reworkings of the classics that borrowed the vocabulary of avant-garde performance, contextualised within the familiarity of the cultural environment of Soho, New York.

The RSVP Cycles

RSVP methodology is based on training that uses a cyclical model of creativity that can be transferable skills used in different disciplines. Resources (R) are an essential starting point referring to the material used for improvisation and the emotional and physical resources performers use to work individually or in a group. The scores (S) are at the centre of The RSVP Cycles describing the process. Halprin defines scores "symbolisation of processes extending overtime" and "instructions for the work". The term 'Valuaction' (V) is action-focused; it joins two words to suggest looking for a value in the scores (actions), "a process of dynamically responding to work based on values". 'Performance' (P) refers to results through the improvisation process "setting the work in motion".[29] The RSVP Cycles are annotations (using examples of musical scores) of creative process development; they are not fixed results but transitions from which to create action, that can be artistic, but it can be any human creative action. As Halprin observes, through "processes, exploration, chance, openness, emotional states and irrationality", the scores are vehicles for the continuous transformation of the material and function.[30] Lawrence Halprin's theory is based on the idea that the creative process is visible through scores in space as a process recording. He poses a question about the energy of group creation processes, how does it influence human action in life and all fields of art? Anna extended her approach to dance training as a healing practice working with people with AIDS and cancer, becoming an influential force in dance therapy throughout the following decades.

By the late 1970s, the theatre groups devising performances in Quebec, who initially rebelled against text-driven theatre and formalising French plays-based repertoire, were dissatisfied with the loose and unstructured ambiguity of group creations. The practice was based on the group creation of a text, not a performance. Devised performance was significant in Quebec as cultural self-discovery and reconfirmation of national identity. It was an alternative to central cultural hegemony. In 1978 a teacher from Quebec City at Conservatoire d'art

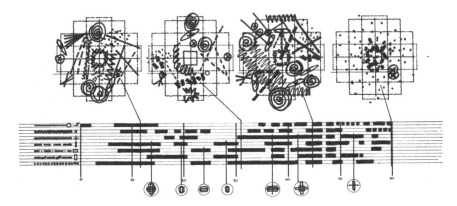

FIGURE 3.2 Lawrence Halprin's scoring system for landscape and movement design – Motation

Lawrence Halprin Collection, The Architectural Archives, University of Pennsylvania

FIGURE 3.3 Lawrence Halprin's Landscape design based on RSVP Cycles integrating space and movement from 1972

Lawrence Halprin Collection, The Architectural Archives, University of Pennsylvania

dramatique de Quebec, Jaques Lessard, himself an actor, went to study in San Francisco with Anna Halprin to find new pedagogy for collaborative performance. Lessard saw that the group theatre in the 1970s lacked constructive creative method and pedagogy for devising practice. Lessard wanted to see a methodology to produce more stable artistic results that could be considered creative pedagogy. They were looking for a more structured work model, a pedagogy for group creation beyond a set of actors' free improvisations and group writing of a text. Lessard recognised that RSVP Cycles and dance/environmental design scores could be suitable as a devising method in group creative practice. In 1979 Lessard returned to Quebec City and created a new pedagogy for actors' group practice founded on the adaptation and translation of the RSVP Cycles to theatre devising process suitable in French: Re-P-è-Re:

Ressources (RE)
les Partitions (p)
l'Évaluation (e)
et la Représentation (re)

making them into Repère, or a point of reference for creative work.

A year later, Lessard founded Théâtre Repère company with students from the Conservatoire to explore further pedagogy that now developed out of inter-medial relation between performance, dance, and environment. Lessard observes that: "By cycles, we mean that the process of creation is circular and that even the representation is not an end, a culmination (the end of the straight line), but a period in a work of creation that is never completed, always to be resumed, to improve. It is a dynamic process."[31]

Robert Lepage entered the theatre in the late 1970s once he finished his actor's training at the Conservatoire as a 20-year-old. His professor at the Conservatoire for a pedagogy of actor improvisation was Lessard, and he invited Lepage to join Théâtre Repère in 1980. Being fresh out of the Academy, Lepage did not have much luck with Quebec's official theatre, film, and TV culture. After leaving the Conservatoire, he was not getting any jobs, as several other young actors found themselves without work in the mainstream French Quebecoise Theatre and Film. If you do not fit within a particular casting model as a type and are not in your preferred acting style, you do not get roles in the auditions. By joining Lessard's company, he became part of a group of actors as devisers that allowed him to learn how to use creative Cycles and work in multimedia theatre and collaborative ways which remained integral to his career in theatre. Lepage's involvement with Théâtre Repère subsequently shaped the form and direction of the development of his theatrical style.

Lepage's primary role in Théâtre Repère was not as a performer but as a director. He became responsible for devising new touring national and international projects, working on experimental performativity with a group of actors as a separate wing within Théâtre Repère, exploring personal and collective stories of worlds in-between dreams, memories, reality, and fantasy that were theatrically expressed through visual images. His visual theatre found resonance with Canadian and inter-national audiences in the late 1980s and 1990s. He started performing at international festivals and commissioned production from various co-producers and Quebec and Canadian government arts funding. Lepage's main creative focus is on the inter-medial interaction between the actor, the space (architecture), the lighting, the media, the sound and music, and the physical objects in a visual performance that does not need spoken language to communicate with the audiences.

Robert Lepage's intermediality in theatre is essential for his performance authorship, usually described by critics and scholars as a form that is content or multimedia that caries storytelling. His performance practice is based on the creative methodology of RSVP Cycles. It is about the process of transformation and remediation. From open improvisation on a starting reference (a text, a film, a historical event, dramatic text, etc.) comes a written text, live theatre produc-tion, a cinema and even an online virtual world (the example of a performance that became various media). Each of the remediations retains appropriation from another previous media: the published play is more of a synopsis of stage action as a textual transcript of what happens in a theatre space, and film, although a new Cycle using performance as a starting point, appropriates the medium of theatre within its cinematic language. We can see a live digital performance within the intermedial context of a postmodern interface of visual disciplines within one interdisciplinary field of visual culture as a confluence of performance and cinema, live and visual art, advertising and pop culture. Mirzoeff describes visual culture as being concerned with a visual event where producers interface with visual technology in terms of creation of meaning, information and pleasure.[32] Lepage as a performance author who acts within intermedial connections and plays within contexts of visual culture, also built an audience over time that followed his work and learned to expect theatre experiences resulting from the ongoing development of narrative and to expect him to exist in an environment through intermediality in his theatre.

Intermediality and actor–solo performance

The performance authorship work of Laurie Anderson, a New York multimedia artist, is recognised as pioneering in digital performance practice, known for technical innovation that brings different media together. She created several solo performances that focused on autobiographical material. Anderson responded to a larger body of work, which Goldberg refers to as '"autobiography performance", made by a performance artist who used multimedia possibilities (mainly sound, video, and film) to transform personal material into performance.[33] Anderson used varied artistic roles as "visual artist, composer, poet, photographer, film-maker, electronics whiz, vocalist, and instrumentalist".[34] Blurring the distinction between reality and performance, Anderson was telling stories related to her life and the work she is making, creatively manipulating technology within a simple narrative form. Her performances included music, poetry, and visual images playing with musical instruments as objects, turning physical objects into elec-tronic media. Indeed, she created a new mechanism through a transformation of the violin, a device she had played since childhood, into an audiotape player by replacing "the horse-hair of her violin bow with a recording tap, playing pre-recorded sentences on an audio head mounted in the body of the violin".[35] As a storyteller, she was exploring a new way of communication through the use of digital technologies mixing digital and analogue. As a musical, visual, and performance artist, texts for her performances (solo shows) became very popular and were published as books. In 1980, she recorded *O Superman*, moving into popular culture, becoming the number one hit on the British pop chart. Her music performance art was recorded on seven albums based on her spectacular multimedia stage performances. Anderson worked on the synergy of arts, developing her themes in subsequent performances, music, stage performance, and video from the same material and starting preoccupation. In 1992, Anderson created a solo autobiographical performance as a full-scale digital multimedia spectacle *Nerve Bible* combining her music (playing violin and keyboards), personal stories, poetry, and imagery flashing on video screens as a metaphor for the human body and its decay through ageing.

Lepage, as director-author and actor-author, interconnects different media in particularity cinema and theatre, physical expression and spacial configuration; he is at the centre of inter-media exchange. Working with various media and establishing intermedial relations between them was more of a necessity of working with no money and traditional theatre space than a planned approach and method of practice reflecting the ethos of group creativity in alternative areas. Using existing electronic media in performance was more accessible to manage than with built scenography and complex set design. His first independent production as writer-director-actor of a solo show was *Vinci*; the incorporation of media into performance action was based on the simple use of technology and what is available in the alternative space (for example, schools, warehouses, basements, and small theatre venues) where rehearsals took place along with the creation process. *Vinci* draws together many of Lepage's ways of making visual performances through interplay with media in creating this solo show. The performance interweaves diverse languages of art and function through aesthetic form rather than the content or narrative. To tell his story in solo shows, Lepage invents the alter ego character for the actor-creator to be transposed into the physical environment of the play. Alter ego characters serve as a connecting device within the narratives to link the performer with various dramaturgical materials, either from the past or the present of a performer creating a story. It has a dual presence of being you and not being you; it is a vehicle for telling a story based on your own experiences.

Similarly, in Lepage's second and arguably one of the best autobiographical solo performances, developed in the early 1990s, *Needles and Opium*, Lepage is mixing in space live theatre and the visuality of cinema. His alter ego, with the same name as Lepage, Robert, is brought into a story where various forms of addictions are explored. As starting reference points were Robert's broken heart after losing a loved one, Jean Cocteau's addiction to opium, his poetic creativity and drug addiction to heroin, and the jazz music of Milles Davis. Using Cocteau's film imagery and poetics combined with Davis's music, Lepage tells the story of addiction to love and the pain of losing loved ones. The dreamlike quality of surreal imagery became a structural aspect of his visual dramaturgy. He uses a pastiche of resources from popular culture and mass media to build his performance and achieve performance transformations through the interconnection of media. He makes interwoven events from different characters' lives by combining projections on the cinema-style screen in the background and using the performer's body suspended in the air or the water on a harness. The physical body interacts with Cocteau's surrealistic images and Davis's powerful sound creating intermedial connections. Lepage poetically transformed one object into another; his body, suspended on the harness, is playing with audience perceptions, a reality of being suspended in between the worlds, where he can be a visual-physical metaphor, also becoming a flying object, a machine and human being falling from the sky.

Integrated digital performance technology that have compatible programs allowed Lepage to fully develop digital expression as a creative tool within the live theatre. In the example of 1999, Lepage's fourth solo show, *The Far Side of the Moon*, rehearsed his use of digital multimedia within performance practice in his multidisciplinary space La Casarne in Quebec City. The rehearsal space looked like a technical laboratory, a space with no audience, just a black box where the performance was 'written' through digital technology of different media. In this solo show, Lapage combines other media using the full power of digital performance, having various engineers with computers designing visual material as he improvises. From observation of the rehearsal process, it was evident that he works with several gadgets surrounding him and a team of collaborators – puppeteer, technicians, and designers (video, audio, lights, computer graphics, etc.) are following rehearsals.

> One side was a performing area with multi-purpose screens and a see-through mirror. On the other side was a massive table with various technical gear: video and audio equipment, projectors, and computers. All around space were several references to journeys to the moon: videotapes, the film *Apollo 13*, books and popular magazines from that time, and bunraku-like puppets in very realistic NASA astronaut suits.[36]

Anderson Project, his most technologically elaborate digital performance solo show, developed in 2005, created some landmark performance space design approaches creating a symbiosis of visual image and physical body and transforming them into a storytelling device. The digital performance space environment consists of a transformational stage machine under the stage and in the wings. In the wings different parts of the set design move (platform, objects, tables, etc.). At the rear, a projection green screen is a large cubical in perspective that allows for projected computer-generated images and films, digitally mastered, that create an illusion of a three-dimensional virtual environment. The cubical is called 'panorama' (or 'the landscape' by the tech crew).

> Covered in a special cloth which, thanks to a pneumatic system, can either cling to the interior of its walls or expand towards the exterior, thereby distorting the image projected frontally onto its surface to give the effect of a shell or an eyeball. The magic of this technique enables a mechanised and efficient integration of body and image (thanks to a slight raising of the central part of the structure), restoring the illusion of depth, or rather, a false 3D, with an invisible and rapid transition from one state to another (concavity-convexity); the moving back and forth of the entire panorama on tracks creates an added depth of field to the stage area.[37]

Lepage's advanced use of digital technology in live theatre integrates virtual and physical space with performers, transforming them from one score to another in front of the audience. Methodology of performative pedagogy of opening up the process to the audiences requires performance to be rehearsal and rehearsal to become performance – blurring the difference between the two. Lepage often uses the term for collaborative productions as 'open' or 'public rehearsal', pointing to performances in front of national and international audiences. Learning how to respond as a performer to the audience's presence is essential in developing actors to work within immersive and participatory audience presence.

Conclusion

Replacing text and verbal language with audio-visual images of digital media performance in the 21st century becomes a language connecting with global audiences. It is an expression that communicates through the performers' engagement with space, objects, video, and audio images, free from verbal language. In the case of Lepage, it is essential to note that while the Québécois cultural context, particularly the quest for national identity, inevitably influenced Lepage, his main preoccupation was theatrical language as a communication tool more on a personal level. He adopted the existing discourse of visual language in the broadest sense, appropriating the new 'corporeal language' without political or ideological references to communicate with the international festival theatre circuit via the language of visual culture in digital media.

Visual recorded images introduced into theatre performance in Robert Lepage's theatre are the basis for a dramaturgy that wants to communicate with international audiences without being limited by language or culture, inhibiting the audience's understanding. Lepage's performativity emphasises performance-writing through theatrical elements that can be situated within the tradition of the French director Roger Planchon's *écriture scénique* (scenic writing) or De Marinis's notion of the performance text. The emphasis on *mise en scène* is not on the fixed narrative or character but on the development of a performance, a new theatrical language. Developing from the 1960s and 1970s, most performance groups used film projections (own or found), television sets with video footage, and various not-theatre spatial sites for performance, involving audience participation as in happenings. In the late 1980s and 1990s, the realisation that art and media should not be studied separately within individual development but in the context of differences and co-relations came to preoccupy discourse on media in arts, particularly regarding live performance. Incorporating stage machines to which the performer is attached, film and sound technology into performance space will be facilitated enthusiastically with the digital revolution in the late 1990s when computer technologies became a constituent part of communication in everyday life, from human interactions to doing business, commerce, and manufacturing in the industrialised world. Once the tech language becomes compatible because of audio and visual technology, similarity, the relationship between media and performance, is much easier to establish. Digital technologies offered performers and audiences new challenges, a lasting impact, and ways to express and communicate everyday material. Like mobile phones and social networks, digital performance became central to the everyday experience of theatre art.

As global theatre focuses on international festivals, the performance themes address a global audience's interests and concerns. The interconnectedness of theatre cultures in international festivals uses media of theatre as a form of expression that is familiar to that festival audience goer sharing the same social status and values regardless of national background (referred to as a Davos group – named after the Davos economic forum of rich and powerful multinational companies). Digital technology and online computer existence for a contemporary audience with knowledgeable users are familiar forms of conveying content. In advanced global capitalism, consumers are shopping for the international production of culture as a brand. Digital performance provides visual language that allows that access, as the internet enables global access.

Learning through doing as an experiential approach to education with skills and a professional approach to arts practice, combined with action learning and training research methodologies, was a model that I have been practising in my approach to teaching theatre since 2000. The emphasis has not been only on a specific text as a guide to learning but also equally or even more importantly on students' experience and cultural background in all the relevant social and present-day contexts that surround the moment in which learning occurs. Working in rehearsals and workshops on art practice, it was also necessary, even as a condition, to relate to the experiential side of students' background, considering that you are taking them on a joint creative journey in which they need to establish their presence as a future artist in theatre, film or other performative arts and media. We must accept that there are disciplinary differences, that their specific media drive unique collaboration between artists. Live digital theatre embraces interconnection of media in intermediate performance and for that we need to develop performers training for interdisciplinary performance pedagogy.

Notes

1 See Steve, Dixon. *Digital Performance: A History of New Media in Theatre, Dance, Performance Art, and Installation* (The MIT Press, 2007).
2 Balme, B. Christopher, "Intermediality in the Theatre of Robert Lepage", in Claudia Orenstein and James Peck (eds). *LeCompte, Chong, Lepage*, Vol. 7, *The Great North American Stage Directors* (Methuen Drama, 2021), p. 182.
3 Chapple, Freda and Chiel Kattenbelt (eds). *Intermediality in Theatre and Performance*, IFTR Working Group (Rodopi, 2006), p. 12. See also the edited book by Sarah Bay-Cheng, Chiel Kattenbelt, Andy Lavender and Robin Nelson. *Mapping Intermediality in Performance* (Amsterdam University Press, 2010).
4 Yeung, Heather H. "Reading Kristeva with Kristeva", *Studies in the Literary Imagination*, vol. 47, no. 1 (Spring 2014), p. 111.
5 See Tate website: https://www.tate.org.uk/art/art-terms/b/black-mountain-college/black-mountain-college-school-no-other
6 "John A. Rice (1888–1968) Black Mountain College, Life as a Writer", Students, University, Education, and Faculty, StateUniversity.com; https://education.stateuniversity.com/pages/2369/Rice-John-1888-1968.html#ixzz7YAhDyLxt
7 Jones, Caroline. "Finishing School: John Cage and the Abstract Expressionist Ego", *Critical Inquiry* vol. 19, no. 4 (1993), pp. 628–65, p. 631.
8 Jones, 1993, p. 633.
9 Patterson, David. "Words and Writings", in D. Nicholls (Ed.) *The Cambridge Companion to John Cage* (Cambridge University Press, 2002), pp. 85–99, p. 88.
10 Iddon, Martin, and Philip Thomas. *John Cage's Concert for Piano and Orchestra*, (Oxford University Press, 2020), p. 208.
11 Feisst, Sabina. "John Cage and Improvisation – An Unresolved Relationship", *Musical Improvisation: Art, Education and Society*, vol. 2, no. 5 (2009).
12 Griniuk, Marija. "Performance Pedagogy: Performing *Fluxus Pedagogy* in a Contemporary Lithuanian Context", *Acta Paedagogica Vilnensia*, vol. 44 (2020), pp. 152–163, p. 155.
13 *Flexus Manifesto* in Fluxus Foundation, 2018 on http://fluxusfoundation.com/exhibitions/anti-film-anti-art/fluxus-manifesto-i/
14 Paik, Nam June. "Cybernated Art", in Noah Wardrip-Fruin and Nick Montfort (eds), *New Media Reader* (Cambridge, MA: Cambridge University Press, 2003), p. 229.
15 Paik submitted a report, "Media Planning for the Post Industrial Society—The 21st Century is now only 26 years away", to the Rockefeller Foundation about new media technology and its prevalence in American society, where he predicted the emergence of the "electronic super highway".
    See Nam June Paik, Electronic Superhighway: Continental U.S., Alaska, Hawaii (article) | Khan Academy
16 See Bhabha Homi, *The Location of Culture* (Routledge, 2012).
17 Fusco, Coco. *English is Broken Here: Notes on Cultural Fusion in the Americas* (The New Press, 1995).
18 Martinez Sanchez, Maria. "Helio Oiticica – Visual Arts and Performativity", in A. Dundjerović and L.F. Ramos (eds) *Brazilian Performing Arts* (Abada Editores, 2019), p. 151.
19 Dundjerović, A. "Theatre of Anthropophagy", in A. Dundjerović and L.F. Ramos (eds). *Brazilian Performing Arts* (Abada Editores, 2019), p. 85.
20 Martinez Sanchez, 2019, p. 144.
21 Martinez Sanchez, 2019, p. 146.
22 Martinez Sanchez, 2019, p. 148.
23 Littlewood quoted in Schechner, Richard. *Performance Theory* (Routledge, 2003), p. 212.

24 Schechner, Richard. *Performance Studies: An Introduction* (Routledge, 2002), p. 1.
25 Gordon, David. " The Forty Year Rehearsal: The Wooster Group's Endless Work in Progress", in Claudia Orenstein and James Peck (eds). *LeCompte, Chong, Lepage*, Vol. 7, *The Great North American Stage Directors* (Methuen Drama, 2021), p. 26.
26 Arson, Arnold. "The Wooster Group's L.S.D. (Just the High Points)", *The Drama Review* (TDR) Vol. 29, (MIT, 1985), p. 66.
27 Arson, 1985, p. 71.
28 Gordon, 2021, p. 25.
29 Halprin, Lawrence. *RSVP Cycles* (George Braziller, 1969), p. 1.
30 Halprin, 1969, p. 192.
31 Beauchamp, H. & J.-M. Larrue. "Les cycles Repère: entrevue avec Jacques Lessard, directeur artistique du Théâtre Repère". *L'Annuaire théâtral*, 8 (1990), pp. 131–143, p. 131.
32 Mirzoeff, Nicholas. *An Introduction to Visual Culture* (Routledge, 1999), p. 199.
33 Goldberg, RoseLee. *Performance: Live Art 1909 to the Present* (New York: Harry N. Abrams Inc.; 1979), p. 110.
34 See Anderson web site https://laurieanderson.com/about/
35 Goldberg, 1979, p. 112.
36 Dundjerović, Aleksandar. "Solo-Performance: Lepage as Actor-Author", in Jenn Stephenson (ed.) *Solo Performance* (Toronto: Playwright Canada Press), p. 170.
37 Monteverdi, Annamaria. "The Machinery of Vision in the Theatre of Robert Lepage" *The Scenographer* Milano: Audio Editore, 2021), p. 144; accessed on the website The Machinery of Vision in the Theatre of Robert Lepage – Digital Performance (annam onteverdi.it).

4

DRAMATURGIES

The theories on digital performance culture developed rapidly in the 21st century to become a very deep, complex, and widespread scholarly influence. The use of digital technology and immersive and interactive media, combined with site-specifisc within the live performance, is exemplified through a number of international performance groups such as Dream Think Speak, Punchdrunk, Third Rail Project, Rimini Protokoll, Blast Theory and Station House Opera, to name but a few. It is understandable that there is an interest in digital media culture as it connects a plurality of arts and expressions that share a similar creative methodology and technology. However, this chapter will not engage with or present an account of the various views and positions on digital media culture nor will it delve in-depth into a theoretical analysis. The key concepts in digital performance are based on visual recordings, while screen or projected visual images are based on photography. A starting point for digital media in live performance is founded on the premise that "most screen-based visual images" are not computer-created.[1] They all do justice to a variety of theoretical discourses on digital performance and culture. The theories that help the understanding of live performance, taking place within digital media on screen, will be examined in this chapter. The focus will be on the theories that underpin the performative elements in the dramaturgy of live digital theatre, looking at theories that help to explain the particular use of space-time, liveness, cyber body and image.

The dramaturgy of theatre performance depends on the space where it takes place. The structure in which the interaction between performance and the audience takes place is reflected on the structure of the text, or pre-text as a starting point for a performance. The dramaturgies of live digital theatre depends on a different elements of space-time, imaginary bodies, audience presence and

DOI: 10.4324/9781003275893-5

the image which we will examine in this chapter. We will engage in discussion of the critical theories that influence the thinking about the dramaturgical composition of live digital theatre as relevant to performer, space and audience. These include Philip Auslander's 'liveness' in performance presence, Michel Foucault's 'heterotopia', and Gilles Deleuze's 'the fold' and 'crystals of time', and valuable deliberations on photographic image through Walter Benjamin's and Roland Barthes's observations, The concept of *transtopia* will be introduced into the dramaturgy of live digital theatre as a system of in-between presence in a location that is a socially constructed communication sphere, as both physical and digital space or a virtual computer generated platform for human interphase. In theatre performance, there is an agreement between the audience and the performers who accept to be together within *transtopic* locations in cyberspace and cyber time. For example, on Zoom live theatre, as the simplest hybrid form of physical and digital existence in cyberspace.

Transtopic Space-Time

There are also, probably in every culture, in every civilisation, real places—places that do exist and that are formed in the very founding of society which are something like counter-sites, a kind of effectively enacted utopia in which the real sites, all the other real sites that can be found within the culture, are simultaneously represented, contested, and inverted. Places of this kind are outside of all places, even though it may be possible to indicate their location in reality. Because these places are absolutely different from all the sites that they reflect and speak about, I shall call them, by way of contrast to utopias, heterotopias.[2]

In live digital theatre, the relationship to space-time is structured differently from the existence of physical theatre in space and time. In live theatre as a physical experience, space is three-dimensional and time is progressive and linear with a specific duration outlining the performance. The use of digital media technology in performance introduces cinema and the presence, on computer screen, of two-dimensional non-location cyberspaces and temporality as a constellation of an experience of time with a plurality of uses – compressed, elongated or regressive (as opposed to progressive and linear). As observed by Bay-Cheng in discussing Alice Rayner's elaboration of shifting from material performance into cyberspace, "Performance in cyberspace occupies no place, but rather ontologically exists only in a time, the perpetual now. In this sense, time is the most dynamic yet intractable element of digital theatre and performance."[3] The dramaturgies of live digital performance offers more possibilities for cinema and theatre to conflate enabling the transformation of space-time through the editing of material on computer screens, projections and video monitors, and the ability to present events simultaneously, as past and memory. In performance, space-time images relate to the audiences' experience of mediatised visual culture, to which they are exposed through daily use of computer technology and social networking. The established relations with their experience configure the immersion of the audience into the artwork. In juxtaposing live performance with digital images in multimedia performance, performance authors undoubtedly produce a unique experience for the audience of different space-time relations. In live digital theatre, this experience of space-time is based on an environment in which constructed cultural and social relations point to a familiar location for the audience, but not necessarily to the physical place where the performer is situated, which could be somewhere else in the world. This reflects the duality in digital performance between real and virtual computer-created space-time dimensions.

In the era of digital culture, heterotopia, as Foucault's articulation of another space, has applicability to an understanding of place within the duality of physical and cyberspace. Foucault's heterotopia is a 'placeless place', a place outside of all places, an impossible, unimaginable space that is simultaneously an accurate site. This space exists outside of all other spaces, somewhat defining his open concept of heterotopia. Yet, this undeveloped idea is flexible to interpretation, generating an enormous impact on literature and film studies from practitioners, including performers, artists and filmmakers. In the 21st century, globalism and digital technology have created a typology of new heterotopian spaces.[4] For Foucault, heterotopias exist in every culture and founding society,

> which are something like counter-sites, a kind of effectively enacted utopia in which the real sites, all the other real sites that can be found within the culture, are simultaneously represented, contested, and inverted....Because these places are different from all the sites that they reflect and speak about, I shall call them, by way of contrast to utopias, heterotopias.[5]

Foucault uses mirrors of "these quite other sites, these heterotopias" that serve as a collective experience.[6] A mirror as 'placeless place' is a utopian site where one sees a reflection of oneself where one is not, a gaze back at self from a place where one is absent, as Foucault puts it, "a virtual space that opens up behind the surface...But it is also a heterotopia in so far as the mirror does exist in reality."[7]

Foucault's concept of heterotopia as a 'placeless place' is based on a fictional representation within the text.[8] Other examples of heterotopia sites that distinguish themselves from what is outside included prisons, gardens, cemeteries, Turkish baths and brothels. In the digital era, heterotopia repositions from the physical space to a heterotopia in a multiplicity of other spaces that simultaneously exist and are present within the digital environment of online cyberspace or virtual computer-created environment. However, in Telepresence performance, where the mediation is through the screen, live action in digital space and the live spectators' presence (their living room or a public location) conflate to become a site for the digital duality that exists in transition. The term digital transtopia can be used for the transition between two special 'reals' in the process of transition in a digital dislocation. In this sense, the meaning of the term is not part of the theories of transness, as Howard Chaing's 'transtopia' points to the interconnection of transgender differences and sex transformation as used in politics of identity categories within the context of cross-cultural transgender disciplines.[9] However, digital transtopia's viewpoint on space is similar to that of transgender transformation on the physical body in 'transtopia'. In our progressively virtual techno culture, *transtopia* transitions between two locations being in neither but in between. It brings together heterotopia and virtual environments as cohabitants in one experience that can be simultaneously unified and disjointed. In the dramaturgy of live digital theatre, a *transtopic* place brings together binarity. In live performance with a mediated visual presence or in telepresence it refers to the split into one operational system of simultaneous existence in a duality of locations. The performer is in the same physical space-time with the audience, communicating online yet dislocated from that space-time in another placeless place within the real or virtual space.

In *transtopia* transitions from one topos – physical location into another topos – the digital cyber location is a simultaneous in-between process where topos exist symbiotically, being overlayered one on another. In transtopia physical (real) and digital (virtual real) space/time perception is socially constructed, connected as part of one bio-sphere.[10] Transtopia understands that all human space is a reproduction of social relations, an idea put forward by the French Marxist sociologist and philosopher Henri Lefebvre. For him, space is made through forces of a dialectical unity of oppositions. Human space is constituted by complex forms of social and political parties that dominate and impose physical materiality through everyday practice and perception. In everyday interactions Human relations within dominant power structures create a unique presence. Lefebvre observes that the social tropes engender space, making it simultaneously abstract and real, concrete through objectification in the same way as commodity or money.[11] "If space embodies social relationships, how and why does it do so? And what relationships are they?"[12] For Lefebvre, "Social space contains – and assigns (more or less) appropriate place to – the social relations of reproduction."[13] Within Lefebvre's conceptualisation of social space, meta space in virtual reality is also a perception of a socially constructed space, with digital platform providers who create virtual reality, content control and allow internet access that exerts Foucault's biopower by administrating competence and financial ability to engage with technology.

Transtopia is not bound by historical time. Fredric Jameson describes postmodern culture as affecting historical time on a collective level, abandoning it for a 'pastiche' of an artificial past. Historicism made of "the random cannibalisation of all the styles of the past, the play of random stylistic allusion…with a whole historically original consumers' appetite for a world transformed into sheer images of itself and for pseudo-events and 'spectacles'."[14] In addition, postmodern critical theory asserts that the text is positioned within a network of relations to other texts (Kristeva's intertextuality). In live digital theatre, this pastiche and the network of connections to other *texts*, as media or socio-cultural information, are embedded within the dramaturgical form of performance that can simultaneously access and use a plurality of media and popular references. The postmodern concept of pastiche is essentially an underpinning approach to structure and organisation of dramaturgies in live digital theatre. Henri Bergson, a French philosopher established a process philosophy that favours motion and change. He recognises real 'objective' time (clock) and what he calls 'duration' time as the most relevant to our experience of lived time, rather than the mathematical time used throughout the history of the material world. As time-image is interpreted by our subjective experiences of it, it relates to our perception of time duration, which we cannot control, to make it shorter or longer. Time flows as an action, where past and future merge into the present as a memory of the past and a desire for the future.[15] For Bergson, the actual image of an object in our perception is more accurate than a virtual image of an object coming from memory, as representation is always virtual. Memories are mobile; they come down from the past to interfere with the perception of the present and action. This is a dynamic process progressing in time.[16] Critical re-interpretation of Bergson's time came from another French philosopher in the second part of the 20th century, Gilles Deleuze, who related Bergsonian thinking to the cinema. Space-time in live digital theatre has a cinematic quality. Deleuze relates time-image to the cinematic use of time. This has an impact on visuality in live digital theatre, which structures and organises visuality following cinematic principles. Deleuze reuses Bergson's three time-images: recognition, recollection, and dream, making Bergson's concepts foundational for developing his philosophy as described in the seminal book *Cinema 2: Time-Image*.[17] For example, an allusion to a mug on a table in the present moment is an actual image recognised in memory through a visual image of a mug known from the past. This is pairing virtual and actual images through recognition-image of the actual image of a mug in the present. The existence is in the real-time of the observation. Recollection-image has a deeper relation to memory through subjectivity. An actual image's temporal and spiritual subjective perception is loosely connected to the present. Recollection-image intervenes in memory recognition. The relation of the recollection to the actual image is seen in film in the use of camera movement and flashback (flashback being famous as a conventional device in a film's narrative where a story cannot be told from the present) as a shortcut that moves from the present to the past as a virtual image. Time in the present is infused with time from the past that has temporal presence. Finally, dream-image (or fantasy) is removed from any connection with the present situation; we are submerged in the exterior and interior world of sensations of memory – fantasy. A dream has no relation to specific recollection images; it is fluid and amorphous. Virtual images become actual, with no connection to the present, but instead to the actualised subconscious. In cinema, montages of hallucination and dream-like states, used in one segment or scattered throughout the film, represent a surreal and poetic transformation of images as a cinematic abstraction actualised through the metamorphosis of events and objects. In dream-image, time and relation to space are structured as a virtual faculty of fantasy with its materiality. Deleuze's 'crystals of time' is a metaphor for different states of time-image in film. Diverse images merge to condense, like crystals, the temporal relation between images of events. For Deleuze, the 'crystal-image' in cinema in representing time is enabled by the exchange between actual and virtual images. For live digital theatre, Deleuze's definition of an image in cinema is relevant: "The purely optical and sound situation (description) is an actual image, but one which, instead of extending into movement, links up with a virtual image and forms a circuit with it."[18] That duality of actual/virtual is reversible. In the section 'The Crystals of Time', Deleuze points out that film unites the real with a recollection of images saying that "the cinema does not just present images, it surrounds them with a world. This is why, early on, it looked for bigger circuits that would unite an actual image with recollection images, dream images and world-images."[19] Another important aspect of live digital theatre's dramaturgies is over-layering and its rhizomatic structure. Deleuze's and Guattari's concept of 'rhizome' as describing relations is linked to the idea of a plant that grows underground as its roots develop through paths and connections that can start from small parts as a starting point and develop structures. The rhizomatic structure as the grouping of things is how dramaturgical composition in live digital theatre uses space-time-based events. Multiple horizontal systems of structures have a plurality of connections, not linear, where different actions with no specific direction can interact.

Deleuze's 'crystals of time' in the visual quality in live digital theatre refers to the use of an image that is in the present with an instilled past/future. In live digital theatre, the duality in existence and reversibility of actual/virtual images 'crystals of time', defines the time-space relationship between performance and audiences. In addition, since the 1970s, relating the interpretation of recollection – dream-world images coming from memory – as the ability to reinvoke mental images of past action or what is stored in the unconscious had a substantial influence on the development of multimedia theatre and particularly on interdisciplinary visuality in performance arts. Personal memory became material for making collaborative creative and autobiographical performances, as pointed out in the intermediality of performance in Schechner's Performance Group, Elisabeth LeCompte, Anderson and Lepage's theatre practice.

Cyborgs: The Imaginary Bodies

The position of the body in the dramaturgy of live digital theatre is both a physical and computer-manipulated presence. The Body or Cyborg is a central focus of the action on screen or stage. The performers' physicality is combined with a computer and in a Zoom live production the image of the body can be manipulated through computer visual effects. The tradition of combining humans and machines is an integral part of the digital performance discourse. In the last part of the 20th century, the relation between technology and the human body can be understood as the integration of organic – living and synthetic – mechanical, as a technological extension of the human body into the environment where the fictional imaginary sees the body mixed with a machine. The cyborg is one of these mixes as a *cybernetic organism*. As McAuley writes, there is also a recognition that the body is no longer perceived in Western culture as a part of man that needs to be

> disciplined and controlled by the reason or seen simply as the material container for mind or spirit; it is now increasingly perceived to be at the centre of a complex web of interrelationships with every aspect of the individual's being and with the world surrounding that individual.[20]

From a collective perception, this is a tectonic shift in Western thinking after centuries of interpreting nature and culture, human behaviour and technology as incompatible, in opposition and lacking standard connections to what a human being is. Even Chaos Theory was concerned with irregular and unpredictable events where stability moves into instability, to find through media, science and computer technology, cybernetics, "how the couplings of contemporary technologies and the body break down the barriers between nature and culture, human and technology".[21]

With the popularisation and advancement of digital media, the focus on contemporary technology's mix of computer and body became the dominant factor favouring artificial intelligence as the next big step in human development. Posthuman performance, as a popular exploration of the discourse of robotics and cybernetics, has an evolutionary view on the synthesis of the biological organic (human) and mechanical information code (digital) where human consciousness transgresses into "the binary code of cyberspace".[22] Michel Serres, an influential French philosopher and writer, argues that human beings are shaped by experiences of communicating and existing within the new digital technology.[23] In the Higher Education sector, the expansion of the internet and the establishment of a digital learning environment produced an epistemological shift in the transfer of knowledge, from knowledge accessible through live education in academia to online information transmitted over the internet. If we look at the heterotopia in Foucault's socio-cultural sites, we can see that its purpose is to repurpose and create the possibilities for new 'other space' – such as digital – in institutions such as schools, universities, hospitals, and libraries. Serres's point is that concentration of knowledge (books) and order (regulation of people) within one space, a classroom or a library, is disordered, 'deluded and expanded' in digital space to achieve diversified global influences.[24] However, Foucault 'other spaces' are not symbolical representations, but concrete spaces, multiform, polyvalent and multifunctioning in different systems simultaneously. The duality of 'real' and 'online' is not just simplistically mirroring these experiences, but allows exponential growth, as in the metaverse that is accessed through augmented reality, virtual reality and mixed reality both as a 2D and 3D experience.

In live digital theatre, as experienced on Zoom live theatre, the dramaturgies of performance responds to digital technology that allows the possibility of making other realities. Zoom live theatre is a combination of film, video and live performance for the audience viewing at home, working on a computer or TV screen as a 2D experience. The performers' body (image usually focused on the head and mid-shot) is a central system for the structure and organization of the dramaturgical composition. As explored in Chapters 2 and 3, in live digital theatre, the body is the locus of all aspects of performance art and intermediality in visual representation. The presence of the live body is also contested terrain, particularly within the notion of a performer as a cyborg in live digital theatre. Mediated through a computer, the body can merge with the digital manifestation of a self – avatar. In the scholarship on performance from the last quarter of the 20th century, the topic of body memory and remembering, particularly within postmodern thought, inspires distrust. From the 19th century onwaards, memory was trusted as a bastion for keeping the past, a keystone for modelling subjectivity and identity, connecting past and present. Memory became the debris of fragmented identity, not trusted and unreliable as storage of past realities. In Postmodernism, the view of the body that contains memory is fragile and vulnerable, with the potential to succumb to outside influences – social and cultural – that could transform it and shape it into whatever the present moment dictates.

In digital performance, the place of memory relates to the presentation of time as a deliberate 'placing memory' within the process of re-positioning the past in a collectively agreed view from a present moment. However, the global interphase of different cultures within the digital theatre exchange means that the notion of what is remembered may become problematic and cause misrepresentation. Outside of collective memories, often within a national construction of identity, the imperfection of memory becomes an essential device in the performers' storytelling. How a character/actor remembers and forgets the past is a powerful tool for narration with all the fragility and vulnerability of fact and accuracy. Performative memory is a narrative of personal use of memory that can be used for subjectification of personal history as an interpretation based on the present circumstances in which one is experiencing remembering. In digital performance, technology provides a location where body memory, as remembered events, can be situated, coexist and even shape the present moment from which one is entering the act of repositioning the past. Fundamentally, using cinematic visualisation, digital theatre juxtaposes fluidity and imperfection of memory to live through a body of the performer as an authentic experience of here and now not only as a thematic and structural device but also as a way that digital performance is inherently organised.

The Hollywood film industry adopted the image of a body as a robot or cyborg, mixing human characteristics with a machine, thus producing a superior being that could potentially endanger human existence. For Dixon, "The cyborg, like the robot, arouses fears and fascinations" as being able to connect to com-municational networks independently.[25] Ridley Scott's 1982 sci-fi film *Blade Runner*, based on an adaptation of the 1968 novel *Do Androids Dream of Electric Sheep?* by Philip K. Dick, depicts a dystopian future in 2019 Los Angeles. It is a postmodern, dehumanised, dying city run by computers and media. Now considered a cult film, the film shows a future where human replicants are bio-engineered by a powerful (above politicians and state) corporation and sent to work in space colonies. A fugitive group of replicants escapes on Earth, and Deckard, played by Harrison Ford, is an ex-policeman hired to hunt and kill androids. As a sci-fi film, it predicted some of the new technologies that would play an essential part in our lives; for example, robots and AI, advanced emotion-sensing lie detectors and intelligent homes with integrated systems from entertainment to kitchen units. Visual images (polaroid photographs) are a central focus in Deckard's investigation of replicants. Reliance on photos as the embodiment of memory relates to today's posting of pictures on Instagram and Facebook. Parker observes that the range of robots/cyborgs has a wide span from

> Frankenstein's monster or *Star Trek's* Borg to reliance on eyeglasses or hear-ing aids, to literal prosthetic limb extensions and internal mechanical valve replacements; to conceptual interfaces such as 'smart' weaponry that 'thinks', or the augmentation of non-human bodies such as insects that are mechani-cally augmented. The cyborg has emerged in fiction, popular culture, sci-ence, the military, and in daily life, as a representation of the often tangled line between bodies and technology.[26]

With the boom in the advancement of the internet in the 1990s, digital tech-nology developed PC webcams. This was a breakthrough in video communica-tion. By the 2000s, development of high-speed internet and video telephony (videoconferencing) technology allowed for a better technological quality of communication. In 2003 Skype launched video calls, from PC to PC, that became affordable and soon commonplace for domestic use in transnational communication. The use of technology for live online theatre was in the experimental stage at the start of 2000s as video call communication was not technically compatible with rehearsals and performances because of the poor quality of sound and image and lack of internet speed. Tom Gordon explains the basis for the research project that started in 2016, 'Immersive Telepresence in Theatre project', as an online course between Coventry University, UK and Tampere University in Finland.

> Telepresence (or telematics) is a process by which the participant can interact, life-sized, with other participants in remote spaces by use of high-speed internet connections, differing from virtual reality in that it allows the user to access a real space in real-time without being physically present.[27]

Telepresence allowed participants in this joint project from two geographically distant locations (the UK and Finland) to collaborate by offering workshops, lectures and rehearsing a play without physically being together. However, this experiment required an understanding of how the principles of telepresence function in order to adapt teaching and actors' training to the new performance platform to enable bringing together technology and education consultation.[28] These experiments in telepresence used in performance practice education provide an understanding of connecting participants from two remotes spaces in real-time and physical presence in digital space. Giannachi points out that virtual reality "in the case of telepresence, is the remediated merging of two real locations".[29] In 1980, Marvin Minsky, a pioneer of AI, referred to this term in his essay "Telepresence" to explain the teleoperation system used to remote control physical objects through the manipulationof robots, creating a remote-controlled mechanical hand that feels like our own.[30]

Interactive depictions using webcam video technology in live events (including recorded elements) allow a live connection with the audience on an online platform. Glasner observes that telepresence performance

> redefines space's role in performance with telepresence both as an emerging model of corporeality and as a spatiotemporal structure. Telepresence as a specific form of embodiment replaces real proximity between the performing and perceiving bodies with their visual representation and, thereby, transforms the role of the physical performing body in performance art.[31]

In rehearsals, technology could be used as part of the methodology for creating artefacts on video through background images, editing and manipulation of represented sequences. Performers telling a story by shooting a self-made video on a personal smartphone to share their emotions in a direct reality situation or connecting live to audiences is a powerful new way to share subjective and unique content with audiences. It gives immediacy and emotional impact to immersive performances because direct emotions, situations and narratives are captured without the intermediary of a film or video crew or stage space that distances the audience from the intimacy of the physical action.

In popular culture Hollywood also presented telecommunication through telepresence as a connection device within the imaginary of sci-fi movies. The video call within a sci-fi context was part of the collective imagination in the latter part of the 20th century. In the television series *Star Trek* in 1966, Captain James who is on a different planet from his crew, presents his full-body voice and action remotely to others (his crew), extending the idea of telepresence. In Stanley Kubrick's *2001 Space Odyssey* (1968), the robot is taking over control and is more powerful and intelligent than the humans. In another part of the film, there is a scene that takes place in a communication cubicle in a space station; a video call to Earth is made over a TV screen. The father talks about his young daughter's birthday, which he will miss, on screen. *Blade Runner* presents a video call for critical communications in a scene when Deckard talks to Rachael (a replicant with whom he will be emotionally involved) using videophone technology, talking live on a phone built on a medium size TV screen.

The Brazilian visionary author and director Rodolpho Vasquez accidentally began experimenting with cyborg theatre in 2009, bringing standard digital technology that people would use in everyday life use into performance.

> Once a friend of mine asked me if I knew something about cyborg theatre. I said: I haven't got the faintest idea! This challenged me, and I started studying cyborg theory and the digital and AI revolution we live through – the internet, smart mobile phones, genetic engineering, and so on. I was fascinated. I started observing how much our daily lives changed with mobile phones and the internet and how we became cyborgs in our world. It is impossible to live nowadays without all these sophisticated technological devices. But theatre was not yet contaminated by this reality. And for me, theatre and society are just one thing. Theatre suddenly became an old-fashioned gentleman who refused to use a cell phone. So, cyborg theatre became the evident reaction to this approach from the past. And if theatre wanted to connect to society, this old-fashioned gentleman should not decide what theatre should be. And then, in 2009, we created the first cyborg performance. No tremendous technological effort. Just internet, mobiles and phone interactions. This changed my understanding of theatre.[32]

In their first cyborg performance, "Hypothesis for Love and Truth", the audience was asked to keep their mobile phones on. The performers called the audience, connected to internet sex, and ordered pizza during the performance. It was an early exploration of telepresence in connecting remotely to locations other than the one they were present in. Rodolfo explains that from the beginning the group understood "that the traditional concept of space was not enough for cyborg theatre. Cyberspace became our new space for theatre research."[33]

Liveness: Audience Presence

In his seminal concept of Liveness, Philip Auslander established in 1999 that "Live performance now often incorporates mediatisation to the degree that the live event itself is a product of media technologies."[34] This assertation was made before digital media culture started to be dominated by live online communication, before we could have live online performances on digital media using the communication platform Zoom. The presence of a live audience is essential to the development of dramaturgy in live digital theatre. The liveness and presence implied the gathering of people as an act of communal participation, reconfirming the collective narrative that provides group identity (for a tribe or a nation).

Ancient Greek performance space had the same public, social and cultural function, facilitating the gathering of people, communicating and reconfirming the dominant cultural narrative. The present day Mass Media is a meeting place as Ancient Greek theatre was, means of communication using technology (TV, Radio, Internet, Newspapers, Journals), electronic, printed, and digital (social networking apps) as a public space to pass information or stories. Starting from the 1960s, the Canadian philosopher Marshal McLuhan in his communication theory famously proclaimed that "the medium is the message, drawing attention to television and the role of mediation, where the content of the medium makes us overlook the character of the medium, and that the scope "of any medium is always another medium."[35] Expanding from McLuhan's theory, the central characteristic of digital media is the ability to represent one medium in another, defined by Bolter and Grusin in 2000 as 'remediation', both on the level of content and form.[36] One consequence of remediation, for example, appropriating content and the form from one medium (novel) into another (film), is the assertion that digital performance on an aesthetic level has to take the role of mediation into account. The use of a medium that filters encounters between the audience (viewer) and the performance (work of art). Following this, Giannachi points out that it must be remembered that the medium of virtual theatre (which, due to the technical scope of 2004 when the book came out, referred to digital performance rather than to the advanced use of virtual computer technology as in the metaverse) and performance is always subject to a process of remediates. "In other words, the medium of virtual theatre is always also its content, and this content is always also inclusive of other media."[37]

By the 1990s, new technologies had taken over all aspects of society. The internet boom of the 1990s, advancements in digital telephone technology, and webcams meant that these new technologies became an essential part of information and communication processes, from business, manufacturing and commercial activities to everyday life in the industrialised world. The history of video calls (Zoom, Teams, Skype and Webex) follows this trajectory in video call communication. By the 2000s the development of high-speed internet and video telephony (videoconferencing) technology allowed communication that could now be used inexpensively (although it was available since the 1970s, and in 1994 there was QuickCam, the first webcam). It was not until 2003 that Skype launched video calls, from PC to PC, and it became affordable and commonplace for domestic use for transnational communication. Still, it was not part of recognised communication in business and a platform for meetings until much later, as technology was not vital to support the signal. With online platforms and apps, video calls started to form an essential part of communication using WhatsApp, Apple's FaceTime, Viber, Facebook, TikTok and Instagram to connect with a high-resolution video image to smartphones, tablets, and PCs. Now computer technology is able to remediate live to a real-time and space experience.

Culture responded with a no less revolutionary use of digital technology for its actions. Arts, aesthetics and creativity are influenced by digital technology affecting film, videos, visual and performing arts. The digital revolution created a

FIGURE 4.1 *Epidaurus Theatre*, Greece
Photo by Maria Jose Martinez Sanchez

digital divide, which became part of the performance artists' response to the imposition of Western financial dominance onto the rest of the world. On the other hand, online productions gave global presence and the ability to capture live art, which had previously been relegated to alternative spaces with a physically present audience, to artists with access to internet infrastructure. The widespread influence of science gave rise to the term 'third culture' coined by John Brockman in 1995.[38] The marriage of art and science pointed to an ever-faster process of change that is direct without the need for a 'middleman' to communicate to the public. The third culture's directness is even more facilitated in digital times through social networking. Digital technology creates a culture within online platforms that directly addresses the public and gives access to the possibility of making a cultural and educational impact. Digital technology profoundly influenced education and had an impact on youth theatre and the Higher Education sector. Since 2009, the online platform Digital Theatre + has served as a learning tool that provides support for pedagogy through access to the experience by showing students' primary sources – productions, essays and commentaries.

In 1999, a provocative book titled *Liveness: Performance in Mediatized Culture* as a starting point posed a question: What is the place of live performance within the realm of mediatised cultural experiences, and what is the relevance of live experience in a world dominated by mass media? The author Philip Auslander begins his examination with the question of the relevance of live performance within the context of media technology. Historical and cultural factors have opposed the relationship between live and media performance in theatre and television or film. However, Auslander recognises these distinctions, but he "argues against intrinsic opposition and in favour of a view that emphasises the mutual dependence of the live and the mediatised and that challenges the traditional assumption that the live preceeds the mediatised."[39] In response to the dismissal of recordings of live images as not being honest, Auslander concludes that "if the mediatised image can be recreated in a live setting, it must have been 'real' to begin with."[40]

The development of intelligent technology brought change by allowing social networking to be an essential part of mass communication and mixing live and mediate. It pushed the discussion on live mediatised to another level beyond material reality into a plurality of different realities, starting with virtual reality. In 1987, virtual reality became all-encompassing, coming out of Jaron Lanier's company Visual Programming Lab, where technological devices for virtual reality were developed. By the 1990s, the public had started to have access to virtual reality gadgets, and foremost ample research industrial innovators such as MIT, NASA, and SEGA got into VR technology. By 2016–17, there had been an explosion of VR products that became mass-market commodities and part of various art experiments and audience experiences. By 2019, playing with immersive technology in theatre performance, using VR and augmented reality and mixed reality (a combination of all three realities) had become part of productions bringing mainstream theatre organisations, digital technology labs and the film industry together.[41] Auslander's analysis can be extended to the presence of digital within live performance as the making of another reality that compliments what is 'real' with multiple media realities that combine live performance with different types of real (Virtual and Augmented). Using mediatised reality for special effects and more intimate relationship between actors and audiences makes them part of one experience for the audience. However, the perception of the difference between live and recorded is factual and palpable up to the global events caused by the Covid-19 pandemic. Up to the paradigm shift with the pandemic, the difference had to do more with liveness being located in temporality, explicitly concerning a time-space problem and not dependent on mediatised forms.

Auslander understands liveness as the binary opposition between live and mediatised only in a historical and cultural context, not aesthetic or creative.

Mediatised had to be live if nothing more than as a basis before it became a mediatised experience. The division is the result of the commodification of the production of art and the cultural economy. Auslander's concept of live and mediatised performances, where the emphasis is not on the opposition, but on the relationship of mutual dependence, is an essential concept for live digital theatre. How does liveness impact on the actors' live performances online? It is a live performance, but is it a different kind of liveness? What does it mean to be made alive in digital cyberspace?

A theatre performance is an act of live interaction and experience of being there and now for actors and the audience. The dramaturgy for live digital theatre has the treatment of the there and now within digital media technology. Historically, live performance is defined through the audience being physically and temporarily co-present with the performers. Liveness in performance expanded with the advancement of new developments in communication to include the experience of listening/watching material recorded live in the new emergent technologies. It is also referent to websites that become live, ready for viewers of the content to engage with them.[42] The development of online and internet raised liveness into the digital world, where it can relate to two new forms: 'online liveness' and 'group liveness', as proposed by Nick Couldry.

> Online liveness: social co-presence on various scales from small groups in chat rooms to huge international audiences for breaking news on major Websites;... Group liveness: the "liveness" of a mobile group of friends who are in continuous contact via their mobile phones through calls and texting.[43]

Liveness is central to communication in online productions. It creates environments that are not physically there, but are present through telepresence (telematics). Telepresence theatre performances developed by the higher education sector in performing and visual arts (particularly in the UK's Coventry University since 2015) are enabled by digital technology that allows performers in two remote locations to appear simultaneously in one rehearsal/performance space as part of the exact physical location. The physical artwork is created across some form of virtual reality that provides a unified presence in a distant area with the source of physical action located remotely. Giannachi points out that virtual reality "in the case of telepresence, is the remediated merging of two real locations".[44] Telepresence has been extended with the internet and high-quality video conferencing to give a remote physical presence for communication and collaboration between different locations.

Telepresence in performance can bring viewers into the live event by combining film/video projections and theatre. Cormac Power proposes three modes of presence: *the fictional*, in which "fictional entities present on the stage" and unfold in front of an audience as it is now; *the auratic*, where the notion of an aura is central to relating to the presence that transcends the fictional and its immediate representation (as in the work of Artaud and Grotowski); and the *literal mode*, which refers to the body on stage. For Power, the stage is an environment of 'appearance and disappearance' of presence.[45] Telepresence in digital space correlates to Power's observations; however, now it is displaced from location and has multiple possibilities, through digital technology, to manipulate, construct, edit and distort. Telepresence adds a multi-layered mode of presence. As a popular platform for making performances live on screen, Zoom theatre was a form of telepresence.

Before live digital theatre, communication technology was used within multimedia theatre to bring video and audio technology into the performance space. In the 1960s, the Fluxus movement, and the work of John Cage, as was pointed out in Chapter 3, promoted the use of multidisciplinary and everyday objects in performance art, with the application of video technology becoming central to their artistic expression. As with Andy Warhol and Nam June Paik, bringing video cameras and technology into the performance space opened the possibility for different (more stable than happenings and installations but also inexpensive) levels of communication and representation. As well, intermediacy in Lepage's solo shows, also discussed in Chapter 3, brought video and telephone communication into the live performance, wherein one character on the stage would have a conversation (recorded) with another character in a different location (an international call in another time zone). From the 1980s onwards, with the customisation of personal computers, new opportunities for digital performance communication emerged. Live digital theatre has evaded performance space and temporality in its relationship to theatrical liveness. However, as it also exists on a screen, it has the intimacy and immediacy of bringing viewers into the event itself, having relevancy to TV liveness. The phenomenon of a different kind of liveness in telepresence is that it can be physical and digital simultaneously.

The Image

Since live digital theatre takes place on screen (usually a computer), it combines theatre with cinematic qualities. It is essential to understand how the image functions within visual dramaturgy. As pointed out before, the theoretical discussion about digital theatre and performance in live physical theatre is vibrant and open to different influences and interpretations, from exploration of the impact of digital technology on live theatre to more complex discursive discussions on history, cultural signification, communication, dramaturgy and digitalisation/archiving.[46] Live digital theatre is based on the visual image, but it can also be recorded, founded on photography. As Dixon points out,

> Performers use a range of media in their work from photographic stills to film, video, and digital media, and the significant aesthetic and technological differences between them are marked. But their common link is a lens-based optical recording technology, that is to say, a photographic system.[47]

The photographic or mediatised image is a close interpretation of what can be considered a reference to the real. That representation of the world outside, the photographic image, can also be understood as a collection of data or textual material. The photographic image, by default, becomes the text and could be seen through varied theories and interpretations relevant to textual analysis. These theoretic interpretations could be translatable to the study of photographic systems. With digital media culture, the difference between photos of real and digitally created mediatised images has become increasingly blurred. As pointed out in the previous chapters, the influence of performance art on theatre placed socio-cultural, visual and textual referencing on the same interpretative level as performative images.

The liberation of the visual image in theatre as a visual text can be seen through the debate on photography as a visual medium. This inspired philosophers such as Walter Benjamin and Roland Barthes and is essential to the overall discussion of digital performance mediums. Roland Barthes is an influential French social and literary critic whose most important work on photography, *Camera Lucida*, sets up photography as constitutive of the self.[48] Barthes points out that a photograph exists while the photo materially corresponds with what is photographed and the subjective fictional account of the photo that is within the constructed narrative. As an event that is reproduced, photography cannot be captured after the fact, and the event is over; it is a moment simultaneously set in the past and present. As a dramaturgical unit in live digital theatre, the captured image has fundamentally the same quality as a photo in capturing events. A digital image is at the moment in time; depending on the fictional narrative frame of a viewer, it creates creating the context for its understanding. Barthes observes, "What the Photograph reproduces to infinity has occurred only once: the Photograph mechanically repeats what could never be repeated existentially. In the Photograph, the event is never transcended for the sake of something else."[49] Barthes positions photography, not as a means of reproduction, but as a reference to a real presence captured in an image. "Photography is indifferent to all intermediaries; it does not invent; it is authentication itself....Every photograph is a certificate of presence."[50] Barthes' idea is that "the photograph shows a reality of the past, of something dead in time, the referent itself appears once again live to us."[51] With digital cameras, photography and video provide a control of the image that surpasses Barthes's notion of reality and creates a sense of reality that does not necessarily correspond to the materiality of what is the real object or captured event, thus locating the image in a perpetual present. Natural photography can now be digitally manipulated to create its reality, as in virtual reality, engaging the audience in the real-time moment when the recording occurred.

In 1936, the Marxist philosopher Walter Benjamin established the influential theoretical perspective, which became relevant to the formation of digital arts and culture theory, *The Work of Art in the Age of Mechanical Reproduction*.[52] His work attracted different interpretations from various disciplines pertinent to today's society and culture. Principally, Benjamin posited that in the work of art, in the age of mechanical reproduction, the term 'aura' of the work of art fades. Benjamin claims that if nature is reproduced, it loses its 'auratic' elements:

> Even the most perfect reproduction of a work of art is lacking in one element: its presence in time and space, its unique existence at the place where it happens to be…The presence of the original is the prerequisite to the concept of authenticity.[53]

Mechanical reproduction – recorded and screen/projected – be it film, photography and, by extension, electronic media and digital performance weakened liveness and presence in reproducing the work of art. However, this Marxist thinking that providing multiple reproductions would dilute originality, subjects the very nature of art to mass production driven by monetary values.

In contrast, digital reproduction loses its conceptual distinction. With developments in digital media culture, the question of ownership of digitally produced images has become problematic. Who can own an idea that exists in cyberspace? It is impossible to make this distinction in any digital virtual and electronic medium. Digital performance is often in the same position: being an original and a reproduction. In the present day context, works of art transform their communication and form of presentation. Everyone is globally involved in reproduction with ready-made art with the World Wide Web as disseminator. The result of art on the World Wide Web has to speak to universality. Categories of originality and authenticity are foregrounded by global consciousness; copy and similarity become acceptable in communication. Unlike the physical world, there can not be only one material artefact in the digital world. Recently, the Covid and Post-Covid world reality places significant importance on social and cultural interactions within digital media contexts. This has led to the popularity of ownership over digital art being established through the NFT model – non-fungible token. NFT comes out of Cryptocurrency as a monetary value for a digital asset. It allows "creators the authority to rent digital artworks out, to sell them or display them how they wish."[54]

Conclusion

As pointed out in Chapter 2 in the discussion of evolution through performance art and in Chapter 3 in various pedagogies, including cyber theatre, this chapter must set up the relevant theoretical parameters for the contextualisation of dramaturgical structures of live digital theatre. Live digital theatre is an interdisciplinary meeting place of theatre, film, performance, architecture and computer technology. Film/video is presented (traditionally) on a two-dimensional spatial object (screen) that has its spatial reality introduced into a three-dimensional space (a room with people watching). A screen is accessible for viewing, replacing our present space/time physical reality while we engage with what is visuality present on the screen. There is no universal time but a subjective experience of time as a different system of temporality. Just as in the viewing/presenting system, there are other processes – spectators in real-time, time on screen, time of performed events on the screen, time digitally or physically manipulated (slow or fast), time of live performance, time of geographical location (in Zoom live theatre). In addition, temporality systems have different tempos and rhythms to which events respond. As Agacinski points out, awareness of time "cannot be separated from different empirical contents that structure it".[55] In media, time is compressed and accelerated; it exists through technology that facilitates the relationship between personal subjective experience and group experience of the globalisation of time.

The dramaturgy of live digital theatre is a unique dramaturgy, where performance is constructed through new realities on the screen within its use of actor, space and audience. Digital media culture is presented and experienced in various ways, but cyberspace and metaspace are more complex and versatile than the engagement with the physical experience of space. Biopower asserts control and governing knowledge from centres through the administration of technology. At the same time, the other side of this bipolar equation becomes a relaxed approach to a creative process that only needs Zoom and WhatsApp apps on a computer or smartphone at the start. Live digital theatre transformed gatekeeping of making theatre in a building and made creative performance practice more inclusive and diversified. Information is communicated now through a tablet or a smartphone rather than through massive library structures and classroom buildings. Accessible digital technology allows the distribution of information everywhere, giving it a broad, global outreach.

Similarly, the transtopic site for live digital theatre is a heterotopia, as locating space in a 'placeless place' that can be delivered globally without any boundaries. Digital mediated technology introduced another reality into live theatre and the presence of not only 2 D, but multipolar and directional possibilities of locations where illusion on screen becomes a representation of something real – there and now. In live Zoom theatre, dramaturgy has to respond to the absence of a physical performer who creates the presence of a cyborg body on a digital screen. It also needs to understand the particular relation of space-time-action as in film, with the live theatre audience following the performance event immersed at the moment in the video communication process.

Apart from watching theatre performances online and providing a game engine as a computer platform that allows playing adventure games, virtual theatre can also be an interface between live performance and computer-simulated reality. The system of dramaturgical structures has to look into the trajectory of space, time and action to consider the different kinds of existence in which they exist. For example, in online Zoom live theatre, there is the presence of all dialectical conditions of reproduction. The control of social space within digital platforms became more evident in cyberspace. As technological devices mediate between the audience and the performance, the ownership of the production facilities and digital technology platform extend the control.

Notes

1 Dixon, Steve. *Digital Performance: A History of New Media in Theater, Dance, Performance Art, and Installation* (MIT Press, 2007), p. 115.
2 Foucault, Michel. Translated from the French by Jay Miskowiec. "*Of Other Spaces: Utopias and Heterotopias*", *Architecture/Mouvement/Continuité* (October, 1984), p. 4. See https://web.mit.edu/allanmc/www/foucault1.pdf
3 Bay-Cheng, Sarah. "Temporality", in Andy Lavender, Robin Nelson, Chiel Kattenbelt and Sarah Bay-Cheng, *Mapping Intermediality in Performance* (Amsterdam University Press, 2010), p. 85.
4 Ferdinand, S. et al. (eds). *Heterotopia in the Twenty-First Century* (London: Routledge, 2020).
5 Foucault, Michel, and Jay Miskowiec. "Of Other Spaces", *diacritics* vol. 16, no. 1 (1986), pp. 22–27, p. 24.
6 Foucault, 1986, p. 24.
7 Ibid.
8 Foucault's analysis comes from interpreting literature from authors such as Sade, Flaubert, Berg and Blanchot.
9 Chiang, Howard. *Transtopia in the Sinophone Pacific* (Columbia University Press, 2021).
10 This idea of the biosphere in physical/digital transtopia and Chiang's "transtopia" as relevant to the transgender body's position is embodied in live digital theatre telepresence.
11 Capitalism has created abstract spaces such as world of commodities – banks and business centres.
12 Lefebvre, Henry. "The Production of Space" Chapter XII, in Jen Jack Gieseking et al. (eds), *The People, Place, and Space Reader* (Routledge, 2014), p. 289.
13 Lefebvre, 2014, p. 289.
14 Jameson, Fredric. *Postmodernism, or The Cultural Logic of Late Capitalism* (Duke University Press, 1991), pp. 65–66.
15 See Bergson, Henri. *Time and Free Will: An Essay on the Immediate Data of Consciousness* (1889, New York: Grey Rabbit Publishing, 2019).
16 See Bergson, Henri. *Matter and Memory* (1896; MIT – Zone Books, 1991).
17 See Deleuze, Gilles. *Cinema 2: Time-Image* (Athlone Press, 1989), pp. 44–68.
18 Deleuze, 1989, p. 47
19 Deleuze, 1989, p. 68.
20 McAuley, Gay. *Space in Performance* (The University of Michigan Press, 2000), p. 120.
21 See web Open Textbook, Media Studies 101, "Part Three: Production and Structure Technology and the Body"(2013), https://opentextbc.ca/mediastudies101/chapter/technology-and-the-body/
22 Remshardt, Ralf. "Posthuman", in Andy Lavender, Robin Nelson, Chiel Kattenbelt and Sarah Bay-Cheng (eds), *Mapping Intermediality in Performance* (Amsterdam University Press, 2010), p. 145.
23 Serres, Michel. Translated by Daniel W. Smith. *Thumbelina: The Culture and Technology of Millennials* (London: Rowman & Littlefield, 2014); Serres, Michel. *Hominescence* (1st edn 2001; Paris: Le Pommier, 2014).
24 Serres, 2014, p. 12.
25 Dixon, 2007, p. 312.
26 Parker-Starbuck, Jenifer. "Introduction: Why Cyborg Theatre", *Cyborg Theatre* (Palgrave Macmillan, 2011), p. 12.
27 Gorman, T., M. Kanninen & T. Syrja. "There is a World Elsewhere: Rehearsing and Training through Immersive Telepresence", *Theatre, Dance and Performance Training*, vol. 10, no. 2 (Taylor and Francis, 2019).
28 Gorman et al., 2019.
29 Giannachi, Gabriella. *Virtual Theatres* (Abingdon: Routledge, 2004), p. 10.

30 Minsky, Marvin. "Telepresence". *Omni Magazine* (June 1980). See https://web.media.mit.edu/~minsky/papers/Telepresence.html. The concept of telepresence, shortened to presence, before Minsky's remote robotics, appeared in different discourses such as the first article of Andre Bazin's film theory, "The Evolution of Film Language", *Vingt ans de cinema à Venise* (Paris, 1952), Erving Goffman's sociology, *The Presentation of Self in Everyday Life* (New York: Doubleday Anchor Books, 1959), and in the writing of John Short, Ederyn Williams and Bruce Christie on social telecommunications, *The Social Psychology of Telecommunications* (London: John Wiley & Sons,1976).
31 Glesner, J. "Internet Performances as Site-Specific Art", *Body Space and Technology* vol. 3, no.1 (2002).
32 Rodolfo Vasquez, personal online interview, February 2022.
33 Rodolfo Vasquez, personal interview January 2022.
34 Auslander, Philip. *Liveness: Performance in a Mediatized Culture* (Taylor & Francis Group, 2008), p. 25.
35 McLuhan, Marshal. *Understanding Media: The Extension of Man* (London Arts Paperback, 1987 [1964]), p. 13.
36 See Bolter J. and R. Grusin. *Remediation: Understanding New Media* (Cambridge, MA: MIT Press, 2000).
37 Giannachi, 2004, p. 5.
38 See Brockman, John. *The Third Culture* (Simon and Schuster, 1995).
39 Auslander, Philip. *Live Performance in Mediatized Culture* (Routledge, 1999), p. 11.
40 Auslander, 1999, pp. 38–39.
41 We will return to this discussion of interdisciplinary media coming together in digital theatre space in chapter 8 on Zoom live digital theatre.
42 See Auslander, Philip. "Digital Liveness: A Historico-Philosophical Perspective", *PAJ: A Journal of Performance and Art*, vol. 34, no. 3 (2012).
43 Couldry, Nick. "Liveness, 'Reality' and the Mediated Habitus from Television to the Mobile Phone", *The Communication Review* 7 (2004), pp. 356–7.
44 Giannachi, 2004, p. 10.
45 Power, Cormac. *Presence in Play: A Critique of Theories of Presence in the Theatre* (Amsterdam: Rodopi, 2008), p. 201.
46 Notably the works of: Dixon, Steven. *Digital Performance* (Massachusetts Institute of Technology, 2007); Cameron, David et al. *Drama and Digital Arts Cultures* (Bloomsbury Methuen Drama, 2017); Giannachi, Gabriela and Kaye, Nick. *Performing Presence: Between the Live and the Simulated* (Manchester University Press, 2011); Santi, Tony ed. *Documenting Performance* (Bloomsbury Methuen Drama, 2017); Masura, Nigel. *Digital Theatre: The Making and Meaning of Live Mediated Performance* (Palgrave Macmillan 2020); Radosavljevic, Duska. *Aural/Oral Dramaturgies: Theatre in the Digital Age* (Routledge 2022).
47 Dixon, 2007, p. 116.
48 Roland Barthes, *Camera Lucida* (New York: Hill &Wang, 1981).
49 Barthes, 1981, p. 4.
50 Barthes, 1981, p. 87.
51 Dixon, 2007, p. 120.
52 Benjamin, Walter, *The Work of Art in the Age of Mechanical Reproduction*, trans. Harry Zorn (London: Pimlico, 1999 [1936]), pp. 211–245.
53 Benjamin, 1999, p. 214.
54 Fitzsimons, Elena. "NTF Art" in *99dsigns*. See https://99designs.co.uk/blog/web-digital/nft-art/
55 Agacinski, Sylviane. *Time Passing* (New York: Columbia University Press, 2003), p. 33.

5

DIGITAL AGORA

All theatre is communal and political, representing a particular perception and depiction of its time, society and culture. For example, The entertainment industry in contemporary mainstream theatre in London's West End is also political as it operates within the established codes of the dominant cultural groups within a social hierarchy that reflects and reconfirms shared political narratives of the empowered. Community theatre focused on social activism is also political as it gives agency to the audience members in the performance and empowers them to share their own values and beliefs. From the roots of theatre rituals to contemporary experimental forms, theatre is interconnected to the audiences' socio-cultural and political circumstances that define what theatre is as an art form. Ancient Greece brought people together through the narratives of theatre plays (either satire of contemporary society or Gods that evoked the characters' tragic destiny) that had the political function of reflecting audiences' beliefs and values. A social gathering was the essence of an agora, a literary marketplace, which was Ancient Athens's way of social communication. As an open space, an agora was a meeting ground that brought people together to exchange relevant information, goods and stories. Within the political context, the agora served as a place for public debate and engagement with the political life and democratic life of a community. It was like an ancient online platform for trade and socialising, for arts, information and political debate. Ancient theatre facilitated the gathering of people to entertain, reengage and reconfirm the dominant cultural narrative and shared beliefs. Theatre was a local event that had meaning for its community. The numerous contexts of agoras provide the epistemology for various public fora of political theatre, which over time became very defined as theatre with a clear political message. For example, Soviet agitprop extended into image-driven political sketches in the work of Red Ladder Company, Joanne Littlewood's Theatre Workshop was theatre for community learning,

DOI: 10.4324/9781003275893-6

Augusto Boal's theatre forum created social awareness and empoweredness, and Bread and Puppet Theatre used grotesque political puppetry. The epistemology of political theatre provided the necessary ground for the development of applied theatre. Therefore, all political theatre is part of applied performance.

One of the crucial elements that developed applied performance pedagogy was what Thompson refers to as 'social theatre', understanding theatre through its social function and engagement with problematic social issues. Namely, Theatre in Education and Community Theatre used applied performance pedagogy as a collective vehicle to address social pressures and themes relevant to the issues of their local community. If we extend agoras to *digital agoras*, we signify the awareness of online global gathering through live online theatre. Our community migrated from local to international. Shifting the creative practices of applied theatre into live digital theatre created conditions for applied global performance. A digital agora is a form that demonstrated its relevance in applied performance during the Covid-19 pandemic lockdown. As online performances for community theatre became a digital agora, live digital theatre started to bring people together to assemble as an international community connected through the internet and digital platforms. Zoom live theatre became an influential, affordable and user-friendly way of replacing live physical with live digital. Digital live communication replaced community physical communication.

Digital platforms allowed gathering and provided a model for community theatre that would operate under applied performance as the companies needed to keep connections with their audiences throughout the pandemic. The use of Zoom as a platform for live digital theatre was a cure for the collective separation and distancing between people in a lockdown that, at the beginning, amounted to house arrest imposed upon communities by governments worldwide. This chapter examines applied performance pedagogy and how it transgresses into online live communication in education and theatre productions. The influence of global applied performance pedagogy on live digital theatre, mainly on Zoom live theatre, is examined. The chapter looks into the testimonials from *Good Theatre for Good Causes*, a series of transnational community productions by Red Curtain International from India, and *The Art of Fear*, an international production created by Os Satiros Theatre from Brazil. These are examples of the shift from a local to a global approach to the creative practice and pedagogy of applied performance through live digital theatre.

Politics of Applied Digital Media Performance

In digital media culture, the local-global are not adverse, they become one functional unit that interacts one with another, with numerous local providers sharing global information and services. Watching films on Netflix is both local – a specific region with language and cultural context – and global, – internationally accessible and understandable. If applied performance was initially local, the international lockdown pushed it into live digital theatre within the context of an applied global performance. The questions of ownership, who controls the content in applied theatre, and whether its outcome is artistic or has a specific social function were elevated to the international arena. Local-global Anthony Jackson, in a seminal edited book on "Theatre in Education," positions TIE against the background of a border *applied theatre* practice, posing the question about identity of applied performance: 'Is it Education or Theatre?' He points to the duality prompted by tensions in funding conditions "while the Arts Council preferred not to fund work undertaken in school hours…school governors and head teachers saw any activity undertaken by a professional theatre company as 'entertainment'…not educational, and not a priority grant-aid".[1] In line with Jackson's position in his discussion on TIE's *Education or Theatre*, the question can be extended to whether it is *Art or Applied*. In live digital theatre, the concept of aesthetics and making art is inherited as a problematic territory when referencing applied performance methodology. How can social theatre with an educational or community purpose have aesthetic values and be perceived as theatre art?

FIGURE 5.1 The Trial of Harold Pinter (2006). Kolectiv Theatre. Kragujevac, Serbia

The applied idea of socially engaged art goes against the more conservative understanding of art entertainemnt, its purpose, cultural and historical conditions, and audience experiences. As White points out:

> Applied theatre is complex territory for academic aesthetics because (...) it takes for granted a heteronomy, a connection with that which surrounds it, whereas much of literary aesthetics is concerned with the autonomy of aesthetic judgements and of the art that gives rise to them.[2]

In applied theatre, the audience's participation is in response to a shared interest in social issues and challenges that leads to a transformative experience. White observes, "The language of aesthetics is tuned to the fully consummated experiences that viewers, readers and spectators have of completed works, not to the difficulties and conflicts of extended engagement with non-professional participants."[3] As pointed out before, applied performances and performances in artistic theatres shared the participatory role of the audience as an immersive experience. Applied performance and theatre performance share these performative elements outlined in Schechner's *Performance Studies*.

Moreover, applied global performance exists within a plurality of inter-theatrical connections. Jacky Bratton looked into the network of performance connections from a historiographic approach and presented the term inter-theatricality, which conceptualises "the mesh of connections between all kinds of theatre texts, and between texts and their users", who carry with them into the theatre memories of other performances; including "dances, spectacles, plays and songs".[4] Inter-theatricality focuses on the possibilities of shaping performance through other performances, essentially how performances draw one from another, creating citations and shared vocabulary, which allows performance realisation. "Inter-theatrical citationality thickens present performance by mediating it with other performances, and in the same way—at the same time?—prepares future performances."[5] Inter-theatricality can be applied to the analysis of digital performance because of the mosaic of references and the mash of plurality of connections that are part of the interdisciplinary processes and practices in live digital theatre. The applied global performance exists in that matrix of relationships and the majority of references to different disciplines, art forms, cultural frameworks, and social conventions. Fluidity in live digital theatre can be seen through the interaction of 'texts' as media. Texts can become any cultural object, such as digital performance, film, video, photo images, music, and web platforms, to name a few. All these media are referential to each other. Audience involvement in digital performance (live/recorded in space or on-screen) is based on shared social and cultural contexts that recognise previous knowledge of other performance material and citations.

Let us look into the context of alternative theatre – populist, community, and radical political theatre in Britain in the 1970s and 1980s, particularly in the work of playwright and theoretician John McGrath and his collective *7:84 Theatre*

Company, one of the most influential alternative companies in the UK. As Bez Kershaw points out in this period, companies "extended the language of performance aesthetics, and they can be sub-grouped according to their interests in four main aspects of style, (a) the visual and physical, (b) the environmental, (c) the musical, (d) the improvisational."[6] McGrath was a socialist who used theatre as a political tool in the 1970s in addressing working-class communities by applying Marxist analysis to criticise evident social and economic inequality and the collapse of British identity as an imperial colonial power with fading global relevance. The Soviet avant-garde also informed his concept of popular theatre in the 1920s, and agit-prop performances, whose purpose was to bring an unmistakable message in a way workers and those present could understand and relate to. However, McGrath's focus was on localism and community interests; by working with his company in Scotland, they picked up on the prevailing dominant forces that would impact the global economy in the future. The discovery and development of oil in the North Sea and the wealth that accompanied 'Scottish oil' promised economic and political power. However, the ownership and exploitation of the land by the ruling class was centralised in the 1973 devised play *The Cheviot, the Stag and the Black, Black Oil* which used Scotland's Scottish history of oppression and its rural landscape to contest the capitalist push to grab land and sea. This could be an excellent example of early applied performance in which interdisciplinary and visual elements were combined with music, space fragmentation, crude humour, with a direct address to the audience about a topic that was very relevant to their lives at that present moment. McGrath set up the characteristics of what a working-class audience likes to see in a show, which became the aesthetic formalisation of his popular theatre form. It can be seen that his popular theatre relates to the aestheticism of contemporary online performance language.

In his book, *A Good Night Out*, McGrath outlines nine differences between popular and folk performance (what working-class audiences like) and mainstream high art (what he calls middle-class or bourgeoise theatre).[7] The first difference is *directness*, an approach to the audience that points to the message and clearly points out what the play is saying to the audience. The second is *comedy*; the working-class audience responds with laughter to jokes about the world they live in. Therefore, comedy needs to be new, perceptive, and related to their lives. The third is *music*. The working-class audience likes to be entertained by music which is live, popular and contains good melody and harmony from folk tradition. Next are *emotions*; the fourth difference is that the working-class audience likes to engage with a strong emotional narrative. Fifth, *variety* of forms using different types of performative expressions within one show, switching quickly from "a singer to a comedian, to a juggler, to a band, to a chorus number, to a conjurer, to a sing-along, to bingo, to wrestling, to strip-tease, and then back again to a singer, and a comedian and a grand 'Altogether' finale…"[8] A sixth difference is the use of the *effect*; the working-class audience wants moment-to-moment exciting entertainment. If it is boring, they will disconnect from the performance and make that known. Seventh is *immediacy*, where the subject matter, the topic of the performance, is much closer to the working-class audience's lives, experiences and interests, drawing on material that communicates these sources to the audience in the best possible way. Eighth is localism which relates to familiarity with a place, recognising characters and events that are local to audiences. Ninth is also localism, but one that relates to the sense of identity, and unity in understanding that the performer "cares enough about being in that place with that audience and knows something about them."[9] McGrath's characteristics or 'differences' of popular – folk theatre, delivered in a lecture to Cambridge students, are also elements of the practice of applied performance: directness, immediacy and localism regarding audience involvement; comedy, music and variety in terms of performing; and effect and emotions as a way of how the specific narrative (message) is delivered.

Applied Theatre as Educational Model and Performance Studies

In the last decades of the 20th century, applied performance developed as an educational model for learning and teaching though the use of drama. Drama was established as an educational tool for participatory and experiential learning, and teachers – actors as actants of instructional performance. The emphasis was on a specific practice pedagogical model as a guide to understanding, which emphasises establishing learning material appropriate to the students' experience and cultural background. While working in rehearsals and workshops on art practice, it was necessary, even as a condition, to relate to the experiential site for students, taking into consideration that they are taken on a joint creative journey in which they need to establish their presence. The educational thinking used in working on live digital theatre with students was similar. However, the critical difference was in the methodology of performance practice related to the physical space and actor (student), which now have digital cyber presence, working within the parameters of a computer screen and performing in front of the camera for the audience on Zoom live theatre. This new live digital theatre required a different methodology to connect performance studies and applied performance.

With the Covid-19 pandemic, the paradigm of live digital performance, is that it can be both performance practice and pedagogy, shifted toward a more developed use of applied performance in digital theatre, as digital platforms became essential for the operational capabilities of lecturers and students in teaching and training in performance practice and making. Digital pedagogies originated from distance learning (correspondence) which saw a significant development in the 1970s through telecourses and the spread of community colleges. In 2020, live online performance was required so that theatre education could remain operative in universities and creative industries. It was a simple question of survival. Digital technology, computer devices and online file sharing allow video and audio conferencing to provide solutions for creative practices. The performance had to adapt to the new circumstances using tools of digital communication. Discovering ways to resolve representation in live online productions required an understanding of all the influences of visual and performance art and multimedia as physically live theatre encounters were impossible. In practice, the pedagogy explored pre-Covid in the Centre for Interdisciplinary Performative Arts at Royal Birmingham Conservatoire, learning through doing live joint meetings and co-creative processes, was essential for learning performance practice. It was not difficult to switch to live digital theatre once online media and performance techniques and the differences between physical and digital processes were understood on a methodological level as relevant to digital media performance.[10]

It is important to make a distinction between the performative contexts of applied theatre and professional theatre as part of the entertainment/art industry, as a creative process that makes theatre for audience engagement and enjoyment. Scholars accept that the primary aim of applied theatre is education. It functions as community-based theatre practice, outside conventional professional theatres. It can be developed by marginalised communities or as a part of drama in education or therapy. It often exists without a traditional theatre building (usually proscenium arch and auditorium), trained professional actors, dramatic text or an audience that pays for often costly tickets.[11] Applied theatre is an umbrella that comprises working practices of Theatre in Education, Popular and Folk Theatre, Community Theatre, Children and Youth Theatre, Theatre for Health Therapy, Theatre for Development, Theatre in prison, museum and heritage performance, Political Theatre, Street/outdoor performance (including dance and visual arts), even Installation and site-specific community events. All these different art forms can have an applied theatre function as actants that influences attitudes and can contribute to the political climate of social change.[12] Applied theatre is also about learning to use innovative theatre techniques as a creative methodology.

How is this educational and social transformation method used in the online applied theatre that emerged in 2020 due to community restrictions on live physical contacts? What was its relevant impact during this short period?

Like performance research, applied theatre came out of the educational context. It was set up in the 1990s in the UK and Australia as a university education training and research discipline. It is an umbrella term for diverse practices using "the power of theatre in making a difference in the human life span".[13] Indeed, existing as a non-traditional theatrical practice, the reason for doing theatre applied is very distinct. Drama theatre mechanisms can be applied to any activity where theatre can be applied as a method to achieve individual and group transformation towards desired objectives, where performance is not the aim, but a vehicle for some other primary objects. For a long time, theatre practitioners used their skills and worked in community, education and therapeutic contexts. For example, learning a language, dealing with mental health issues, understanding social problems, celebrating community, in post-war conflict reconciliation, business training etc. In addition, the use of space is, to a certain extent, different from a traditional theatre, played in spaces that are not usually used for theatre performances. Space can become initiation, a trigger as a community site for applied theatre to take place. Space can be any outdoor environment or an alternative site such as an abandoned church, a museum, a prison, an empty warehouse, a pub or a community hall. Space can also be an ordinary black box theatre.

Another ideological difference between the cultural industry, where professional theatre is mainly dramatic text-based, and traditional applied performance is the freedom to re-textualise the text or the devising process using not a dramatic text but a group text that results from collective themes and concerns. Typically, applied theatre creates its textual base, devised through group work on a problem or an important event in the community, which is used as material in making the play. As well, the audiences are different. Applied performance benefits the actors who take part, but also its community as it directly addresses the audience's interests. It is also common practice for applied theatre to use community and nonprofessional performers. In drama schools and universities, training and learning for applied theatre typically requires a different set of skills from those required of acting students. Although applied theatre students use theatre-based techniques to address various social issues as art facilitators, they do not perceive themselves as actors in the traditional sense of stage or television acting. Acting in an applied theatre requires a direct address and participatory engagement of the audience and is part of the skills and training needed from the applied performer.

In the 1960s, performance studies and multimedia led to cross-disciplinary performance, where the boundaries between what is considered traditional theatre and what is experimental or experiential and outside of conventional theatre were blurred. Applied theatre in the 1990s inherited a performance studies approach concerning acting, text, space, audience and visual audio imagery. As observed before, Richard Schechner's research practice was established within the context of performance theory and performance studies that operated outside traditional theatre.[14] As observed in Chapter 3, Schechner's The Performance Group, which later became The Wooster Group, developed this performance experience as the totality of the artistic process, which used various intermedial practice methodologies and pedagogies. Stepping outside art theatre, applied theatre entered an area occupied by performance studies within the broad spectrum of social contexts and real-life situations, developing a matrix of a multiplicity of performance forms of practices, i.e. educational, therapy, youth etc.[15] We can say that applied performance, using the broad range of performative expressions, became an integral part of performance studies. In the early 2000s, the scope of applied theatre was further broadened and deepened with the inclusion of digital media.

A significant educational development was the use of performance pedagogy as a teaching and learning method that extends its scope to what is happening in the classroom. A teaching environment similar to what is going on in the rehearsal room becomes central to teaching and learning. In performance pedagogy, a teacher is an actor/facilitator, students are actors/audience, and effective teaching relies on a model of performance techniques.[16] Students are actors in the classroom, rehearsing their ideas, systems of beliefs, cultures, and personal backgrounds. Performative pedagogy became contextualised between pedagogy and performance theories, taking over the essential qualities of performance, emphasising processes and embedded learning through action. In the 1960s, the work of the Brazilian Paolo Freire's 'Pedagogy of the Oppressed,' a theory of education as thoroughly engaging participants through empowerment and participatory method, incorporated the needs of the poor and marginalised communities in the process of becoming self-aware through education. In a capitalist structure, raising consciousness was a way to empower people to represent their interests and improve their socio-economic position. Freire believed he was giving the oppressed their freedom through a different approach to education. Freire's pedagogy was created based on his first-hand experience with illiterate adults from farms and workers in Brazil. In collaboration with them, he identified their interests and created an action plan that served their interests, undermining existing power structures. In 1970, Freire's book was published under the same title as his method, and he extended his practice, developed with illiterate farmers and labourers, to work with students, giving them the right to take responsibility for their education. For Freire, education supports the dominant power structures in society, maintaining the status quo of exploitation, and his model of pedagogy enables the oppressed towards liberation. Similarly, critical pedagogy is based on dominant power as a social construct demeaning and marginalising others (of different cultural or racial backgrounds). As Warren and Fassett point out, "The foundation of critical race theory and cultural studies means that we infuse all course content with issues of power, refusing to allow matters of race and difference to be marginalised."[17]

A ground-breaking development in applied performance came with Freire's student, Augusto Boal, who developed his educational approach as a model through performance work with disfranchised communities. He used it to set up theatre techniques that revolutionised applied performance as a tool for social, cultural and political transformation.[18] Within the social, cultural and political matrix, education relates to the centre that occupies the position of power on the *inside*, that is divided on the mainstream and the periphery *outside* (social centre–periphery model), which is distant from the centre of power and decision making. Following Marxist analysis, this is the typical economically and politically disempowered position of those from the outside looking in. With live online productions taking place internationally, live digital theatre established a new pedagogy and diverse ways of existing in digital space as a live performance and communicating with audiences, which shifted power relations significantly away from a system of traditional cultural gatekeepers (venue politics, funding bodies, institutional structures, various levels of control of the subject matter etc.). Communication platforms like Zoom, social networking apps like WhatsApp, and media sharing YouTube became instrumental in shifting the power structure from the centre to the periphery. Communities on the social edge that would not necessarily have had access to performance as a public arena within the physical theatre space now use digital media to be empowered on the same level as the centre or mainstream production companies. So, in the context of Freire's pedagogy and Boal's ethos of applied performance, online live production has allowed access to art and education both to performance makers and audiences (and students) without the restrictions set up by those who control what content can be done and, even more so, who is allowed to present content. To clarify, if the community or group of performers is willing and digitally capable, they can put a digital performance as a live online production in digital space without any financial constraints or the need to have costly access to the physical theatre space and audiences. Access to funding is the mechanism of financial control that the centre imposes on the periphery, reframed in the case of live digital theatre.

Throughout the 1980s and 1990s, the concept of performance pedagogies started to shape into practice and theories of what is happening in the rehearsal/classroom. Locating oneself in a situation where the matrix of relationships with students, other colleagues, educational policies, traditions, and the creative practice construct performance pedagogies through interactive learning made within a classroom environment is an approach consistent with performance studies. Pineau points out, "Performance studies scholars and practitioners locate themselves as embodied researchers: listening, observing, reflecting, theorising, interpreting, and representing human communication through the medium of their own and others' experiencing their bodies."[19] As a consequence, the performance model was articulated as an instructional metaphor and a pedagogical method. Pineau observes that various scholars appropriated performance, creating new ways of looking at reality, which coincides with the post-modern world view.[20] Performance pedagogies and techniques migrated from an arts experience to an education learning method, emerging for teachers as "both explanatory metaphor and qualitative research method".[21] Indeed, the interdisciplinary qualities of performance studies appeared like a tool that could branch into different disciplines. Methodologies in performance pedagogies work separately from the sense of the established academic authority, where the lecturer is the bearer of knowledge. Instead, the performance focuses on body and inclusivity that builds its interpretation through the audience (students) and performers (teachers as actors) models. Bringing performance into pedagogy allowed for a more open and flexible approach to learning by introducing performance techniques such as open improvisation, character work, stage presence, scene writing, use of media, and a critical approach to the material. For John Warren, the body in the educational context of a classroom/rehearsal setting has to be encouraged and not silenced. It "performs as a site marked by a political, ideological, and historical inscription

(…) serves education as a highly-informed source of experiential knowledge that can, through performative engagement, act as a canvas for creating alternative possibilities through bodily play."[22]

Working with students on video art performance in May 2020 *We Will Meet Again at Rick's*, had the characteristics of a digital applied performance.[23] Due to the lockdown, everything had to migrate online, and the teaching method of group devising had to be adapted to live digital theatre. In the beginning, no connections were established with applied theatre or video performance, but the traditional approach to physical space within could not be used soon into the process. A group-based method of devising was used. Live digital theatre used the characteristics of applied theatre by positioning the actors to personalise the material related to the community's concerns. The subject matter was central to how a group of students/performers were united in their devising process. The theatre/film adaptation of *Casablanca* became a starting reference point for the live group devising process, where rehearsals took place online. To kick start the process, the focus was on themes that students could recognise as familiar and could relate to, such as waiting or wanting to escape, being stuck in one place, isolation, and being separated from loved ones. Another reference point was a famous British song from the Second World War, "We'll meet again" (1939), performed by Vera Lynn, about people being separated by war. This song was noted in the Queen's speech on April 5, 2020 on the hardship of Coronavirus: "we will be with our friends again; we will be with our families again; we will meet again".[24] In this way, film and song provided emotional content from which students could start relating their experiences of separation during the Coronavirus lockdown. As director/deviser of the project, the author went through the same process of subjectivising and telling his circumstances to the situation of waiting and separation. A vital performative context that digital performance provides as part of the role of theatre in times of Covid-19 is the mission to respond to social circumstances of isolation and closure of public life, imposed imprisonment in a form that is not that different from house arrest.

Testimonial 1: *Good Theatre for Good Causes*

Sumit Lai Roy, Red Curtain International productions, India

We started as a local English theatre group: *The Red Curtain*, in Kolkata, India, in April 1969. More than 50 years ago. In those years, we've done over 50 productions, ranging from plays by the global greats like Shakespeare, Shaw, and Stoppard to Indian playwrights like Vijay Tendulkar and Manjula Padmanabhan, and Mahesh Dattani. In 2020, we became *The Red Curtain International* once the pandemic forced us to create theatre online. In three months, we found we had raised more money for the causes we chose to support than we had done in three years of doing productions in Kolkata.

Though we are based in Kolkata, India, as an English theatre company, during the pandemic, we grew into becoming *The Red Curtain International* with a global family of performers and audiences from six continents through our frequent productions and theatre festivals. Theatre without borders. Our performance actors and audiences meet in real-time on a live online platform. Every performance is different. As good theatre should be. Though we are now a global production company, we have local communities at heart in our stories. We encourage cross-cultural productions where teams work seamlessly across continents. But they are inspired by stories from their geographies. We seem to have built what Dundjerović refers to as 'digital agora' without even knowing the word's meaning! Yes, we can now use the term 'digital agora' confidently. We have a family across six continents by bringing people together, performers and audience, from six continents through our production.

We are a global production company but with local communities at our heart in our stories. We have created a theatre community without borders, a Good The@tre Family of thespians, and audiences who support *good theatre for good causes*. The@tre without Borders. We are apolitical by nature. We see ourselves as global citizens. We are not opposed to the "boundaries imposed by the first world". We ignore them. If that is political activism, I guess we are politically active. We believe every human has the right to be the best they can be. And those who are better off should help those not so well off.

Fortunately, founder members active in 1969 were now spread across the globe, and we were able to organise three global theatre festivals between November 2020 and September 2021. (We are currently planning our fourth, in September 2022, which will include physical, digital, and phygital plays.) To enable this to happen smoothly, we are now a registered non-profit in the USA, where two more founder members, Paul Lopez and Radha Iyengar, live. Being originally based only in India gives us a global perspective. India has a vast English-speaking population. 125 million people. The second-largest population in the world. The level of tech-savviness is also very high. If you look at the CEOs of most global tech giants, they are Indian. That's because of the high level of education in Engineering and Management Sciences. Technology is second nature to most Indian college graduates. So is English.

The Indian diaspora is enormous. Over 40 million people of Indian origin are now spread across the globe. And they have mingled with people of other communities. It's quite a convenient global network. India has more than 14 official languages. So, while we are used to English, we are also used to accepting those who use other languages. Fortunately, technology has made sub-titling theatre done in any language relatively easy. We transitioned quickly to bringing productions in Portuguese, Spanish, Farsi, Mandarin and Tamil to global audiences.

We look forward to giving theatre in more languages a worldwide platform and reaching out to international communities in countries where actors and audiences would not have access to physical theatre in a building and cultural capitals.

We continue to dedicate ourselves to doing *good the@tre for good causes* with *The Good The@tre Family* from around the world that has gathered around us. I fell in love with theatre when I was 16 going on 17, in 1969. A school friend was tired of playing women's roles in an all-boys school in Kolkata. So since we had a bit of a gap after completing our 'Senior Cambridge School Leaving Exams' and the start of college, he chose to do a play where participants could also be from a 'sister' school. Proceeds would be given to a charitable cause since we would all be joining college soon. He needed a Stage Manager, and I agreed. Three days before the opening night, the second lead chose to leave for the USA for further studies. Since I was the only person who knew the lines and the moves, having been the prompter at all rehearsals, the role was thrust upon me. The applause of that opening night still rings in my ears. Even more life-changing was the sincere thank you speech by a lady in a blue-bordered sari, who accepted the show's proceeds. She said, "You boys and girls are doing good work. You should keep doing it." The world knows that lady as Mother Teresa now. And that's why The Red Curtain keeps doing good theatre for good causes.

All of us who run *The Red Curtain International* have day jobs. But in all our cases, being involved in theatre has helped our professional careers.

My personal experience with applied theatre started when I chose to create a career for myself of growing people who grow brands. Having learned about growing brands at Ogilvy for 14 years, I started using theatre workshop principles to help practising advertising professionals grow brands. They knew – and earned – on the job, and our techniques to understand the characters we play in theatre helped them better understand their audiences. Learning by Earning is a model I have been operating since 1991, and I have been doing this online since 1996. I've been 'applying theatre' for business training since 1996. You run the workshops/assignments online. No lectures, no theory, you learn-by-doing, or, in my case, you learn-by-earning. So when the pandemic closed down theatres, it was easy for me to see that theatre could continue online. Now that theatres are opening up, we find that Phygital The@tre is completely changing the economics of theatre positively. Anything one can do in the *metaspace* can be done in this digital meet-space or metaspace. Geography has become history.

I can see why online live theatre requires a new approach to pedagogy, but the advantage is that you can adapt any pedagogy that you use in 'meatspace' to online. There are some techniques you can use online that you can adapt to 'metaspace' as well. For example 'Live translations', 'Breakout Rooms', 'Virtual Backgrounds', and 'Virtual Avatars'... Our first online play, *Three Men In A Boat + Monty* (April 2020), had actors from three continents performing simultaneously. Naturally, that helped us attract an audience from those geographies. A global Indian diaspora helped. Family and friends of the actors were spread across the world. While theatres were shut down, they could watch the performance from their homes.

Testimonial 2: *The Art of Facing Fear*

Rodolpho Vasquez, Os Satiros Theatre, Brazil

As soon as the isolation period started in São Paulo (March 2020), our theatre company, Os Satyros, started transmitting Ivam Cabral′s solo performance *Todos os sonhos do Mundo* (All the dreams of the world) on Instagram. Two weeks later, we were invited by a ticket sales agency to explore the possibilities of the Zoom app platform. In June, we started performing on this platform. Simultaneously, other Brazilian companies started similar research. The Culture Secretaries of the state and the city of Sao Paulo saw these performances. They were supposed to direct some funds for culture from the second semester of 2020 on, and they decided that digital theatre would be the best way to help companies and artists to maintain their activities. They opened several calls for theatre artists to develop their work on digital platforms, and the result was that we had a big theatre production in this format for almost two years. Later on, despite Bolsonaro's resistance, Congress decided to dedicate massive funding for artists from the federal budget. And online theatre got even more resources.

It was an exciting learning process for us as performers, our students in Performance School that our theatre runs, and our audiences. We didn't have any experience with digital platforms at all. We had to learn how to do it while creating our art to be shown to the audience. We didn't have support from all of the theatre community. Many critics and artists criticised our effort and said it would never be theatre.

On the other hand, I was in SP Escola de Teatro as a pedagogical coordinator for the directing course. We could not stop teaching. So we learnt how to do it at the same time that we had to teach it. How to teach something that you are learning how to do? This was a considerable challenge. Everything was unclear, but we had to find alternatives; otherwise, our school could be closed by the state. It was a question of survival also.

With digital theatre, archiving is exceptionally easy and cheap to save the performances, the chats, and the interaction with the audience. So, we can say we have registered our history in a way never seen before. Of course, it is an entirely different experience to watch it after it happened because it is not alive anymore. It is a fragment of an incident. But it gives us a document for research and teaching purposes and historical evidence of what theatre looked like in this terrible period.

We had many experiences with artists from all over Brazil and abroad. We worked with Brazilian teenagers in youth theatre from the countryside. We taught them how to use Zoom theatre and act in this environment. It was remarkable how easy it was for them to understand this new way of theatre. It was fun and natural for them. They had no prejudice against it. At the same time, we rehearsed and performed with artists living under terrible conditions. For example, we had an actress from Iran who was afraid of being taken to jail, as women are not allowed to perform. And she had no veil! She was a brave artist who found a way to express herself on a digital platform. Or the Congolese actor who was a refugee in a camp in south Kenya for nine years. He had the opportunity to go back to the stage using Zoom. Living under challenging conditions, he found a way of performing his art to people worldwide.

I hope we don't forget the possibilities digital theatre can bring us for the future. We have to look at the pedagogical process differently in digital live online performance. First, we must get our traditional theatre background as a reference. So, physical theatre training is just a part of the creative process. On the other hand, we must open space for digitality, technology, new paradigms and research in a new technological world. And the younger generation is much more equipped to face this challenge than the old theatre tradition can think. And, of course, you need theoretical support, given by the cyborg theory studies and the techno presence discussions. We are only prepared to create these new pedagogies by combining these efforts (the tradition, the technological research, and critical technological theoretical support).

The pandemic sped up the technological revolution we are now experiencing. Telemedicine has already proved its outstanding contribution to the benefit of society. Tele-education and telework as well. Why should theatre ignore this potential for its expression? Online theatre will never replace physical theatre. It is just another way of manifesting theatre. And there is nothing wrong with theatre occupying this technological space. Theatre has never been ashamed of occupying churches, prisons, schools, and hospitals. The Internet will not stop it at all. I can say from my own experience that I could have never imagined I would make friends from all over the planet during those two years. I met terrific artists from many different realities and crafts with a simple click. And not only artists but also critics and audiences. We must consider how this global community theatre can help artists in danger when they live in authoritarian regimes or under natural catastrophes.

In the Zoom theatre online performance *Art of Facing Fear*, Os Satiros's production with European, Asian and African partners, actors were asked to improvise based on songs and culturally specific elements from their home country. They created dances with this song or music and brought these elements into rehearsal. Following this, they get objects one can dance with and interact with within parallel instructions using Zoom technology to make a digital performance space. For example, learning to open and close cameras corresponds to entering – going on stage and exiting – leaving the scene. They are asked to improvise in the groups of two with a camera opening – entrance and closing – exits, and depending on the subject of improvisation, they are put into small units that can create mini performances of 4–5 people.

We had already finished the run of *The Art of Facing Fear* (TAOFF) when we received an invitation to participate in an online festival in India. It was October 2020, and we thought: Was it possible? An online festival? Then we called all the actors back and performed for Indian audiences. It was a fantastic experience. It was the Red Curtain Festival. From Red Curtain Production, the festival organiser, Sumit, invited us to make a new production with actors from all continents. It was a considerable challenge. And then we met American Young Hozier and probably

Edinburgh Fringe shortly. It is extraordinary to think that theatre can overcome all borders and create an artistic experience for people worldwide. And the most exciting aspect: it is democratic. It doesn't cost the fortunes it would cost for a live performance to cross oceans. You can perform from your home. You can watch it from your home. The question of theatrical space is completely turned upside down. And it makes the theatre a viable art for anyone anywhere.

TAOFF created a global political activist performance that responded to the threat of Covid and the government's use of the pandemic to impose their agenda of control and restrictions. In the beginning, TAOFF meant so much to us in Brazil. We were living under the threat of a coup d'état from our president, and, at the same time, we had a fear of a global pandemic. We were threatened daily by our president, who called artists the vagabonds of society. It was oppressive, and the performance had this perspective.

However, as soon as we started the other versions of the performance, with actors from different countries and continents, we noticed it was a metaphor for many different situations. For example, TAOFF became a protest connected to Black Lives Matter and Trump's government in the USA. In other countries in Africa and Asia, it was a potent symbol of resistance for the artists who lived under authoritarian regimes. In Europe, it brought fear to the extreme-right movement. In each reality, TAOFF got different readings about the tragic moment we were living.

Conclusion

These two examples give us an overview of the use of applied performance within live digital theatre. Learning by doing and through experience emphasising the creative process was essential for the benefit of applied performance pedagogy in live digital theatre. As established within the scope of the performance pedagogy, the framework necessitates teachers and workshop-rehearsal facilitators to re-evaluate their lesson plans, activities, and assigned work beyond the set text. Applied performance is the immediacy of the relationship between the subject being explored, student and teacher. It requires a more collaborative approach with students/actors so that both teacher and student have invested equal interests in the educational process. In addition, applied global performance relies on a group of artists coming together from different parts of the world to collaborate on live interaction, experimentation, and adaptation of culturally diverse material.

Applied performance influenced live Zoom theatre through creative practice. Based on the examples from India and Brazil, it can be seen that applied global performance occupies its own production culture that depends on a different set of relationships, such as working in the studio, creating work in a physical space and developing within the personal area (alone in a room) in front of a camera and computer, collaborating on digital artefacts and visual effects, connectivity through Internet and apps with other people forging another type of connection as a workplace in a cyber world through the digital video communication tools. Applied performance is central to storytelling through the creative process of local communities.

Under lockdown circumstances, the live digital theatre became a method that facilitated an applied global performance, working on social transformation from separation to unification over online versions. The performance enabled gathering people, creating a digital agora and bringing people together in online shows assembled around the performance. By doing so, live digital theatre performed a social role. It also cured the collective separation and distancing imposed upon communities. The gathering function eliminated implied differences between creating theatre performance as art and making performance an act of social theatre. Therefore, professional theatre, communities, and drama schools alike used live online productions to communicate and connect as performers and audiences that became part of live communication. The performative context provided by live online shows made the versatility of applied performance central to developing a pedagogical experience within the new conditions.

Live digital theatre is a fragmented online performance that takes place in a viewers private area (home) connecting several different users and exchanging information and inputs. Because there is no physical presence in one given location, as there would be in a rehearsal or classroom, but the work between student/actor and teacher/student happens in a digital space, it is essential to nourish interactivity and student response, which continuously allows the flow of communication. Applied Digital performance pedagogies, like any other teaching and learning experience, cannot support one side of communication, which eventually becomes deadening. In his experience with live online physical training during the Covid-19 pandemic, Aquilina points out that developing digital pedagogies as a teaching method does not surprise the process of finding tools for cultural transmission. He points out that he "wanted to find ways in which students remain connected and engaged while working online, and where they could bring in a degree of attention and commitment to the proceedings".[25]

When the shift to online teaching and training took place in May 2020 due to Covid-19, there was a need to transition to online communication. Video and audio online conferencing apps replaced physical one-space live encounters with digital cyberspace liveness. The inclusion of online teaching, live theatre and, more importantly, pedagogical work on performance practice did not counteract the values of collaborative process-oriented work or the ways of devising, improvising, and teaching how to work as a group. As Aquilina observes in an essay detailing his experience of physical theatre online, online communication platforms are "A tool, therefore,...never an end in itself but an instrument that exists to function concerning an objective to which it is assigned."[26] It was not about exploring digital technology but about using another way of live communication with co-creation between a group of performers and computer technology as a collaborative tool in creative practice and pedagogy.

Notes

1 Jackson, Anthony and Chris Vine. *Learning through Theatre* (Routledge, 2013, 3rd edition), p.32.
2 White, Gareth. *Applied Theatre: Aesthetics: Aesthetics* (Bloomsbury Publishing Plc, 2015), p.23.
3 White, 2015, p. 45.
4 Bratton, Jacky. *New Readings in Theatre History* (Cambridge: Cambridge University Press, 2003), pp.37–38. The term "intertextuality" exists in the work of most eloquent post-structuralist theorists such as Roland Barthes, and Julie Kristeva. We will not develop this further here, other than to note that the term refers to the interpretation of a text as a dynamic site where relational processes with other textual works with similar interconnection are the focus of analysis.
5 Bloom, Gina and all, "Ophelia's Intertheatricality, or, How Performance Is History", *Theatre Journal*, vol. 65, no. 2 (May 2013), pp. 165–182, p.169.
6 Kershaw, Baz. *The Politics of Performance: Radical Theatre As Cultural Intervention* (Taylor & Francis Group, 1992), p.139.
7 McGrath, John. *A Good Night Out. Popular Theatre: Audience, Class and Form* (London: Eyre Methuen, 1981).
8 McGrath, 1995, p.211.
9 McGrath, 1995, p.213.
10 In response to teaching performance practice, I introduced the pedagogy of reflective practice (Bolton, Gillie. *Reflective Practice*, Sage Publications, 2010) and experiential learning (Beard, Collin and John Wilson. *The Power of Experiential Learning: A Handbook for Trainers and Educators*, Kogan Page, 2002) and by bringing action learning and student-centred teaching (Atkinson, Robert et al. "Learning from Examples: Instructional Principles from the Worked Examples Research", *Review of Educational Research* vol. 70, no. 2, pp. 181–214, 2000) with ongoing assessment feedback for students' practical work, I centralised the process and rehearsal/workshop (classroom) learning environment.
11 For the critical concepts in applied theatre, see seminal books by Thompson, James. *Applied Theatre: Bewilderment and Beyond* (Peter Lang, 2003) and Nicolson, Hellen. *Applied Drama: The Gift of Theatre* (Palgrave, 2005).
12 The central reference point for applied theatre in the West (Europe, Australia, USA) came from Agusto Boal, the Brazilian theatre visionary, director, activist and theorist who established the theatre method of the Oppressed, empowering the audience to analyse and perform in problematic created situations made to provoke a response that invitee spectators to perform offering a solution that can help them change their everyday conditions. See book Boal, Agusto. *The Theatre of the Oppressed* (published in English in 1985).
13 Taylor, Peter. "Applied Theatre/Drama: An E-debate in 2004. Viewpoints", *Research in Drama and Education*, vol. 11, no. 1, p.93.
14 Schechner, Richard. *Performance Studies: Introduction* (Routledge, 2002).
15 Schechner, Richard. *Performance Theory* (Routledge, 2003).
16 Pineau, Elyse Lamm, "Teaching Is Performance: Reconceptualizing a Problematic Metaphor", *American Educational Research Journal*, vol. 31, no. 1 (Spring, 1994), pp. 3–25, p.4.
17 Warren, Deanna and John Fassett. *Naming a Critical Communication Pedagogy* (SAGE, 2004) p. 421.
18 See Freire Paolo, *Pedagogy of the Oppressed* first published in 1970 (Penguin, 2017).
19 Pineau, 1994, pp. 3–21.
20 Turner set up performance as part of anthropology in investigating social drama, Bauman as verbal art, Schechner established performance for expressing cultural identity, and Gofman's sociology positioned performance of self in everyday life.

21 Pineau, 1994.
22 Warren, John. "The Body Politic: Performance, Pedagogy, and the Power of Enfleshment." *Text and Performance Quarterly 19* (1999), pp. 257–266, p. 257.
23 See Chapter 8 for the full elaboration on the case study *We Will Meet Again at Rick's.*
24 The Queen's Speech on Coronavirus: Full recording of Her Majesty's address streamed live on 5 April 2020, accessed on https://www.youtube.com/watch?v=2klmuggOElE
25 Aquilina, Stefan. "Physical Training Online: Transitioning Towards Digital Pedagogies", *Theatre, Dance and Performance Training*, vol. 13, no. 1 (2022), pp. 6–21, p. 8.
26 Aquilian, 2022, p. 9

PART 2
Pedagogical Praxis

6

INTERMEDIAL PRACTICES

Digital Media Performance in Live Theatre

The chapters in Part 2 explore *Pedagogical Praxis*, how live digital theatre operates in practice, based on performance case studies developed since 2008 through the work of my collaborative group Kolectiv Theatre with students and professional performers. Kolectiv Theatre has been co-creating projects with national (UK) and international (Ireland, Spain, Romania, Serbia, Iran, and Russia) partners. I founded in 2000, Kolectiv Theatre within the Higher Education context (first at Liverpool Hope University and after at Manchester University, University College Cork and Birmingham City University) to explore interdisciplinary and international theatre practices and pedagogies. Its objective was to further students' learning through practice engagement and experience by collaborating with professionals following creative industry standards and investigating innovative performance practice methodology and pedagogies. Our examples of practice are grouped chronologically, from the inclusion of digital media into live theatre, to live performance coming into online digital platforms, and finally, an assessment of post-digital theatre in a hybrid of live physical and digital performance – Phygital and implication of theatre in metaverse and meta-space. An account of performative pedagogies and embodied practices for live digital theatre and the creative methodology and audience experience for Zoom live theatre as new artistic forms and expressions. A traditional approach to teaching and learning of practice in HE drama schools and conservatoires, generally in the training of actors, directors, writers, and performance authors and makers, does not include pedagogies of multimedia and digital arts as the critical impact on how performance is created. Interdisciplinary performative pedagogies are not part of the creative process where students are exposed to different media and digital practices; arts disciplines are still approached separately as in the 1970s with electronic media such as acting for television, video, theatre (building with stage), radio and film.

DOI: 10.4324/9781003275893-8

With the Covid-19 pandemic, communication technology and computers aimed to overcome the obstacles to theatre live performance. These conditions broadened the concept of liveness and pushed the boundaries of liveness and contemporary creative practice in theatre. With the existing restrictions on social contacts and our need to find ways to overcome them, we had to think of the type of video conferencing, telepresence systems explored previously, or any online digital platform (for example, WhatsApp, Instagram, Facebook, etc.) and look for the relativity of these digital communicational concepts to liveness in performance art and theatre. A need to discover new pedagogy led to the development of the wholly novel idea of live online performance based on experiences of Telepresence and Digital Video Communication.

The chapter six focuses on the pedagogies of digital multimedia performance and intermedia relationships. The presence of actor and audience in digital media performance in recent years, as Vanhoutten observes, is evidenced in "a continuous network of embodied states of presence that is increasingly defined according to participation and agency, rather than physical co-presence".[1] We will see how the involvement of digital technologies changes actors' approaches to text that is now re-mediatised through different communication channels, not only physical/vocal actors' delivery.

Looking at digital media performance being used in live onstage performance we discuss examples of three case studies that explore creative practice and pedagogy of live digital theatre. The relevance of these case studies is in exploring physical theatre space as a site and forum for mediatising visual content within that space, working with interdisciplinary actors and immersive promenade relations with the audience. The methodology of Zoom Live Theatre can be seen to come out of digital media performance in the areas such as performer working with a camera, use of space on a computer or television screen, relation with an interactive audience whose presence is known and acknowledged telepresence of performers' physical and private space. Three performances are examples of co-productions with various theatre venues, festivals in different countries, and audiences' languages, and working with performers whose experiences and levels range from experienced professionals to student actors and beginners. These are the theatre productions I directed and devised from 2008 to 2015 as projects exploring interrelationships between the performers and the digital media and their mediatised presence on computer-generated images on the projection screen and space with audience immersion in site-specific locations. The performer's action in these projects was at the centre of the creative process, with inter-mediality in productions as an outcome of the interconnection of digital media brought into the physical environment. The projects were: *The Orchard Cycle* (2008–2011, Kolectiv Theatre, in the UK, Iran and Serbia), *The Club New World Order* (2009–2010, Kolectiv Theatre, Drama at Manchester University and Knajzevsko Srpski Teatar, Royal Court Theatre, Serbia), and *Death of a Salesman* (2013–2015, Kolectiv Theatre, Drama and Theatre, University College Cork,

Everyman Theatre, Cork Ireland and Belgrade Drama Theatre, Serbia). We will focus on examples from the performance-making practice of how digital multimedia impacts the collaboration of performers within an intermedial creative context. This chapter will also investigate the creative processes, pedagogical methodologies, actors' required training, and behind the performance practice of these projects. The recorded film and video agency, sound and visual images within live performances have equal balance with the performers' actions and storytelling. A performer can communicate to an audience live and through an intermedial environment. There is a need for interdisciplinary performative practice pedagogy to set up an examination of actors' performance at the centre of intermedial theatre experience. This process is generally neglected in conservatoire and drama school training.

There are two groups of the intermedial experimental practice research project in which case studies will be explored. The first one focuses on the immersive and digital multimedia on-site location relating to non-theatre spaces: *The Orchard Cycle* based on *The Chery Orchard* by A. Chekhov and *The Club New World Order*, a collage of texts from a selection of Pinter's one acts plays, Muller's *Hamletmachine* and Plato's *The Death of Socrates*. The other group relates to adaptation of stage text for multimedia cinematic theatre exploring theatre stage through the example of *Death of a Salesman* by Arthur Miller. These experiments examine the theatrical language of visual and physical expressivity and the influence of multimedia on performance making. In both experimental production groups, we can see the progression of physical theatre space into promenade site-specific multimedia collage (in *Orchard* and *World Order*) and digital performance into the intermedial experience (in *Salesman).*

As elaborated in Chapter 3, intermediality in theatre resulted in the creation of performance practice and pedagogy based on models developed in Black Mountain College by John Cage, Anna Halprin in San Francisco Dance Workshop and Robert Lepage with Theatre Repere and Ex Machina, actors training techniques, and Elizabeth LeCompte Wooster Group's montage of live and visual events. The intermedial pedagogical models developed in studios and through rehearsals for performer training used creative practice from visual and live arts, dance traditions, performance arts, and multidisciplinary theatre and not training from traditional drama schools and conservatoire actors' education. This results from a production outcome where performance does not serve a written text and actors are not interpreters of characters developed in the text. Instead, production is aligned with performance art, creating an experience and performance event through the actor-author. Projects depend on physical and mediated reality from the actor's interconnection with media and the transformation of action and space. Physical presence and digital visual projections provided context for telling the stories. All three research projects had pedagogical objectives, exploring methods of practice in creating the aestheticism of live multimedia performance through digital technology and the best ways ensembles of actors can embrace it without experience in multimedia, and groups of performers with various skills in different stages of their careers.

The Orchard Cycle (based on A. Chekhov, *The Cherry Orchard*), Liverpool Capital of Culture (2008, Liverpool, UK); 27th FAJR International Theatre Festival (2009, Teheran, Iran;) JoakimInterfest – International Theatre Festival (2009, Kragujevac, Serbia); Studio, Lawry Theatre (2010, Manchester, UK)

Contexts: Hyperreal Orchard

The Orchard Cycle is an immersive site-specific performance based on Anton Chekhov's play *The Cherry Orchard* that developed through Four Cycles, following methodologies of RSVP Cycles and Robert Lepage's intermedial performance making. Interdisciplinary performative pedagogies focus on space for performance in how space is transposed from a site-specific location to mediatised reality created through various visual projections. It was essential to develop pedagogy to help actors respond to the environment and create relationships with other actors/characters by drawing inspiration and energy embodied within that location.

The project took place from November 2008 to June 2010. The actors who had just finished London Acting Studio training joined Kolectiv Theatre Ltd. The way of working was close to the ensemble as they all studied together in the same school and have developed a 'generational' and joint communal approach to acting. It was traditional stage theatre training with little understanding of the use of the digital media creation process. The origins of *The Orchard Cycle* was the 2008 Liverpool Capital of Culture, as a performance event taking place in one of several cultural activities that happened all around the city in alternative locations.

FIGURE 6.1 *Cherry Orchard* (2009) Kolectiv Theatre. Teheran, Iran

Initially, the performance was presented in a gamekeeper's lodge in Sefton Park, Liverpool.

In January 2009, at the Fajr Festival in Teheran, I directed in collaboration with Atila Pesyani and the Bazi theatre group from Teheran bilingual promenade site-specific performance. It was part of an international programme as co-creation on the new version/cycle between my company from the UK and a leading Iranian theatre group that included the following members in the production: Atilla, his daughter Setareh Pesyani, and actors Sahar Dolatshahi and Naz Shademan. The production was performed bilingually in English and Farsi to an audience that followed the action through various spaces in a building of Theatre House in Teheran. In October 2009, at the Serbian international theatre festival Joakiminterfest, we performed in the House of Youth Arts (Dom Omladine) using similar relations developed in Teheran, adapting to new circumstances of the space and audience. Finally, we used the building of Lawry Studio Theatre in June 2010, adapting locations to our environment by using visual projected reality, creating an intermedial experience for actors and the audience.

Development: Immersive Site and Digital Media as Text for Performance

The textual adaptation of the narrative in Chekhov's play for the First Cycle in Liverpool came from actors creating life stories of their characters based on multiple perspectives as interviews leading to a set of soliloquies about living in the most beautiful orchard that will now be sold as there is no money to maintain the estate. One of the starting reference points of this project was the characters' personal stories that are not in the text but are indicated by their actions and some lines indicating what their dreams were and what they wanted to do once the orchard was not there anymore. *The Orchard*, as a new text, gave voice to other characters in the play through their monologues developed by actors playing those characters to offer views on their life, what their dreams are and what they want to live but do not, and how their reality differs. The space, a house, was fragmented into different rooms with an interactive approach to audiences that were taken on a promenade. In a new narrative, the house was the central estate from the play, which is now turned into a model home for the new cottages that will be built, The personal stories created by performers who developed characters based on themselves transpired as an essential activity, a dream, of either running away from the space, from entrapment of the *Orchard* or possessing it, controlling and destroying it.

The beginning of the research project focused on a location, a cottage and an orchard as sites where the characters' stories take place. In the dramaturgical approach, we started from the end of the play, where the orchard is being cut down to build summer cottages. The spaces for performance were linked through the play's awareness of a present-day supra narrative emphasising tensions between the past as represented in the location and its recent utterance. The story unfolds throughout the space as a remembrance of what once the orchard was for all characters, not only the story of the main character Ranevskya. This was a plurality of stories from perceptions of different characters. It was a polyvalent focus on narrative. The outdoor scenes were performed in the cottage garden, indicating a road opposite the house leading to Sefton Park as the location for the cherry orchard. Action and space helped us define the overall narrative of the performance we wanted to communicate and the performance form of the piece that translated Chekhov's play into the new environment. We set the whole performance in the context of summer cottages as the story of the main house that will become one of the summer cottages built at the end of the play once the orchard is sold and cut. We agreed that the audience would be taken on the promenade of a model summer cottage (a gamekeeper's cottage on the edge of Sefton Park, referred to as the model cottage built from the orchard being cut down). The audience had a function of potential buyers. At the beginning of the narrative, we start with the estate agent taking the audience through different rooms in which each fragmented scene took place as a memory of the location, as a story told by the house of what it was before it became a house. The tour distanced the audience from the play's action and focused on the movement of the performance within a present-day property sale.[2]

Once we determined fixed resources – personal stories developed by actors as authors relating to a site that is in some form of transition, with audiences' immersion and promenade and performance reflecting different socio-political and cultural circumstances, we moved to the 2nd Cycle. The Scores were transferable into *The Orchard* for Teheran production. The critical elements of the Teheran Cycle were to include space as a site of a building that was under reconstruction, which was a location that was a new cottage that was being refurbished. The collaborators from Iran joined the co-creation creating a now bilingual performance in English and Farsi. In addition, there were a set of installation images of the orchard in the courtyard of the building with pink and white flickering Christmas-type lights suggesting a cherry tree in blossom with an open fire in a barrel. In the 3rd Cycle in Kragujevac, where the production was in Serbian and English, the outdoor scene was played in a courtyard. The narrative shift reflected the performance's site, a grand 19th-century villa. The space was used as an actual site for the main house of the estate that would now be demolished to build space for new cottages at the end. Changing the location initiated a different approach to the story, and actors had to accommodate their approach to characters responding to a set of new circumstances coming from a site. Finally, the performance in Manchester as the 4th Cycle transposes a site-specific location into a studio theatre. It uses digital media to create various visual references to past events in the mediatised play *The Cherry Orchard*. The outdoor scene was set up through live video projections of a film that showed characters in the past within the actual cherry orchard setting. The audio landscape supported play on memory, where characters on the stage appeared as part of the video and audio hidden stories from the Estate.

Objectives and Methodology: Remediating 'Orchard'

The objective of this project was to re-mediate text through the site, where immersive space 'tells' a story of the orchard. We wanted to explore how location and digital media can influence performers' actions and how to live. Media presence is incorporated into dramaturgy and provides space/media context for the play's narrative. It was also important to create each new cycle in response to a different location as an audience promenade: an estate house in Liverpool, a building under reconstruction in Teheran, a 19th-century villa now house of culture in Kragujevac (Serbia) and Lowrey's studio using the whole of the theatre building in Manchester. The use of these locations was essential as it allowed for interaction between space and action and life, and mediated in creating a dramaturgy of the play. Pedagogically each of the Cycles had a different set of tasks and required training from actors to respond to the specificities of the performance.

The methodologies of practice and training used in this process were drawn from John Cage's group improvisation applying imperfection of found environment as random influences outside of artist intentions as a *flexible* and identifying group of possibilities for each performance element that could be *fixed*. For example, the house or building where the performance as a site-specific promenade would take place became a fixed element of the *Orchard Cycle*. In contrast, rooms in the house/building and exterior space were flexible for limiting personal in-group improvisation to adaptation to random factors. The critical method of open rehearsal came from Lawrence and Anna Halprin's RSVP Cycles, appropriated through the actor-author writing of performance text, physical action, the transformation of space, body, objects and physical and media resources.. For Lepage's devising process,

> space is equal to score (performers' interaction with resources in the space). [...] The actor-creator of scores is a writer in space. Scores are small, improvised scenes that are not connected to any narrative but can be rearranged and edited depending on the images and dramaturgically interesting material they produce.[3]

Immersed in site and interactivity with other performers based on the event in the space and a character responding to stimuli and not following the fixed text, actors used the creative viewpoint methodology initially developed by choreographer Marie Overlie. Viewpoint pedagogy uses six essential elements on stage: space, shape, time, emotion, movement and story. Theatre director and educator Anne Bogart elaborated these into nine physical and five vocal viewpoints. Our training in the *Orchard Cycle* provided context for actors' observations. Viewpoint exercises provide an opportunity for training and creativity that places the performer at the centre of the observation process, allowing a group of actors in an ensemble "to practice creating fiction together daily using the tools of time and space".[4]

As a site-specific performance, *Orchard Cycle* seemed as if it had been created for each separate space and venue in which it was presented and not superposed to the physical conditions of an existing location. One of the first tasks for the group was to establish how the action score relates to a different space. The work method was group creativity, where I facilitated the process by organising scores and providing overall direction. Still, actors as a group were responsible collectively for all the elements (set, costume, props) of the creative process. The rehearsal process was about learning to interpret different physical environments, including the one created by media through projections which became part of the performers' scores. We moved to another location, trying to adapt to the site and figure it out. What different areas within the house tell us about the events relating to the production? How do we perform within this new environment and include space, media and audience within the dramaturgy of our performance? The fixed elements in the project needed to be reworked into improvisational material relevant to a new setting.

The actors were learning how to work in an immersive site-specific and mediated environment using video cameras and video projections, which then was translated into the dramaturgical development of the performance. Following are exercises used to develop actors' presence within space-time conditions of immersive site-specific and media performance. In the workshop and rehearsal process, the practices used in all cycles were about the appropriation of space in *character interactions in a public space* through the re-enactment of the events from the play. The objective of the exercise is to free the actors from the circumstances that exist in the play and allow characters to interact in various circumstances beyond the story found in the text. Sudley House is a historic estate house in Liverpool built in 1824 belonging to a wealthy Victorian merchant belonging now to Liverpool Museums.[5] As an authentic site, this house was the closest to what we can get to the house in Cherry Orchard, which was probably built around the same period. The actors had to interact with each other and the public as if they were in the estate house of Cherry Orchard, using furniture, dressed in costumes they had chosen for their characters living in all the space of Sudley House from the vast entrance hall and period drawing room to dining room and library. There was no time limit to exercise, and actors were supposed to be characters living in any improvised situations. As characters were based on actors who wrote their personal stories in monologues, actors were not characters; they lived them as their alter-egos. The exercise in Sudley House was interrupted by security, who asked us to leave but not before the characters had a chance to live and interact in space for a considerable time. Similar, *live character interaction in a public space* took place in the Grand Bazaar in Tehran as part of rehearsals for the 2nd Cycle that premiered at the Fadjr Festival—being the central indoor shopping place in Teheran with a wide range of goods for sale, including jewellery and famous Persian rugs. The task was for each actor to buy or negotiate a price for an object relevant to their character, and improvise what their character would do and how they would interact if they were in the Bazaar as the site location.

Another exercise that the group developed was using time as *live durational time*. The dramaturgy in Chekov's play is based on actual events separated into four acts which correspond to our four events within different sites within the existing house where actors are together with the audience. Each event took real-time action, with the characters performing in a memory alive in a space while the audience was taken on a tour of a prospective property. Dramaturgically this was time as a remembrance that exists within the tour time of the audience. The task for actors/students was to live in a site as in durational performance, to accept that they were there 24 hours and not only for the length of the scene. This involves the creation of various physical actions that each performer had to engage individuals with within their own space. Actors developed multiple events around the main event in act one, which was the reception of Ranevskaya returning from France to her estate. As the site was a house and the audience was on a promenade, there was no stage, off-stage, or auditorium; the whole place was one lived experience for the audience and actors. The relationship with the exercise on time was also with the audience, who was recognised as another person participating in the scene. Therefore, the address would also include them as participants in the situation. The audience was moving through the house, and the task was to keep the character continuously wherever one may be. Even if not physically in the room where the audience is, as the action is happening simultaneously in different rooms actor had to live as a character even without an audience present. This approach to engagement with time was used for all four events in the performance.

The media exercise involving the creation of a *virtual past on camera* through film and visual images was relevant for the 4th Cycle in Lowry. The event 'walking in the field' from act 2, taking place in the field that leads towards the cherry orchard in the distance was conceptualised in a mediated environment in a studio where the film characters appear as video projections and simultaneously live on stage in studio space without seating area in Lowry. Interplay was created between the performers' live presence and their mediatised presence. The events presented in the film are from the past described in the background of the narrative of Chekhov's play but developed by actors into short stories. Video projection of the cherry orchard in blossom, the pond at the bottom of the garden, the ghost of Ranevskya's little son who drowned some years ago, a love relationship between young Anya (Ranevskya's younger daughter) and Trofimov (the eternal student living on the estate) before she left for France, Lopakhin (now a wealthy merchant who will buy the Orchard to destroy it and built cottages) as a child growing up in poverty and domestic violence, were juxtaposed to the same characters in the 'walking in the filed' re-mediatising story through the double presence using the intermediality of live performance and film creating a hyperreal experience. Each actor made their stories by using a camera, working with each other in filming. Learning to work with a camera and use it to perform and capture performance was part of the workshop. At the same time performing in the mediated space with a video projection of themselves required interface with the video as another acting partner in the scene.

Summary of Outcomes

The performers involved in the devising process incorporated different physical and digital locations when we performed in the Lowry studios. Actors and space were the central pedagogical focus in different *Orchard Cycles*. Actors and performance space became critical elements in the participatory relationship with the audience. Digital images supported the audience experience, which was central in both pieces. The different media and the performative context of the site-specific location emphasised audience participation. The audience and actors were part of the same physical space, and spectators played a role (buyers of cottages) within the performance supra-narrative. One of the critical outcomes came from the audience feedback (in our open talks after the show as part of the R&D workshop process) and a comment that they felt that their experience of the performance was super real, as if they were part of a TV drama or virtual reality as the action was taking place all around them, with no separation on auditorium and stage, in a space where actors are just a meter away from the audience. Pedagogically, actors had to work on a close-up, film relationship with the audience, similar to Zoom live digital theatre camera shots. The relationship with the present audience showing an intimate space where a performer is physically based.

The Club New World Order (based on a collage of texts from H. Pinter's one-act plays Party Time, New World and One for the Road, Plato's Socrates Death and Heiner Muller's HAMLETMACHINE) 2009–2011 seasons in Knjazevsko Srpski Teatar (Serbian Royal Court Theatre, Kragujevac, Serbia)

Contexts: From Fragmented Theatre Space to Intermedial Presence

The Club New World Order is a collage of dramatic texts, live theatre and digital media within performance spaces of a 19th-century neo-baroque theatre building used as an architectural site. A fragmentary site-specific promenade throughout the building was used to provide a performance space where the live action was interconnected with digital media performance. The creative methodology for *The Club* focused on performers' interaction and appropriations of rooms –

locations and audience presence within these locations having different roles. Within the live digital theatre, space and audience have a plurality of implications that are much more complex than with realistic proscenium or fourth-wall theatre audience communication of a story. As mentioned before, the dramaturgy of live digital theatre is simultaneously live theatre, film, and video art. In addition, dramaturgical structure worked as a presence of digital media performance in live theatre through various projections and video installations and live performances within the digital platform since some events were projected while taking place live in an adjunct space to where the audience was located.

The production was undertaken by an ensemble of actors, dancers, musicians, professionals, and students working collaboratively on the creation of performance events that related to several different starting reference points: space for performance in the theatre building, film interactivity with live performance, video projections of digitally created material, and audio landscape. As a contextualisation for performance event, marking ten years from the NATO bombing of Serbia, I was relating to anti-war sentiment. The performance *World Order* is commissioned by Royal Court Theatre Kragujevac (Serbia) and City Council Kragujevac (Serbia) and supported by the University of Manchester and Kolectiv Theatre UK. It premiered in repertory on the June 27, 2009. In this particular case study, I worked on creating a textual collage, an adaptation of Harold Pinter's four one-act plays, organised in the *New World Order Cycle* consisting of *One for the Road* (1984), *Mountain Language* (1988), *New World Order* (1991) and *Party Time* (1991). In addition, the project used textual fragments from Heiner Muller's *Hamletmachine* (1977), a postmodern reiteration of Shakespeare's Hamlet, and *The Death of Socrates* by Plato (-400BC).

In a mediatised culture, reality in digital technology is equal to the physical experience of truth for audiences familiar with digital social networking. In *The Club New World Order*, digital media and interactivity of media spaces within theatre space have the quality of liveness, modifying the original Auslander's understanding of what is live in real-time events within the mediatised performance. Intermedial performance allows connection here beyond the boundaries of theatre space and somewhere else as other spaces, in transgression between local location and media location. Within live digital theatre, this hybrid connection of equal influences being the in-between location is what we describe in Chapter 5 as Transtopia. However, the performance action was contained within the space of a theatre building with filmed projections to alternative spaces elsewhere for participating audiences without entering cyberspace or the digital world connected through the Internet. *The Club* used digital media within the live theatre performance to develop a site of theatre space to establish an intermedial presence involving incorporating visual and performance art, dance, and digital media. The research project introduced an intermedial approach to acting pedagogy, where the performer must be responsive and interact with an environment consisting of digital media and live theatre.

The audience's body responded to the performance event as a familiar occurrence, both as a location and as an experience they were witnessing. The performance is related to the collective memories and experiences of the audience who went through more than three months of intensive NATO bombing of Serbia in 1999, in which more than 5,000 people lost their lives or were declared missing. The audience did not want to be reminded and again positioned in the same circumstances. The participatory, promenade, site-specific performance experience engaged the audience's memories with their collective freeze response to ongoing decades of threats of sanctions and bombs since flight and aggressiveness are likely ineffective. The hostess inside the hall bears the same name as NATO's bombing operation in Serbia, 'Merciful Angel', in a white dress. The title is projected on her and the images of the bombing. She is fake, masking the truth that Pinter calls for. The VIP lounge hostess represents a manufactured reality conceived for the public by the leading world powers to justify the actions taken against sovereign states.

Apart from my role as a researcher, examining pedagogies of multimedia performance, I directed, adapted, and created a design vision in collaboration with the group of performers. In 2008, we wanted to experiment with the pedagogy of collaborative performance using multimedia and site-based performativity within a more defined location for intermedial explorations. Using the experience of Brazilian collaborative theatre, which I explored in 2008 as part of the Leverhulme Fellowship and applying it to a state ensemble of actors, I wanted to see how they would respond to the new multimedia group theatre performance pedagogy. Inspired by the work of the Wooster Group, the fundamental idea of textual and media collage is relevant to the experience of the audience's social-cultural context. Again Lepage's working from scores (location, text, sound, video, visual projection, TV screen, music, physical expression) was the primary pedagogical approach to interrelating all the elements within the intermedial presentation in a performance space. In this way, digital technology serves as an intermedial connection between different art forms, such as performance art, visual art, dramatic text, dance, music, etc., to create multiple events coming together within the audience's experience.

Objectives and Methodology

The objective of the performance research project in Serbia was to develop a living environment in a whole theatre building as a location combining physical sites with live digital projections. It was also a second Cycle developed in 2009, created from the exploration of the first version produced initially in John Thaw Studio with acting students at The University of Manchester as a first Cycle in 2006. The performance space was approached as an architectural site; the performance was articulated as a promenade where the audience could experience an experiential spatial journey. The actors had to learn how to perform with each other and interact with physical locations in the building and the digital environment introduced in various fragmented spaces throughout the building.

The participants were not exposed before to interdisciplinary performance making. 2006 was Pinter's year, and as a celebration of his 2005 Nobel prize for literature, I adapted and directed with acting students a multimedia promenade performance *Playing Pinter* produced by the Drama and Screen Studies Department, where I was a Senior Lecturer. We used the John Thaw studio and the whole building of the Martin Harris Centre, University of Manchester, as our site for performance. The objective was to expose acting students to multimedia performance using performance and visual arts references and site-specific and promenade aestheticism. The innovation with this performance was the emphasis on performativity rather than dramatic text consisting of an intermedial and physical embodiment of performance space inhabited by different hypermedia expressions. Alongside digital performance, which facilitated the quality of media presence, the actors were developing live performances integrated within the totality of the performance experience. Inspired by this experiment, I decided to transfer the approach to multimedia pedagogy into ensemble theatre in Serbia, pushing the boundaries with actors in Serbia of what can be considered intemedial theatre and what can be allowed within performance space.

Through the experience of being in the same space in various locations in theatre, the audience shared the physical space with the performers and were assigned a role; they were the new members who had just joined the exclusive club *The New World Order*, witnesses of torture, and people from a village waiting to see their loved ones imprisoned. The audience experience before they entered the production was essential for the performative context. Serbia's social and cultural context in 2009 influenced the formation and interpretation of the project's narrative. It was relevant to the shape of an overall performance action and how the audience interacted based on that familiarity with context. The relevance of 10 years from the NATO bombing with bombed-out buildings still visible left as apocalyptic monuments, economic corruption, political instability and the influence of various social clubs promoting exclusivity and elitism for a group to socialise was an everyday reality for those living in Kragujevac. Pinter's criticism of American imperialism, and imposed values of the now-defunct new world order, were central to the themes around which the multimedia performance was organised.

The creative method used by the Wooster Group was essential for making this production and creating performance through a montage of sites' physical locations, video art, cinematic projections and a mix of recorded and live action. Digital technology allowed us to create interactive videos and bring visual projection into different locations, live music mixed with recorded sounds, to introduce characters on television screens performing alongside actors. It was an exercise *in creating a textual montage of sites. The Club* presented a task in front of an ensemble actor trained to work on a text and director's concept, to become an author of its performance that uses text as much as other production elements in creative practice. Referring to Lepage's approach to working with actors, that actor is an author of performance and not an interpreter, the initiated pedagogy was to use textual starting points from Pinter, Muller, and Plato, as well as incorporating Brazilian axe drumming, visual quotations from Marina Abramovich, installation performance art *Balkan Bones*, digital video art installation editing the Iraq and Bosnian wars and incorporating live streaming of events taking place outside the theatre into the action on stage.

Exercises in *Intermedial Score Making* reflected a mix of Wooster Group montage with Lepage's approach to scores using live and media performance elements. Using montage, each textual fragment was related to space for the group of actors to develop an intermedial score within the theatre building. Working on the score included a specific role given to the audience members. The actors had to establish relationships with the audience present depending on the situation, participants in a Club as VIP guests; people in a village who are protesting; prisoners, and a theatre audience watching a play about interrogation that at some point becomes a reality show; tourists observing freak shows for their entertainment. In an audience promenade we travelled from the theatre restaurant/bar to various locations in the theatre building, except for the 300-seat auditorium that was not used – it remained visibly empty during the promenade with the lights on. We wanted to question reality: did the event book the theatre for the Club, and this is all real, or is this a theatre act? The resources are given to each group doing a score – text, location, video and film projection, audio, objects, and audience presence. Each group of actors plays with the material given and finds a way to communicate textual fragments through various intermedial connections.

It was an exercise in *repurposing the site as an alternative space*. At the same time, the site-specific use of the whole theatre, a 19th-century Neo-Baroque building, provided a physical location that both complemented and contrasted with the digital aesthetics of the performance. Each area within the theatre became an alternative space for events with *The Club*. The unification between fragmented and different scores/locations was by digital visual/auditory imagery and a camera filming live events in another part of the building and projecting for the audience while in another score/location. The performance started from the gallery with a bar in front of a theatre auditorium. It progressed through a promenade into the backstage area. Under stage corridors, to a set workshop adjunct to the theatre, outside on the city square consisting of the cathedral and townhouse in front of a main entrance to the theatre, to finish on the proscenium stage where both actors and audience were together, finishing video and audio installation referring to bombing and recent America led wars with a waltz danced by actors involving the audience. The whole theatre building, including its urban context, became a performative space for the production.

Summary of Outcomes

Pedagogy consisted of creating group improvisations and sets of games in which actors and non-actors could engage. Also, performing with video content, with a material projected or shown on a television screen as a partner, required different performance techniques. The image, being the primary communication device, consists of a plurality of elements – words (text), visual, physical, audio, and music. The performer has to be aware of all these elements coming together with which he has to work. The practice model was novel as it expanded the fixed boundaries of state theatre with the ensemble, initiating more of a group creative dynamics and pedagogies relevant to experimental theatre. Apart from actors from Serbia, the innovative team and I involved musicians from the UK and a video installation artist from Brazil. The multimedia aspect of the performance was also reflected in the multicultural approach, where creative group dynamics were explored as a way of making theatre.

The primary and most significant difference was in the approach to performative pedagogy, where practice methodology required the use of parallel simultaneous spaces, physical and digital. For example, the performers were in the space with the audience but at the same time interacting with actors on screen who were in a different space, similar to the Zoom theatre experience. Despite talented and competent actors, the Kragujevac ensemble lacked performance versatility and the ability to work in non-textual, devised and multimedia ways. In addition to the ensemble, I incorporated acting students, local musicians and jazz club dancers within this new versatile group. They joined the ensemble as associates for the production. The work process provided a unique working experience in learning methodology that combines the interaction of different media with live performance. As the group of performers were experienced within a traditional theatre setting and trained in Stanislavsky's realism, this was a new way of experiencing theatre-making as a collaborative creative founded on shared actor ownership of performance based on individual and group improvisation and creation of performance text through the use of different media. This dynamic of the creative process is what live digital theatre requires from performers, playing with multiple references from being in a transtopic presence and intermedial incorporation of physical and digital worlds.

Death of a Salesman by Arthur Miller, 2013–2015, Everyman Theatre, Cork, Ireland and Belgrade Drama Theatre, Belgrade, Serbia

Context: Remediating Theatre through Cinema Language

The research project *Death of a Salesman* was a case study that examines the live performance framed within digital media as visual (film) and audio (music) design.

FIGURE 6.2 *Death of a Salesman* (2013) Kolectiv Theatre. Everyman Theatre, Cork, Ireland.

This case study was the most relevant to interdisciplinary performative pedagogies of the live digital theatre experience with Zoom live theatre, as it combined filmed and theatre performances.

The performance interconnected on-screen presence with the live theatre play, incorporating digital media in visual projection and electronic music performed live on stage. The project focused on Miller's dramatic text without significant interference with its dramatic content made for a proscenium stage. We created digital filmed performances that transform traditional theatre expression into intermedial aestheticism. A pedagogically novel concept in this performance essentially is making a film of past events as a memory that intersects the present moment of live performance. This was not a theatre performance using visual projections, but digital film and live digital music edited together with live performers' action. The pedagogical focus was on exploring with a cast of mainly young and student actors' ways to perfor in the mixed physical, live digital and pre-recorded event. We recorded a film, and the actors interacted on stage with it. Live digital theatre integrated recorded videos, mix of audio and live music with live performance following dramaturgical divided within Miller's play between present moment (live) and memories/fantasise (recorded) The videos feature fragments of memories and imaginary events in the life of Willy Lowman.

The production took place in May 2013 at the Everyman Palace Theatre (Cork, Ireland), co-produced by the Drama and Theatre Department of University College Cork. The production took place within the Irish National Festival called 'The Gathering Ireland 2013'. It was a cultural initiative in Ireland to promote projects that would mobilise the Irish diaspora to return to Ireland and participate in organised activities. Throughout the year, The Gathering had over 5,000 events organised by communities, other cultural groups and families, considered to be People's projects. The digital multimedia performance was undertaken by professional and community actors, students from the University of Cork (Drama, Music and Arts schools), a local custom designer, a scenographer, and a lighting designer. This was a professional production frame involving two American actors who joined the project and several students for whom this was a learning experience.

Objective and Methodology: Magnifying Live through Digital Experience

I directed and adapted for digital theatre a 1947 Miller's stage play that questioned the validity of the American dream to contextualise it into a contemporary fake belief in celebrity culture, money, and the Club mentality belonging to political and business elite. The objective was to translate text into visual dramaturgy within a digital performance frame using digital video film that would cover over 50% of the action with the play. There were three performance scores: video film, live performance, and original music, both live and recorded. I was manipulating those scores into events. Conceptually, I wanted to create a cinema theatre that would integrate live performance with media projection, bringing live sound and recordings to follow the performance development of having live musicians on stage. My objective as an editor and facilitator of different media, combined with my role as a pedagogue, was to communicate digital performance practice to students who were part of the show and those who were observing the rehearsal process. Learning and teaching actors how to use digital performance and intermediality was an essential objective of this project. In addition, integrating international and local actors and actors with different skills and abilities into one performance group was a challenge. Finding a methodology that could help unite all these other skills and experiences within one performance language was one of the critical tasks I had to develop.

To develop this digital performance, I set up a collaboration between the drama department – where I was the head of the programme – and the artistic director of the Everyman Palace Theatre, looking for ways to connect actors' training with established professional theatres in the city of Cork. In addition, the central role of Willy Loman, around whom the whole narrative is centred, was performed by American actor and acting professor Paddy Cronin, crucial pedagogical support in the project. He came to Ireland for Gathering and was essential in putting this project together between the Everyman Palace and the Drama Department. Cronin's input into learning how to respond to stage and film expression for students and young actors was invaluable. As a collaborator, he led the actors within the group while I worked externally as an outside eye. The play *Death of a Salesman* was organised around three focal points; first, the play was seen as a solo performance of the main character Willy Loman a day before he would commit suicide. Second, all the memories for Willy that he is reliving as an actual event were filmed and projected on screens as digitally mastered videos. And third, live scenes performed by actors on stage were used to connect the other two worlds of memory of the past and fantasies in the present moment. The outcome was a production where the digital elements constituted half of the performance.

The methodology I used in creating this performance was based on Lepage's use of multimedia as alternative text to establish the presence of the dramatic text used as a starting point. I adapted the text of *Death of a Salesman* through media – audiovisual and audio. Dramaturgy was based on the interrelation between present and past in Willy Lauman's hallucinations. The performance was continuously interacting between recorded and live action as the play developed through communication between past and present. The role of the sound, as recorded in live audio, was to trigger the memory and give the emotional context for the performance actions.

The stage had in the background four big projection screens in the shape of sails, covering the whole of the backstage but allowing spaces in between. The material used was a gauze that allowed the vision of objects and people positioned behind them with the appropriate light. The proscenium consisted of objects and necessary set pieces that reference the aesthetics of the film *Dogville* by Lars Von Trier. These digital projections defined the intermedial aesthetics of performance space, which were central to the performance experience. In addition, the pedagogy of digital performance of recorded scenes of memory that were integrated with live performance requires that the performers interact on stage with the pre-recorded memories as they are taking place now.

As the cast was made up of professionals and students, I set up several workshops where more experienced actors showed the students how to act in front of the camera and capture the materials for digital video editing. I also set up workshops with video editors who showed the actors how to work.

In addition, the devising methodology consisted of four phases:

1. Filming – recording a video film of the memorable scenes in the studio, which is approximately half of the play.
2. Digital editing – film scenes were digitally mastered, inputting the graphical backgrounds related to the live performance scenes, particularly environments and performance spaces associated with the live performed events.
3. Montage – the integration of the live and recorded events where actors on stage performed together with those recorded on a screen.
4. Audio – working sound and music into film and live performance, where the music was introduced live into the performance action. In many sections of the performance, the music was spontaneous and improvisational, following the themes and rhythm of stage action.

Summary of Outcomes

In intermedial practices Live physical actions were synchronised with performance space and digital media, particularly film and music. The montaging of digital and live performances provided a pedagogical environment where digital visual arts, music and acting students could create within the learning environment they mutually created. All four phases were organically connected and, as a process, depended on accomplishing one step before moving to another. For the video editor to digitally master the recorded film, it was important for actors to record the memory scenes. And actors on stage who performed live needed to interact with fully developed video projections to do the scenes involving memory. The actors on screen were not the same as the ones performing live, but they were performing the same characters at different times of their lives. The music had to come as the last phase because the musicians were following the live-action in the space. Pedagogically, the influence of the creative methods of John Cage and Merce Cunningham was instrumental in the relationship between video, live-action and music. The versatility of actors with different skills and experiences exposed to various performance stimuli was an excellent learning opportunity. Several media came into theatre: film, music and dance brought into one multimedia performative expression through digital technology, creating a pedagogical environment where actors could use several skills and develop those that could be important for their future careers. Montage of intermedial elements in the rehearsals happened in a triangle of simultaneous interaction between digital video/audio, live music and performance on stage. Sound, video and light designers were present throughout rehearsals, where different media were composed together, transforming material and adapting to live performance action and music. Live digital theatre necessitates pedagogy enabling actors to develop a live presence through the screen – and with the screen in the space. In Zoom live theatre, the intermedial relation are essential for performance style as the actor communicates through screen live with the audience.

Notes

1 Vanhoutte, Kurt. "Note: Modes of Experience" in Sarah Bay-Cheng et al. (eds.) *Mapping Intermediality in Performance* (Amsterdam University Press, 2010), p. 45.
2 In 2008, there was a significant property crisis in the UK and referring to the destruction of the orchard to build a cottage was a timely message on the suffering caused by capitalist greed-driven markets to burst the property market bubble.
3 Dundjerović, Aleksandar. *Robert Lepage: Performance Practitioners* (Routledge, 2nd ed., 2019), p. 120.
4 Bogart, Anne and Tina Landau. *The Viewpoints Book* (New York: Theatre Communication Group, 2005), p. 17.
5 See the Sudley House website at https://www.liverpoolmuseums.org.uk/sudley-house#section–explore-sudley-house

7

INTERDISCIPLINARY PERFORMATIVE PEDAGOGIES IN *MACBETH PROJETO*

Macbeth Projeto 1–6 (www.macbethprojeto.co.uk) is a research project based on an interdisciplinary performance adaptation through a six parts cyclical devising process of Shakespeare's *Macbeth*. This project investigated how interdisciplinary performative pedagogies and creative methodologies are used in various aspects of live digital theatre, from cinematic to Zoom live theatre. In the earlier chapters, we established Historical, Intermedial, Applied and Dramaturgical impacts on the origins and evolution of live digital theatre. Chapter 6 focused on examples of creative practice by looking at different practice projects relating to digital media performance and site-specific intermediality used in live theatre performances in physical space. Here, we will investigate interdisciplinary pedagogies applicable across various areas of practice that can be experimented with in live digital theatre: performance and visual arts, digital media and technology, architecture and design, live and recorded soundscapes and music and textual analyses. The focus will be on one text as the central character telling a story through the embodiment of practice explores different performative ways of storytelling through Interdisciplinary theatre. We are using Shakespeare's *Macbeth* as a starting point in devising and improvising events, images, themes, and the Macbeth character's interconnectedness with different contemporary artistic and cultural references. We also look at actors' explorations of what is known about the Elizabethan (Shakespeare's) theatre rehearsal tradition and how that collaborative methodology can be used in the dramaturgy of digital media performance. We used installation-design sites to capture and concretise the group's understanding of Shakespeare's text using a plurality of images and textual references that could be used to devise new material and adapted it for augmented reality and live Zoom performance.

Macbeth Projeto 1–6 is a research project that developed from April 2017 to January 2021 through six performance cycles, working with students, professional performers, and artists.[1] The main collaborators on the research project were

DOI: 10.4324/9781003275893-9

Stephen Simms and Dr Maria Sanchez. Stephen Simms experimented as an actor-author and deviser on interdisciplinary performance models, as a performance author being a character of Macbeth and Lady Macbeth simultaneously in a live theatre solo show, and augmented reality and co-creator in the final live Zoom theatre cycle of *Macbeth Projeto*. Dr Maria Sanchez brought her expertise in architectural design and interdisciplinary spatial practices into the project, creating an innovative approach to space based on the migration of art forms – from dramatic text/space to its fragmentation through installation art. The research project was established between the Centre for Interdisciplinary Performing Arts (CIPA), Royal Birmingham Conservatoire, UK, Kolectiv Theatre, UK and Teatro Os Satyros Teatro, Brazil. Each one of the six cycles listed below was characterised by the venue and the digital media used in the process of devising the performance:

- Cycle 1/Cinematic Theatre: The Shell Multimedia studio, Royal Birmingham Conservatoire (Birmingham, 2017)
- Cycle 2/Site-specific and Visual Installation Art: Centrala – Community Arts Centre and Dig-brew Brewery (Digbeth, Birmingham, 2017–18)
- Cycle 3/Multimedia Solo-performance: International Federation of Theatre Research (IFTR) and VUK Theatre (Belgrade, 2018)
- Cycle 4/Interdisciplinary space design: Prague Quadrennial of Performance Design (Prague, 2019)
- Cycle 5/Live and augmented reality performance: AHRC UK-China Creative Industries Partnership in Shanghai Theatre Academy (Shanghai, 2019)
- Cycle 6/Live Zoom performance: online digital production on Zoom platform with Brazilian experimental theatre Teatro Os Satyros (digital space, 2020). The final cycle six was supposed to be done as a theatre bilingual (English and Portuguese) multimedia performance production in Sao Paulo, Brazil, in collaboration with Os Satyros. However, the effects of the C-19 pandemic on global theatre, particularly in the Brazilian community theatre, moved theatre from taking place in a physical space to online production in cyberspace, resulting in the creation of the live Zoom theatre version.

Context: Exploring Interdisciplinary Pedagogies

Macbeth was the last of the four great Shakespeare tragedies, considered to be the shortest play with a reputation of being unfinished. It has abundant religious references: personal anguish, supernatural powers, religious and political conflicts, and questions of faith and morality. It is politically topical for the time, reflecting themes of power related to King James I, namely state stability under threat from rebellions and James I's grand personal ambitions as a ruler of England and Scotland. The play was probably performed for the first time in 1606, although eye-witness accounts place it in 1611 at the Globe Theatre. Being unfinished, it was in the early printed text for the First Folio in 1623 based on theatre scrolls, with editing and revision possibly by Thomas Middleton.[2] Its poetic structure was placed in a five-act dramaturgical form after the 19th century. The poetic images and themes can be seen as scores that can be developed through the actor–author approach. These original conditions in the play allow us to approach *Macbeth* as an open structure text, creating sections and specific themes and imagery that could be adapted as starting points for a hybrid of art forms, media, and cultures. My choice to work with *Macbeth* came from the relation between black culture and African traditions in Brazilian performing arts (significant influence on hybridity and interdisciplinarity through cultural anthropophagy) and supernatural imagery that provided provocation for the exploration of the digital performance. Our approach was that the text depicting an event is a vehicle for investigating rehearsal techniques and exploring the migration of the dramatic text into performance and visual arts in workshops. Early in the rehearsal process after Cycle 1, we focused on an event that provided participatory audience experience and possibilities to create an interactive playground for performers and audience, an interdisciplinary environment bringing digital and physical together. It was a "Feast" in Macbeth's castle celebrating his assession to the throne. It was a party to which the audience was invited and greeted by Macbeth.

Because of these possibilities, the text was a good choice for exploring interdisciplinary pedagogies in live digital theatre. The structural openness of *Macbeth* allowed the appropriation of the collaborative creative process. It was suitable for the devising process using different performative pedagogies within the context of anthropophagic theatre, which at the core has interdisciplinary performativity.

Macbeth Projeto 1–6 (*MP 1–6*) explored the migration of art forms and media into the performance, experimenting with rehearsal methods and incorporating new technologies in devising intermedial digital media performances. This project examined the pedagogical approaches required in the creative process of interdisciplinary performance practices. This pedagogical approach is built up on my previous practice research work in cinema and theatre of Robert Lepage. These experiences collected and published as performance practice research informed my starting approach to interdisciplinary pedagogy investigated within live and digital contexts in *MP 1–6*. The epistemological approach was based on the experience with theatre and cultural anthropophagy in Brazilian collaborative and participatory theatre integrated with Western interdisciplinarity performance as a different knowledge system. Extensive research on Brazilian collaborative theatre and performing arts provided methodological and pedagogical input into the *MP 1–6* research project. The new understanding and insight into collaborative practices and performing arts in Brazil were revised based on the new material generated through practice work on six cycles.[3]

In this practice project, the philosophy of theatre anthropophagy – essential to the collaborative creative process – emerged from Brazilian theatre tradition. Approaches to pedagogical methods of group devising, oral storytelling, dance and physical expression, combined with solid visual expression (location, film, images) and local music were appropriate ways of engaging with experiences of Brazilian theatre culture. Brazilian theatre anthropophagy establishing director-author Ze Celso and his Teatro Oficina underpinned the approach to the diversity of performance practice. Anthropophagy as a cultural movement is rooted in 1920s Brazilian Modernism and the work of poet and playwright Oscar de Andrade. Anthropophagy sought to establish a uniquely Brazilian national culture founded on indigenous, African and non-European influences decolonising it from Western dominance. Ze Celso positions subjectivity in Brazilian theatre as a consequence of anthropophagic relation to others, the others being European conquistadors, and freely using colonial arts and culture as "food" and eating the best parts using them for their creative process. In Brazil, Shakespeare's opus has been firmly linked to anthropophagy as global intercultural otherness and cultural hybridity.[4]

Ever since Orson Welles' production of *Voodoo Macbeth* with an all-black cast in 1936 in New York's Harlem, the text of *Macbeth* has provided connectivity with traditions that could bring different understandings as well as performative and aesthetic qualities to the interpretation of the play. Welles transposed *Macbeth* from Scotland (Shakespeare uses accounts to base his character on Raphael Holinshed's *Chronicles of England, Scotland and Ireland*, 1587, a popular history at his time) to an island resembling Haiti, using the supernatural and witches to connect with African traditions. We wanted to transpose *Macbeth* to the aestheticism of Brazilian black traditions and anthropophagic cultural influence. Via the witches, Shakespeare takes us through a series of events into supernatural ritualistic performativity, such as Brazilian *Candomblé*. *Macbeth* allows us to recreate rituals from different cultures and create images with them. It is in the richness of the visual possibilities that *Macbeth* offers us what is behind the choice of this play. Shakespearean theatrical conventions are based on open bare stage space and performed in daylight. The Elizabethan stage conventions allowed us to transpose the images within Shakespeare's text into a different theatrical space, from site-specific to digital and virtual locations.

Another method explored in all *MP 1–6* was RSVP Cycles, using the score and actor-author approach to devising from a plurality of resources: from textual to multimedia, historical to socio-cultural. An essential part of the RSVP/Repère Cycles method came from the transposition of the play's fragments of text and themes into space for performance – from the non-traditional use of theatre space to digital space. Using performing and visual arts to migrate the dramatic text required us to incorporate strategies from the participatory audience, live digital performance, site-specific, installation, and immersive performance. In Anna Halprin's RSVP Cycles and Lepage's performance transformation, the final product is unknown as the focus is on the change of the ongoing exploratory process.[5] Performance is a rehearsal, and, with audience presence, it becomes an open rehearsal with feedback that influences further narrative development through cycles.

Interdisciplinary performative pedagogies requires participants to adapt to multimedia way of working, to be performance-author and not interpreters, flexible and open to change, and not work towards a fixed product presented on the opening night. This thinking goes against traditional training where the actor must fulfil a set of tasks (objectives and actions) found in the text and given by the director. Therefore, the number of cycles we wanted to develop was unknown at the start of the research project. Instead, each Cycle emerged from the previous performance and with performers/audience insights made on that Cycle. For example, the performance in Cycle 1 had a scene of "the Feast" at Macbeth's castle that became an (R)esource for developing Cycle 2 as a party to celebrate Macbeth becoming a King. Subsequently, performance in Cycle 2, a resource, used space both as an installation and as site-specific for the new Cycle 3, using space as a central element to develop solo performance and write a new text. With the creative method of RSVP Cycles, we were re-editing the version in rehearsals, using an open rehearsal in front of an audience to explore the performativity of practice and pedagogy underpinning the creative process.

In addition to exploring physical and digital space concerning the selected theme was the development of Macbeth's and Lady Macbeth's characters as essential reference points to our adaptation. Starting from Cycle MP2, it became clear that our Macbeth is alone in a very subjective interpretation of the environment and that he is as the protagonist an entertainer, as an entertainer master of ceremony or DJ allowing him open actions to shape events taking place in his party and interacting with a site, visual images and participatory audience (invited to his feast to celebrate him becoming a King). Lady Macbeth increasingly became Macbeth's fantasy, almost an aspect of his alter ego. Lady Macbeth's character is mediated through different cycles as a projection in a water bucket, a contortionist, performed in a solo show by the same actor doing Macbeth, and an augmented reality avatar, the main antagonist. The only other character from the play *Macbeth* was the ghost of Banquo, that haunted Macbeth while he was entertaining his guests (audiences). In Cycle 6, in addition to the character of Macbeth, we focused on the creation of three different Lady Macbeths and the development of the characters of Duncan, Banquo, Witches, and Lady Macduff. Planning a collaboration with Brazilian Theatre Company Os Satyros was fixed from the beginning of the creative research process that would come at the end of our investigation in Cycle 6.

Interdisciplinary *Macbeth* though *Cycles 1–6*

The resources performers can use in live digital theatre (LDT) are similar to the ones for devising performances in physical space. One significant addition is the performer on camera and the representation of action on screen. *Macbeth Projeto* aimed to integrate different types of scores in live and digital performance explored within interdisciplinary pedagogy, relying on knowledge from other disciplines. Our objective was to use performance techniques relevant to the theatre – acting in solo performance, video and film editing, digital design and construction of performance space as installation, multimedia visualisation in interior and exterior, digital image processing, live and recorded music, and immersion of audience presence. From the start, the objective was to digitally archive on a bespoke website, where the process of making and production were open for viewers to examine and see different parts of the development of the multi-art performance. As this case study intended to interrogate pedagogy of practice as a performative enquiry of the migration of dramatic text into performance/visual arts both in a physical and digital space, it was essential to archive the process. The fact that live digital theatre can be recorded and its practices curated at the moment of creation, and that it is a hybrid form, being alive in a digital medium (as a video performance once it stopped being performed live) outside of the temporality of liveness, is very relevant for the preservation of the material and its archiving capabilities.[6]

The discoveries through the research project were personal and arrived at through trial and error from embodied learning. As the interdisciplinarity method brought together various arts and media involved in the *Cycles 1–6*, performers (students) needed to engage in working across different platforms and sharing discoveries through collaboration. It was important through making mistakes to know which direction we were taking, chaos was the impetus/energy for discovery, there was no established system, the way was open. This changes the participants understanding of an initial discipline as they gain new skills and concepts of hybrid mixing within the live digital theatre. Inviting new co-production into the process allowed us to learn a new set of creative circumstances from others in a co-creative process that would infuse our work. Performance was not set up to be only the outcome but also the process of making performance through interdisciplinary collaborative contexts between performer and digital media performance.

Cycle 1: *Cinematic Theatre – Macbeth Obsessions* Shell Studio, Parkside, Birmingham City University, Birmingham, UK

Description

In the first cycle, we worked on the idea of the narrative of *Macbeth* as a visual and physical experience shared with audiences in the format of a group ritual/religious procession. The performance was an open rehearsal involving students and alumina from Acting at Royal Birmingham Conservatoire, and, in the end, the audience was invited to a recorded Q&A session. We tested different ways of telling stories to the audience through fragmented experiences of the dramatic text, using physical and visual images and sound. We explored group improvisation and ritualistic ideas triggered by the dramaturgy of *Macbeth* (witches, ghosts, visions, the prophecy of the future). Reading of Tarot cards came from one of these sessions and became key to the beginning of the performance from Cycle 3 onwards. We also explored the performativity of voodoo and Candomblé.

Objectives

The starting cycle engaged with the fragments of Shakespeare's text and explored a collaboratively created narrative organised around themes of supernatural, witchcraft, ghosts, dreams, madness and ritual procession as a passage from one "real" world into an inner and imaginary world. Questions concerned how to approach Shakespeare's *Macbeth* as a physical and audio/visual experience were shared with audiences? How to explore the format of an open rehearsal through which to test different ways of telling stories?. How to involve the audience in the participatory experience of ritual through a mixture of fragmented dramatic text, perspectives on narrative, and poetic images found in the text of *Macbeth*? These questions also triggered the investigation of visual and spatial dramaturgy.

The underpinning philosophy for Cycle 1 at the start of the creative research project was cultural anthropophagy, which has an actual application to director's theatre in Brazil and was also relevant to Shakespeare's use of various existing materials for his theatre. The founding Brazilian director-authors, such as Zé Celso, Antunes Filho and Gerald Thomas, share approaches to anthropophagy as a "negation" of realism of foreign cultures (colonial) through a "transformation" of the source material.

Methodology

Theatre of anthropophagy is a transformation that results from "eating" other relevant artistic and cultural references. The Brazilian culture of anthropophagy is the meeting of two philosophical systems of thinking about life: the indigenous, through dances, rituals and ceremonies; and the European, through Catholicism and evangelisation of society. Out of this encounter came the idea of mixing influences and "devouring": taking over the properties of a source's arts or culture and making them your own. The theatre of anthropophagy is simultaneously a process of intercultural appropriation and collaborative devising. Anthropophagic theatricality brings to performances a total theatre experience, immediacy and immersion, ritual dance and ceremonies (such as the performing of carnival or Candomblé rituals), and communal sharing. The Brazilian theatre context combines native traditions with elements of anti-realism and the devouring of various artistic and cultural sources.

The creative method and reference point for the work in this cycle and, subsequently, all processes was RSVP/Repère Cycles combined with the experience of collaborative Brazilian anthropophagic theatre. We also wanted to explore Elizabethan rehearsal strategies (using scrolls and group creation) and examine the mix-authorship approach in making Shakespeare's plays. In addition, Orson Welles' production of *Voodoo Macbeth* (1936) became a reference point for our adaptation of the text. In preparation for working with Teatro Os Satyros, we wanted to look into the different cultural appropriations of *Macbeth* in Brazil.

Observations

The output was a 45-minute performance at the Shell Multimedia Studio at Royal Birmingham Conservatoire in front of acting students, staff and invited practitioners and scholars. It was an open rehearsal followed by a Q&A session.

The evaluation process involved reviewing the performance recording and the feedback and suggestions, which indicated to the group possible new developments in the dramaturgical and spatial investigation. The audience's comments about the experience of the procession and the rituals led us into the critical reference points for the second cycle, where the audience's understanding of the procession was translated into how we use promenades to experience space and installation.

After the first cycle, the critical reference points for future development became Act 3 Scene 4 "Feast scene", which was turned into a party at Macbeth's in celebration of him becoming king; the relationship with Lady Macbeth, and the development of Lady Macbeth's story; ghosts, witches and the supernatural, and the exploration of the audience as participants in the narrative of the play. From the group discussions and feedback, it became clear that in future developments, the character of Macbeth would be the one telling the story to the audience in an autobiographical way, using site-specific and visual arts to create an environment for the play.

Cycle 2: Site-specific installation – *Welcome to Macbeth's Party* (Centrala Polish Arts Centre, June 2017, Birmingham), and 1st Friday performance art festival Digbrew Beerhouse (March 2018, Birmingham).

Description

The second cycle consisted of two different performances, each adapting to the performance environment and creating very different outcomes: phase one in Centrala and phase two in Digbrew. In this cycle, we explored space as a central focus of rehearsal methodology as site-specific events and installation performances using text as an inspiration and starting point for video art, smell scape, physical expression, cinematic projection, live music, contortionism, and film projections. The space for performance in Centrala and Digbrew became the score around which the devising process took place. The performance was

FIGURE 7.1 *Macbeth Projeto* Cycle 2. The Party. Centrala Arts Centre. Birmingham, UK

participatory, where the audience as guests were invited to a party at Macbeth's home, a feast, to celebrate him becoming king.

Phase 1 was performed at Centrala Arts Centre as part of the Digbeth First Friday Festival, adapting the centre's two floors to situate a selection of critical events taken from the text to co-create an immersive experience involving sound and video design by Dani Blanco and smell scape by Jieling Xiao for the audience.

Phase 2 adapted *Macbeth* to the spatial narrative of Digbrew (a brewery in Digbeth, Birmingham), which was integrated into the performance of *Macbeth*. Maria J.M. Sanchez brought the spatial configuration of the brewery to not only the dramaturgy of the narrative but also all its sensory and immersive audience experience, the wooden table where they were seated, temperature and the strong smell-scape (smell of yeast and beer fermentation).

Objectives

The research enquiry in this cycle was: How can a dramatic text be presented as a performative spatial experience? How can installation and visual arts methods enhance the immersive experience of theatre?

In *Macbeth Projeto*, space was an active element in devising. We observed how the conflicts shaped the piece, or perhaps, as Pearson says, we achieved "studied indifference". In other words, in both spaces – Centrala and Digbrew – it seemed

FIGURE 7.2 *Macbeth Projeto* Cycle 2. Fragmented installation at Centrala Arts Centre. Birmingham, UK

like the piece had been created for that particular space, not just superposed to an existing reality.

The dramatic action became an essential performance element in the architectural space within this cycle. The architect Bernard Tschumi defines interaction between space and action as when "architectural spaces and programs can become interdependent and fully condition each other's existence".[7] The interdependence between the site and the dramaturgy of *Macbeth* emerged during the devising process.

In investigating where the dramatic action is situated, we examined theatrical space, which has proved essential in discussion on place and how contemporary performance practices respond to construction of place.[8] In his book *Postdramatic Theatre*, Hans-Thies Lehmann highlighted the importance of space in the dramaturgical process of the new theatre since the 1960s that shifts from text to new technologies, images and sound.[9] Lepage's work, from the 1990s, was characterised by the use of multi-media projection in space, with spatiality becoming the main performance element.[10] The practice of using non-theatrical spaces by companies such as Shunt and Punchdrunk has pointed to the use of sites and architectural spaces as part of the play's dramaturgy or performative event.[11]

Spaces have memories that are kept within them. These memories impact the future events that take place inside them. The existing link between memories and spaces occurs through two processes: the first occurs when the performance location is designed for host-specific actions. The clearest example of action defining space is the Greek civic space, where spaces, used for gathering became a site for theatre, and are designed based on the civic rights and religious rituals that generate them, as in Richard Schechner's definition: "rituals are collective memories encoded into actions".[12] The second process takes place through the creation of collective memories in space – usually through events or festivals that are transmitted from one generation to another.

Methodology

In this cycle, we worked in the spaces of Centrala and Digbrew in Birmingham, using an instalation and a site-specific methodology. In the phase staged in Centrala, the objective was to present a fragmented narrative of *Macbeth*, gathering images and ritualistic sequences that emerged from the text to create a spatial dramaturgy. This dramaturgy with solid visual elements, spatial narratives and objects was presented at Centrala, a space with an industrial character. The piece had limited text; however, dramaturgy sought to re-enact the stories from one segment of the play *Macbeth* through a plurality of spatial and mediated perception and body exploration. The text migrated into an art installation.

In the case of the phase in Digbrew, location materiality with metal constructions for brewing in a warehouse, the smell of beer, the presence of a large silver tank and the echoing sound constituted such a powerful atmosphere that it

FIGURE 7.3 *Macbeth Projeto* Cycle 2. Site-specific installation at Digbrew. Birmingham, UK

provided an environment in which performance had to adapt. The performance space was materialised, not just through the objective space but through the concept that generated the whole environment involving a music concert where Stephen Simms, as Macbeth hosting a party, was singing and narrating his version of Shakespeare's story in a style of Lauri Anderson's music performance solo shows, with a silent Lady Macbeth as a contortionist suspended in the air. The space was in transformation. It was in the process of making that related to its original use. A brewery is an industrial space with its own spatial and programmatic needs. We superposed a narrative of *Macbeth* onto this space, and, in this way, we articulated a dialogue between the brewing process and our dramaturgy.

Observations

Phase 1 was an arts event and an installation. Phase 2 was a site-specific performance.

This cycle established the foundations of a paper presented at IFTR (International Federation of Theatre Research). Cycle 2 gave us the opportunity of experimenting with space, understanding how each of the fragments of *Macbeth* had its own spatial identity. After fragmenting the text and creating audience experiences through different spatial environments that became the embodiment of visual dramaturgy, we conceptualised the role of each of the images in the space and how each created a perception in the audience. In the evaluation of cycle two, we synthesised the experiences made in the different spatial

FIGURE 7.4 *Macbeth Projeto* Cycle 2. Macbeth and Lady Macbeth. Digbrew. Birmingham, UK

environments to bring them back together in a traditional theatre space in cycle three, finding equivalents and analogies. The experience of talking to the audience after Cycle 2 about the contortionist that represented Lady Macbeth led us to focus on two different narratives within a solo-performance in Cycle 3. We devised two stories told by Macbeth and Lady Macbeth. In this version they are Mac and Beth, a married couple, with the expectations they had from each other, mainly failed ambitions and dreams..

Cycle 3: Multimedia Solo Performance *Mac&Beth @ 4:48* (the Vuk Theatre part of International Federation of Theatre Research IFTR, July 2018, Belgrade, Serbia)

Description

The practice-led research in this cycle, *Mac&Beth @ 4:48*, explored multimedia solo performance using Elizabethan rehearsal techniques and multimedia, allowing the connection between different fragments, forms and experiences through deconstruction and transformation of Shakespeare's original text. Directed and Adapted by Aleksandar Dundjerović, Connecting the solo show adaptation with autobiography in the performance was a central part of the investigation. Stephen Simms plays the

FIGURE 7.5 *Mac&Beth @ 4:48 – Projeto* Cycle 3. Vuk Theatre. Belgrade, Serbia

reducted characters of Macbeth and Lady Macbeth in this cycle. Focusing on the relationship between these two main characters and developing events that preceded Lady Macbeth's suicide was central to the narrative of this cycle.

Cycle 3 combined two projects as references: performance installation *Vacío* (Madrid, 2012), an adaptation of the text *4:48 Psychosis* by Sarah Kane as a physical performance using an inflatable structure and the body; and *Macbeth Projeto* (Cycle 1 and 2, Birmingham, 2017/18) an interdisciplinary solo performance/visual art based on Shakespeare's *Macbeth*. These two projects were the starting point of the performance *Mac&Beth @ 4:48*.

Objectives

The research aims to investigate strategies for mixing visual and performing arts. The research questions are: How can we offer our audiences new experiences combining elements of performance, conceptual and visual arts? How do we define the geographies of performance and live art? What processes and methodologies can we follow to adapt the dramatic text into a multi-sensorial aesthetic performing arts experience? This cycle also offers a new understanding of cross-cultural collaboration that could help other global companies engage in the adaptation and migration of classics through multimedia and plural linguistic performances.

This bubble housed a performer and the performer's body. The process of bringing a visual element, such as the inflatable, which belonged to the language of visual arts, into the performance created a synergy of languages that expanded the visual languages of the project.

Performance and visual art can be presented as two different geographies defined by the language of each artistic medium. In the case of conceptual art, it is the space, texture, and atmosphere combined with the atemporality of the art piece. In theatre, the moving body of the actor, the dramatic text and the temporal line of the dramatic action define its geography.

Methodology

In theatre praxis, it is understood that to create a character, the actor needs to draw on their personal experiences. Ultimately, a character will reflect aspects of the actor's personality and environmental influences. The autobiographical elements of actor-author Stephen Simms provided material for part of the content, where a new meta-context was developed based on a montage of the existing *Macbeth* text, Sara Kane *4:48 Psychosis*, and Sanskrit Poetry from *The Radiance Sutras*. The writing by Simms was done following Shakespeare's scrolls, consisting of text segments and indications of actions.

Mac& Beth @ 4:48 used solo performance as an interdisciplinary installation in which the narrative is fragmented and presented as a multi-sensorial aesthetic

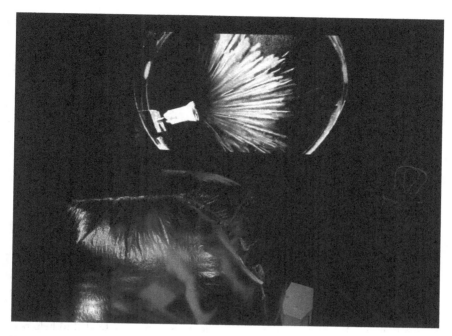

FIGURE 7.6 *Macbeth Projeto* Cycle 3. Macbeth solo performance. Vuk Theatre. Belgrade, Serbia

journey, which provides a new performative experience. Different visual elements (inflatable structure, ropes, projections, buckets, toy soldiers, soundscape, karaoke singing) and the solo-performer are in the space providing the spectator with different narratives emerging from the dramatic text that has mutated into an installation, appropriating performance and visual languages.

Observations

This cycle investigates the transformative and mutational character of the performance, migrating dramatic text into the field of installation art, where the spectator defines their narrative about the artistic sensuousness of the experience. Performance and visual art can be presented as two different geographies defined by the language each creative media uses. In the case of conceptual art, it is the space, texture and atmosphere combined with the atemporality of the art piece. In theatre, the moving body of the actor, the dramatic text and the temporal line of the dramatic action define its geography. The digital art forms within multimedia experience are connected to each other within rhizomatic structures, as non-linear networks without any apparent order.[13] They can be transformed and migrate from one another following different processes, not just through a linear hierarchical process. The non-linear process moved from a creative group activities based on improvisation and collective dynamics to combining popular art forms (stand-up comedy, karaoke and storytelling) with digital visual and installation arts.

The originality of *Mac&Beth @ 4:48* is in developing a performance using the aestheticism of visual and performance arts – *Vacio* (Madrid, 2012) – combined with a text-driven solo show.

Cycle 4: Digital Space Design – *Interdisciplinary Macbeth* Emergence Performance Festival/Prague Industrial Palace (June 2019, Prague Quadrennial of Performance Design, Prague, Czech Republic)

Description

Interdisciplinary Macbeth was a digital performance design site-specific interdisciplinary installation as an immersive experience. The workshop extended into a performance in the main exhibition hall. It resulted from a six-day intensive ten hours workshop-rehearsals led by Aleksandar Dundjerović and Maria J.M. Sanchez, as part of the Result Driven Workshop section of the festival with an international group of 12 performance designers. The outcome, promenade installation, was presented at the Prague Industrial Palace on 12 June 2019. The workshop was intended to help performance designers to engage in devising processes using their own visual and multi-sensorial language and translating it into dramaturgical decisions in the interpretation of imagery in Shakespeare's *Macbeth*. In this workshop, we devised using objects, images, sound and the human body. Starting from the pictures evoked by *Macbeth*, the participants created a series of performative and visual events or installations, using objects, projection, sound and their bodies. This workshop was attended by designers from different parts of the world – China, the USA, Australia, Brazil and the UK – who worked collaboratively with the principal investigators. The participants included students and established professionals from different backgrounds, such as installation, costume, puppetry and theatre design.

Objectives

The objective of *Interdisciplinary Macbeth* was to explore the use of space as the primary tool in devising and working with the space as dramaturgy. Designers are not generally actively involved in the devising process, although it is one of the most popular strategies in performance creation. Directors and performers mostly use devising, but how can a designer create a space through a group process and be actively engaged in developing new performance work?

The starting point was the creative process based on the practice methodologies appropriated by Robert Lepage. Founded on Anna and Lawrence Halprin's RSVP Cycles, this process has group creativity based on a cyclical reworking of starting references at its core. The methodology based on actors' creator improvisation and collective dynamics was applied to performance designers as creators, devising through visual and installation arts. In addition, we used the viewpoints through exploring architectural objects, lighting, and understanding of the configuration of space to respond to it as performers – this innovative approach to working with designers as devisers places the performing area at the centre of creativity.

Methodology

In *Interdisciplinary Macbeth*, the participants walked amongst the audience at the Prague Industrial Palace, inviting the audience to come into a section of the space which had been transformed into a mix-media experience based on the prophecies from the text of *Macbeth*. Through immersion, the audience explored areas where fragments from Shakespeare's *Macbeth* were presented using the performance language of installation, combining visual and performing arts. This work, following collaborative methods, provided new ways of exploring different dramaturgical techniques, creative workshops and strategies, and mixing visual and performing arts. It also offered a new understanding of cross-cultural collaboration that helped to engage in the adaptation of classics through multimedia and plural linguistic performances at a global level.

Observations

This cycle staged themes from Shakespeare using the aesthetic of mixed media, visual and performance arts. The outcome was a series of performative events based on stimuli such as words, themes and images found in the text.

Interdisciplinary Macbeth as part of the Emergence Performance Festival at Prague Quadrennial 19. This unique version of *Macbeth* approached the transformation and adaptation of Shakespeare's *Macbeth* through an immersive installation space. The change was done through digital multimedia techniques involving projection, soundscapes and performance scores in a site-specific installation designed to trigger audience participation.

The outcome of cycle four was the creation of several visual images to develop a future performance narrative, translating the dramatic text's language into the space's performance design using audio-visual elements. This led us to question how to make these images more accessible to broader audiences when staging *Macbeth*. We found the answer in using technologies such as virtual and augmented reality.

Cycle 5: *Live and augmented reality – Macbeth* in *Mixed-Reality* (Shanghai Theatre Academy and International Federation for Theatre Research IFTR, July 2019, Shanghai, China)

Description

Cycle 5 explored mixed live and augmented reality performances. It was part of an R&D project launched by AHRC UK-China Creative Industries Partnership,

FIGURE 7.7 *Macbeth Projeto* Cycle 5. Macbeth VR and AR. Shanghai Theatre Academy, China

and it was presented at IFTR 2019, *Theatre, Performance and Urbanism* in Shanghai. This next step explored mixed media relationships between live performance and augmented reality. The key partners of this funded project were the Centre for Interdisciplinary Performative Arts (CIPA), the Centre for Digital Media Technology (DMT), BCU, and Shanghai Theatre Academy (STA). The collaboration set up a platform for developing more prominent practice research projects between performance/visual arts practitioners, researchers, artists, industry participants and associated creative businesses.

The project explores how augmented reality can be used as an additional devising tool in creating a multimedia performance. The performance and visual arts experience of devising a multimedia performance based on *Macbeth* serves as material to explore a mix of live and augmented reality. Lady Macbeth was created as an avatar in augmented reality. The technical implications were discussed with collaborators from Shanghai, creating a platform for a future more significant development and long-term collaboration between the two institutions and creative industries.

Objectives

How can we develop new ways of doing performative practices through mixed reality experiences, using live performing arts and augmented reality? What happens when we take *Macbeth* as canonical text and transpose it by combining performing and visual arts with new media technology and augmented reality?

The proposed project's central theme is to explore a classical drama text (a case study of Shakespeare's *Macbeth*) using new media technologies to create an augmented reality experience. The creative experiences from Cycle 4 with designers at PQ19 provided an essential collection of images to build on a new Cycle 5. Besides, we experimented with Lady Macbeth's character transposed to augmented reality from the opera *Macbeth* by Giuseppe Verdi. Using the experience of augmented reality games for iPhone and Android, the project explored possible ways to build on the themes and images linked to the text to create a live performance devised to instigate different audience experiences and cultural contexts. With augmented reality, using a phone that superimposes digital images over an actual painting on a phone camera, we investigated bringing audience participation and immersion to another communication level.

The augmented reality within the theatre/performance event will be a way of creating a different reality for the audience that will transform the real space into mediated circumstances. This will substantially impact how the narrative is communicated through a mixture of liveness and technology.

Methodology

We are exploring different ways of using mixed realities as a performative tool employed in the creative process, experimenting with the elements of an augmented reality experience. By sharing best practices and exchanging knowledge with collaborators from the Shanghai Theatre Academy, the project will build on the strengths of both STA and Royal Birmingham Conservatoire in performance practice and creative industry research. Augmented reality will allow us to transpose Shakespeare's world into reality. We will explore the gaming industry as a new way of relating fictional stories to relevant cultural narratives. The augmented reality within the theatre/performance event will be a way of creating a different reality for the audience. This will transform the real space into mediated circumstances and substantially impact how the narrative is communicated through a mixture of liveness and technology. The project will look into developing research questions and opportunities for collaborations across various creative industry sectors: theatre, performing arts and new media, video gaming, and visual and installation arts.

Observations

This cycle explored ways of developing activities through a workshop and symposium to examine the opportunities and challenges of a mix-media approach combining live performance and augmented reality.

A possible outcome of developing an augmented reality platform for live performance is to attract younger audiences by using the technologies available to them to communicate the traditional theatre materials within different cultural contexts (i.e. Shakespeare).

One outcome is establishing and enhancing partnerships and networks between Royal Birmingham Conservatoire and Shanghai Theatre Academy based performance practitioners, researchers, creative businesses and cultural organisations. Another outcome was the exploration of mixed realities as a performative tool in staging a classic text. Augmented reality will allow the transposition of Shakespeare's world into existence, exploring the game industry as a new way of relating fictional stories to relevant cultural narratives.

The possible future developmental stage of the augmented reality platform for live performance would involve video game digital art and video games development designers, including staff with extensive experience in the creative industry. Shanghai Theatre Academy will also bring its connections as a partner hub with the Chinese video gaming industry.

This cycle provided us with an understanding of the potential of the new digital media to represent the dramatic text (*Macbeth*). It led us to a further investigation of the use of video art, integrated with live performance and accessibility to broader audiences through experimental digital platforms.

Cycle 6: Live Zoom Performance – *Macbeth Projecto* (Host: Teatro Os Satyros, December 2020, Sao Paulo, Brazil and Hozier Young Festival of Digital Theatre, online live Zoom digital platform, February 2021, USA)

Participants: External Funding: Satyrianas Festival/Ministry of Culture Brazil/ SESC Brazil

FIGURE 7.8 *Macbeth Projeto* Cycle 6. Macbeth Live Digital Theatre. Collaboration with Os Satyros. Zoom.

The version as live Zoom digital theatre played at the international digital theatre festival hosted online in the USA in February of 2021, receiving an award for collaborative work of the year with Teatro Os Satyros.

Description

Cycle 6 developed over four weeks as a bilingual English and Portuguese performance. The co-creators were Aleksandar Dundjerović, Stephen Simms, and Rodolfo Vasquez. It was a collaboration between the Centre for Interdisciplinary Performing Arts (CIPA), Royal Birmingham Conservatoire (Paul Sadot and Maria Sanchez) and an ensemble of Teatro Os Satyros, Brazil, led by Vasquez (www.satyros.com.br). It was facilitated through computer technology and a live digital theatre using the Zoom platform for rehearsals and production. The concept put forward by Rodolfo Garcia Vasquez, artistic director of Os Satyros and co-director of *Macbeth 6*, is *"tele-co-presence"* as a principle of digital theatre where actors are cyborgs. This refers to actors and the physical audience being present simultaneously but on screen, using a technological extension, to do live encounters. The online platform used for live performance was Zoom. The rehearsals were online with actors in their locations (homes or studios) in different countries (the UK, USA and Brazil) and time zones.

Objective

How could we create a live performance using digital theatre within different cultural contexts? What is our collaborative strategy with a Brazilian partner and their work method, which is different from our practices, particularly as they have extensive experience within the digital theatre? Aleksandar Dundjerović's directing experience is with live theatre performances and multimedia contexts. CIPA has been exploring video art/performance, which was pre-recorded. Directing and devising Cycle 6 demanded critical interrogation of the rehearsal collaboration and interdisciplinary creative strategies.

Teatro Os Satyros has been researching and experimenting with cyber theatre since 2009. They moved into creating live digital theatre once Covid-19 forced all theatres and public life in Sao Paulo to close. The starting idea was to investigate theatre's connection with the technological digital revolution. The platform used was Zoom, which allowed live performance to take place. CIPA had previously experimented with video art/performance and recorded devised performances. Paul Sadot, who worked as a video art editor on *Macbeth*, had extensive experience with this art form.

Methodology

This live Zoom theatre experimental performance uses an interdisciplinary performative pedagogy. Participants had to learn the creative methodology of Zoom theatre, consisting of an exploration of cross-cultural and bilingual live digital performances and a recorded video art collaboration devised by an international cast. Fundamentally, we had three years of experience to draw on while Os Satyros worked within the online live platform that they championed.

Here are the creative methods of different performative pedagogies for the development of scores within live digital theatre.

- Solo performance as a one-person show tells a story to audiences through mediatised performance. In LDT, a solo performance is a score, and the actor is usually alone in front of a camera. Live or recorded in front of the camera; the actor engages in a solo performance in his own physical/digital space. It is important to emphasise that working on a solo performance score is similar to doing it live in a physical theatre when using various resources to devise a performance. The main difference is that this takes place in front of the camera. Therefore space is defined through the performer's actions and the use of a camera (and editing) and processing of digital images.
- Video filming and editing rely, on using a video camera, webcam or smart-phone camera to film live footage and edit in any available apps, for example, adobe rush or I-movie, or even In Shot. It is about the simplicity and immediacy of self-made video, documenting real experience, seeing the world from the inside and capturing authentic emotion, not outside of a professional video crew, or using professional acting techniques. The individual performer uses the video editing as if for home use, making the actor the video's author. These can also relate to a group working together where the tasks of performing, filming and editing are equally shared. The performer introduces the filmed material as part of the live performance on the online platform.
- Self-filming performers on the camera allow the performer to act and film simultaneously. In LDT, it is a combination of performing in front of a camera and direct communication on social platforms. The performer interacts with the camera using it as a resource. The performer can move the camera based on actions. The performer decides what will be in the shot (what type of shot to use), and the physicality and expressivity define what happens in the image.
- The multimedia design of performance space in physical and online digital theatre becomes our only representation of reality. In virtual digital manifestation, the audience and performers do not share the same physical space; the creative team can manipulate how the audience perceives the space. The performance space in LDT is configured as a physical design – in the performing area where the performers develop the action – through digital images – backgrounds, virtual reality, or filters – or encouraging the audience to take part in line online performance and even manipulate their own physical space following a set of directions.

- Lights are an essential score delineating what we can see and how we can interpret and connect the set's atmosphere. A necessary aspect of live digital theatre is that it creates both theatre and film visible environments. The lighting score uses video/film lights, particularly the relationship between the shadow, light and darkness, to denote what is visible. The light communicates the emotional content and the feeling connected to the score. In many ways, it resembles the lights in the painting as fundamentally live digital theatre works through the visual image on the screen.
- Live digital production allows the audience to observe and participate in the development of the performance action. This could be done on camera or through interactions with the performers through the chat. Live digital theatre allows for an open narrative and immersive sensory experience involving audiences.

Observations

The live performance was followed by 146 devices and approximately 300 people globally. It created a new understanding and knowledge of a novel way of making live theatre. About 90 devices followed a post-production Q&A discussion. The audience engaged positively with various questions about the creative process and performance narrative. It was pointed out that this work model can be applied in performing arts, creative industry and education. The Q&A session was recorded and will play an essential part in the future development of the performance. The plan is to develop the next exploratory phase to perform within Teatro Os Satyros' digital theatre repertoire.

A digital livestream is not the same as a live performance in communication with the audience, happening now (time) and in a shared location (space). With the rupture, the closure of all public venues, including film theatres, film studios and production facilities, live and mediatised experience became part of the same operating system. However, the experience of doing live Zoom theatre production of *Macbeth Projecto* in December 2020 as part of a collaboration between the Centre for Interdisciplinary Performative Arts (CIPA) and Brazilian Theatre company Os Satyros provided me with greater insight into how live online performance could work. I decided to bring a full use of Zoom theatre into students' work as a pedagogy that will help students create within a different medium – a live online production. Using a zoom communication platform, Zoom theatre allowed performances to be live and performed live at other times. These can also stay recorded for a limited time for the pre-registered audience. The performance can be fully staged for webcam, and Zoom allowed the fullest computer/tablet/smartphone medium to be explored. In addition, the audience on Zoom can fully participate in the performance by opening their mics, chatting, or being visible on camera. This brings the audience into the event so that the actors can hear you respond to their performance live, in real-time.

Testimonial on Macbeth Projeto 1-6 performance development by actor-author Steven Simms

Stephen Simms's work as actor-author devising from within material and developing the character of Macbeth (also playing the character of Lady Macbeth in Cycles 3 and 5), offers testimonials on the process of working with images and themes and character development by making a very subjective narrative.

Images

The Blood Red Sea

In *Macbeth Projeto* 1 I was taken by the image of the sea being made red with the blood of Macbeth's murder victims from Act 2: Scene 2: Line 61

> MACBETH: "Will all great Neptune's ocean wash this blood
> Clean from my hand? No this my hand will rather
> The multitudinous sees incarnadine,
> Making the green one red."

I found a copy of a black-and-white silent film *Napoleon* by Abel Gance. In this movie there is a scene where Napoleon stands with his back to the audience looking out at the sea. A dramatic and highly romantic image, referencing Caspar David Freidrich's painting of 1817 "Wanderer above the sea of fog". Although a black-and-white movie, various episodes of the film had been tinted in different colours. In this episode the entire screen is tinted red so Napoleon is looking out at the red sea. One is invited into Napoleon's thoughts, to imagine his experience. To me, the image brought up the idea of calmly contemplating suicide by drowning (something which terrifies me). Suicide seemed appropriate as intimated by this image, as I felt it linked Macbeth to Lady Macbeth: she kills herself, and one can imagine that Macbeth believes his fate is sealed when he finds out that Macduff was not of woman born (the witches had prophesied that "none of woman born shall harm Macbeth", Act 4, Scene 1, Line 79): he believes his attempt to fight Macduff will be pointless, and therefore fighting Macduff would be suicide.

This image of the blood red sea was repeated throughout all the various *Macbeth Projeto* cycles and was notably the final image for both the solo show and for the final online Zoom production of MP 6.

Napoleon

The idea of Macbeth as a Napoleon figure lingered in my imagination but did not emerge as part of Macbeth's character until the online *Projeto 6*, in which we further explored some of Macbeth's possible decline into a paranoid and highly disturbed mental state. In the second half of the play Macbeth is more or less isolated on stage: he remains alone while others come to meet him. One can imagine that these visitations may or may not be real.

I invested in buying a Napoleonic hat as part of his costume which in a humorous and also Gothic way was intended to describe his internal madness – the idea of thinking you are Napoleon is a traditional British comic trope for presenting someone who is insane. I thought it also gave the character a pop sexuality reminiscent of British "new romantic" rock groups such as Adam and the Ants. This ambiguous sexual pop-star persona spilled over into his relationship with Banquo and Lady Macbeth as well as the witches.

Disney milieu

For *Projeto* 2, the installation-party version in Centrala, the costume was inspired by the line from Act 3, Scene 4, where Macbeth finds himself terrified at the return of Banquo as a ghost and describes himself as "the baby of a girl". I, therefore, wore as part of the costume a small child's party dress, combined with the Hussar's jacket from *Projeto* 1. This also developed into the karaoke section where we sang Disney songs that you might expect to find at a small girl's birthday party featuring a Disney princess.

This exploration of popular Disney imagery was continued through all the cycles of the *Macbeth Projeto*. The idea that Macbeth starts to live in a parallel time zone, through lack of sleep, was given expression in the use of a talking Mickey Mouse watch – one I had bought many years before on my first visit to Holly-wood – which Macbeth kept fixed to Memphis USA time.

Sleep

Throughout the play Macbeth refers to the fact that he cannot sleep that "Macbeth has murdered sleep". As part of my costume as well as the voodoo passport I wore an empty packet of sleeping pills on a chain around my neck. I related this inability to sleep directly to myself in an attempt to blur the line between my persona as an actor and the invented character of Macbeth. I suffer very badly from jetlag and need to use sleeping pills if I am to get back to a normal state after travelling long distance. The idea, that one might take sleeping pills and still not be able to sleep, which I had some minor experience of, might potentially lead one to feel divorced from reality and that psychosis could ensue through lack of sleep. I felt this was a useful way to explore Macbeth's character as the play progresses when he is sleep-deprived and hallucinations become part of his life. He questions reality and enters dream worlds.

Character development

In *Projeto* 2 and throughout all the following cycles I wanted to explore the slippage between a real person (the real-life embodied experience of myself as an actor), and the fictional character of Macbeth. As part of the background exploration of Macbeth I started to look for parallel inspiration and found it in the life of Elvis Presley who was known as "the king". I wanted to integrate this Elvis persona as part of the "slippage" which would become my "Macbeth". The idea that the audience might be lulled into believing the Stephen–Macbeth–Elvis persona was confusingly "real" on some level, and intrigued me as part of my investigation into the nature of acting. When an audience member met me in the foyer during *Projeto* 3, and I offered to give them a Tarot reading, and blew cigarette smoke into their face, and drank alcohol (ritual voodoo ingredients: tobacco and alcohol), they wouldn't know who I was. When I started the show by describing the fire and safety regulations of the theatre, and then started to talk about my hearing problems brought on by a long-haul flight, and my problems with sleeping, the audience would be unclear where the "actor" ended and the "character" of Macbeth began. This slippage of character, of reality and unreality, I felt echoed Macbeth's slippage into madness through the actions of the play, to where he can't really trust his own mind: Is anything real? The Dagger? Banquo's ghost? The witches? The performance the audience is watching? It also echoes one of the paradoxes of acting: My character is pretend, but his body is real (it's mine), his voice is mine, those tears in my eyes are a genuine physical manifestation, but are they "real"?

Lady Macbeth

Elvis' marriage to Priscilla Presley was seen as a fairytale event, and from the outside, they appeared to have a fairy-tale life in the mansion in Memphis USA. This developed from, and related to, the little girl party princess songs from *Projeto* 2. In *Projeto* 2 (Digbrew version) the song I decided to sing live (not karaoke) was by Elvis's daughter, Lisa Marie Presley and the lyrics describe the fact that in the backyard of the Presley home, Graceland, in Memphis, alongside the grave of Elvis and his mother, there is an empty plot for a grave waiting for Priscilla when she dies. This seemed an engaging image to me, as Macbeth and Lady Macbeth have a dead child that we never see. In the song, Lisa Marie Presley also describes how she keeps her watch set to Memphis time no matter where she is in the world. I, therefore, had Macbeth's talking Mickey Mouse watch set to Memphis time.

In the solo performance as Lady Macbeth I carried a very small white wooden coffin, with straps attached, which I used as a handbag, but which also had a small viewing window in the top through which one imagined Lady Macbeth could see her dead child, which she always carried with her.

When developing *Projeto* 3, the solo show, it occurred to me that we did not know the names of Macbeth or Lady Macbeth only the surname and title. I then realised that one could see in the name Macbeth a compound of a male and female character Mac and Beth, Mac/Beth: the male and the female. This gave rise to the idea of playing both Macbeth and Lady Macbeth as two aspects of the same persona. The idea of split personality was a further expression of the madness that seemed to have overtaken Macbeth's life in the play and tied it to Sarah Kane's play *4:48 Psychosis* as well as her personal life which ended in suicide.

Banquo

The image of Banquo returning as a ghost, not dying when he has been bludgeoned and stabbed, was something that was first explored in *Projeto* 1.

I was particularly inspired by the lines from Act 3, Scene 4, Line 76

> "The times have been
> That when the brains were out, the man would die,
> And there's an end. But now they rise again
> With twenty mortal murders on their crowns"

In *Projeto* 1, the actor playing Banquo was repeatedly attacked, fell down, and re-vivified in a sort of ritual choreographic dance macabre, to come back to haunt Macbeth. This image of the un-dead related to and inspired some of the exploration of voodoo magic and ritual. For part of Macbeth's costume, I created a voodoo passport. Voodoo passport is something that exists, and can be worn as protection when travelling the island of Haiti at night to keep evil spirits and especially the undead away. I wore this around my neck. It was an outward expression of the growing superstition and magical consciousness that I felt grew as part of Macbeth's character throughout the play.

By the time we got to *Projeto* 6 online version, Macbeth had become Banquo's killer-lover, whom Macbeth loves in a homosexual relation, but had to murder in order to stop the prophecy by witches, and he murdered him with his dagger in a highly sensual moment achieved through the use of Zoom theatre by physically holding the computer camera up close and moving it over my body – and although we two actors were separated by thousands of miles, I felt it was experienced by the audience as an intimate, uncomfortable and eroticised exchange, in which I spoke Portuguese and Banquo spoke English. In my scenes with Lady Macbeth, I spoke English and Lady Macbeth spoke Potuguese.

Macbeth's child

If I were to move forward with the project I would like to explore integrating the character of Macbeth's dead child into the characters I would perform, alongside Macbeth and Lady Macbeth.

Stand-up

From *Projeto* 2, Macbeth was a stand-up entertainer. All of the following cycles had a stand-up element to them in terms of direct address to the audience that came to

Macbeth's party. This was inspired after visiting and watching a performance by Robert Lepage. In the performance we saw Lepage on stage with a dolls-house size model of the home he grew up in when he was a child in Canada. I thought it would be fun for Macbeth to have a model of his castle that he could show the audience by using a camera projecting onto a large screen. I made my castle from shoeboxes. I was able to add a comic "reveal" by showing the room that Malcolm stayed in which was covered in blood. This room was actually based on the living room of Elvis's house in Memphis which is all white: white carpets, white furniture, and white walls. I thought it would be funny if this was the room Malcolm was murdered in and therefore would lead to some real problems cleaning up the evidence. This also led to the idea in *Projeto* 6 that Macbeth might have a YouTube channel through which he could demonstrate how to make a model of his house.

This YouTube section was inspired by having to use the computer as the means of delivering our performance, the computer world in which YouTube and Zoom exist, and which had become so familiar to all of us during the world Covid lockdown. It was a way to develop the stand-up comedy popular-entertainment element of the performance, but keeping it native to the computer medium, and the audience's experience of using computers and smart phones.

Body as a resource

In Cycle 4, Prague, I was able to build on the experience of *Projeto* 2, which was part art-installation, and in which I felt I became living sculpture – being discovered "dead" on the toilet, wearing a crown from burger king (referencing Elvis' death); or discovered in a magically lit alcove, seated on a throne, with tarot cards tumbling from my hands (like a living Jungian architype), or appearing like a ghost in a corridor, following an imaginary dagger, revealed to the audience and then suddenly closed off from them.

Working with the designers, I offered myself as a resource. I thought of myself as a Gordon Craig puppet actor, to be controlled by and absorbed into the design. They wrapped my naked torso in plastic film, and using coloured lights, made a video of me struggling in this trap. The film was then projected on one wall of the environment they eventually created – and the images of me were also interrupted and disturbed electronically by the movement and approach of the audience spectators. The videos were also projected onto a throne. This could just be viewed in its throne-room, or the spectators could sit on the throne and become combined with the projected images of my struggling body, thus becoming part of the performative space as actors themselves. I felt that through the projection, I haunted and possessed them, without their knowing, like a ghost.

Zoom theatre – like Prospero's isle

My main recollection of Zoom theatre, *Macbeth Projeto* 6, is how it totally took over my life because my house became the studio and rehearsal room. I wandered alone in my lock-down home, wearing Macbeth costume and make-up, making huge numbers of videos, talking to sound and video editors, and filming myself naked covered in blood in the shower. Most poignantly I recall vividly the moments when rehearsals with my fellow actors in Brazil would end and the Zoom call stopped: I was suddenly alone, back in lockdown. I used to feel incredibly sad. It reminded me of Caliban waking from his dreams, finding himself still a slave on Prospero's island, and longing to dream again. The rehearsals and performance had an incredibly "live" feel. It felt exactly like being in a theatre or rehearsal room. We were together in a different reality: I developed a closeness and a bond with the Brazilian actors and the director, which was emotional and felt totally physical. I hated it when the cameras turned off and they disappeared – like Prospero's spirits at the end of the Masque.

I think this intensity helped to feed into the vividness of the performance: I was living a little like the character, alone in my castle being visited by spirits. In such an unreal world, the idea of living a method-actor existence was not intended, but certainly on reflection it was part of the process.

Conclusion: from cinematic theatre to live Zoom Performance

Exploring visual images and narratives using various creative methods (physical performance, installation and site-specific, solo performance, interdisciplinary, augmented reality performance and Zoom theatre) can provide different performance aesthetics, multi-media and audience experiences. All these various visual explorations found their place on a digital platform, resulting in a website that allowed for work archived and preserved for viewing and future research.

The project has provided a new understanding of the interdisciplinary methodologies and pedagogies implemented in the exploration *of Macbeth Projeto* Cycles. The text became an inter-theatrical reference point for live digital theatre. Together all elements from performance and visual arts allowed the migration of dramatic text into an exploration of interdisciplinary performative pedagogies. The cycles were enabled by a national and international collaborative partnership with the creative industry and festivals as the production interacted with the audiences in different cultural contexts that influenced our artistic development. The audience's participation was an essential part of our explorations with performative creative forms.

- Shell Studio, Parkside, BCU for acting students and staff of Royal Birmingham Conservatoire. This was followed by extensive Q&A feedback in April 2017;
- Centrala Arts Centre, June 2017 and Digbrew Beerhouse (Birmingham), March 2018, for the festival audience as a part of the 1st Friday Community Arts Festival.

- As a solo performance and paper presentation at the International Federation of Theatre Research (IFTR) in Belgrade, 2018, this is a significant theatre conference with over 1,000 performance academics and participants worldwide. The production was presented for three days to more than 600 audience members at the Vuk Theatre, Belgrade. Funding by Belgrade City Arts – (10,000 euros).
- As a six-day Result Driven Workshop with an international group of performance designers whose outcome was presented for a week in the Prague Industrial Palace to the global audiences, practitioners and scholars. This included the presentation of a keynote about our rehearsal process in June 2019 at the Prague Quadrennial (PQ 19) in Prague – (1,500 euros).
- Six-month R&D on mixed media performance, exploring augmented reality and live performance, funded by AHRC in collaboration with acting staff from Shanghai Theatre Academy. Performed in July 2019 at Shanghai Theatre Academy in Shanghai – (£50,000).
- As a video, live performance art using the Zoom online platform as a digital theatre in collaboration with the experimental cyborg theatre company Teatro Os Satyros. (Sao Paulo); live-streamed in December 2020 as live online performance – (3,000 US dollars).

The cultural and production platforms shaped by the audience's experiences and expectations created new performative contexts. The project began a new production context that engaged different audiences: acting students at RBC, local communities and participants in local festivals, international scholarly platforms on performance studies and performance design, AHRC-funded R&D and full live digital collaboration with a professional theatre company. The practice-led interdisciplinary research performance, *Macbeth Projeto*, engages with adaptations of Shakespeare's *Macbeth*, allowing connections between different dramatic forms and experiences through various artistic and theatrical forms. Over three years, we have enabled knowledge transfer through representation at leading international conferences in the performing arts sector. This is also essential for the overall development of the project's impact. In addition, the ability to forge new collaborations with other world-leading researchers gave us new connections and opened up opportunities for future collaborations with our project.

Notes

1 The research performance project development is fully documented on the website www.macbethprojeto.co.uk
2 Dundjerović, Aleksandar "Research context" *Macbeth Projeto* (December 2020). See the website http://macbethprojeto.co.uk/research-context/
3 Since 2007, I have been a visiting professor in the School of Performing Arts, University of Sao Paulo, Brazil. In 2008/9, I was awarded the Leverhulme Research Fellowship to investigate performance practices in Brazilian group theatre devising

processes. During this time, I offered several educational workshops in intermedial digital performance across Brazil (Salvador de Bahia, Rio de Janeiro, Sao Paulo, Curitiba and Porto Alegre). I also explored and learned experimental pedagogical practices with students and performers through mixed arts and media practised in Brazilian theatre-making. My two co-authored books, *Brazilian Collaborative Theatre* (2017) and *Brazilian Performing Arts* (2019), created with leading Brazilian theatre scholar Luis Fernando Ramos were based on an examination of collaborative, anthropophagic theatre and interdisciplinary performing arts in Brazil.

4 Refskou, Anne, Marcelo De Amorium, and Vinicius de Carvalho, *Eating Shakespeare: Cultural Anthropophagy as Global Methodology* (Bloomsbury Academic, 2019).
5 See the section on the RSVP Cycles in Chapter 3.
6 In critical debates around archiving as a research tool, collection depends on the inclusion of material and the exclusion of what is remembered at the point of creating archives. Online digital applied and community theatre might be understood in a context of positioning and repositioning content that is culturally and physically (body presence) significant. One of the essential national (UK) archives for performing arts documentation is the V&A theatre and performance archives, collecting material since 1920. https://www.vam.ac.uk/info/theatre-performance-archives
7 Tschumi, Bernard. *Architecture and Disjunction* (MIT Press, 1996), p. 129.
8 See article by Macauley, David. "The Fate of Place: A Philosophical History", *Environmental Ethics 22* (2000), pp. 219–221.
9 Lehmann, Hans-Theis. *Postdramatic Theatre* (Routledge, 2006).
10 Dundjerović, Aleksandar. *The Theatricality of Robert Lepage* (McGill-Queen's University Press, 2007).
11 Mike Pearson presented the use of space as a site for dramaturgy in the important study *Site-Specific Performance* (Palgrave Macmillan, 2010).
12 Schechner, Richard. *Performance Study: An Introduction* (Routledge, 2002,) p. 52.
13 Deleuze, Gilles and Felix Guattari. *A Thousand Plateaus: Capitalism and Schizophrenia* (University of Minnesota Press, 1988).

8

LIVE THEATRE ON ZOOM

As we have observed throughout the book, in early 2020 Covid-19 triggered the need for a new reality in human communication. This had an impact, particularly in live arts and theatre. Recent developments in digital media did not come out of being artistically different or for theatre performances trying to be more like media-tised forms, digital or games; it was due to the group's live physical interaction in space that could not exist legally. Where can theatre performance practitioners and students go, where do they start, and how can they be alive and connected to their community with no budget to make theatre when everything was stopped? The independent theatre sector migrated online, produced new material, and stayed connected to the audience. Streaming platforms provided a feasible option, and video communication software such as Zoom transformed into a digital *stage* for Zoom theatre performance. Microsoft Teams (hearafter Teams) was used for online classes in higher education, particularly in the UK.

Mainstream theatre communities enhanced the showing of theatre production on online platforms established form 2009 to bring recorded live theatre to international audiences. The Royal National Theatre's response to the pandemic, sponsored by Arts Council England, was to create a series of Livestream broadcasts of previously recorded production to be shared with the world through an already existing scheme under National Theatre Live (NTL – showing live theatre in local cinemas across the UK and internationally). Flo Buckeridge, producer of NTL, points out that due to the closure of live theatre and cinema, they made theatre available free on YouTube, "we created what we called 'National Theatre at Home', and it started in April (2021)."[1] Another example of online digital theatre was provided by Shakespeare's Globe, which agreed to release 40 productions on their web/app, Globe Player Services, for the audience. In London, Hampstead Theatre opened its archive pro-ductions for online streaming from its website in collaboration with *The Guardian*.

DOI: 10.4324/9781003275893-10

Within a worldwide marketplace, theatre and music with other live art that migrated online started to compete for an audience with established film outlets such as Netflix, extending its presence on Instagram, Facebook, and YouTube to produce digital mass media and popular entertainment.

However, the independent theatre sector, small arts companies, and education for practice training in drama and theatre had to reinvent the different approaches to performing practice. In Royal Birmingham Conservatoire, the practice classes in Acting have switched to Teams, lectures, and meetings, as the university was using live online to replace physical communication. For creative practice, the Zoom platform was more flexible, open to international connections and adaptable to the presentation mode that responds to live performers – audience connectivity. On the other hand, Teams for use in live performances was not flexible or open, being restrictive to the HE institution. It was a tool for meetings in enclosed social circumstances (class, workplace, etc.). Advancement in contemporary digital technology and its social implications as platforms for communication and information (knowledge) exchange shifted epistemological inquiry into the digital realm. However, performance practice in cyberspace is not a natural condition for live theatre; digital media is not an alternative for live performance experienced by the audience as *there and now* of a live event. What live Zoom theatre provides is a theatre-like digital space but not a physical theatre experience, of attending a play in an architectural theatre space.

With the shift from live theatre to live online performance during the lockdown, the question of the feasibility of liveness and different kinds of liveness in Zoom Theatre became centralised on providing audiences' participation in the communication process. It offered "social inclusion as it allows vital intersection between performers and audiences" within art communicational structure.[2] Typically, online performance appears within the context of an institutional website or specialised app linked to a company or educational program and represents a set of themes and narratives. In live online production, physical and digital presence is simultaneous as a film on a computer screen, or a television combined with a live theatre performance. Cyberspace became a new location for lack of physical space, and social interaction moved to the digital area as *transtopia*.

The computer screen in live digital theatre became a proscenium stage offering a perception of the world that the viewer is experiencing as if being there and the ability to interpret the images on the screen as truthful. Even though what is presented on the screen may not be a recording of actual or even a reconstruction of someone's interpretation of reality, technologies create environments that appear realistic to our senses. Gabriella Giannachi observes that "the viewer is still reading the screen as if it were presenting an objective view of the world".[3] This apparent faculty of the screen allowed the audience to believe in the authenticity of the experience as being live. In the 21st century, digital technology mastering virtual computer-generated new simulations of reality, according to Jean Baudrillard, is an act of "simulation" that refers to no specific origin or allusion to reality. Baudrillard points out that "Simulation is no longer that of a territory, a referential Being, or a substance. It is the generation by models of real without origin or reality: a hyper-real"[4]. Live Zoom theatre can be seen as a hyperreal that offers an experience of liveness, crossing theatre, computer interactive technology and video/film.

The chapter will establish how essential elements function within live Zoom theatre as live digital theatre. It will show the critical aspects of theatre (live audience, space and performer) that are adapted through video communication platforms as creative resources for performative pedagogies in live digital theatre. The two models of pedagogy for live online production: video choreography and Zoom theatre production, were done as a course at Royal Birmingham Conservatoire as an online practice in 2020 and 2021. The shows were part of an ongoing research project exploring various web applications, video, film and live online telepresence forms in creating performances and exploring actors' training and education. This chapter will explore three case studies: *We'll Meet again at Ricks* as a combination of Zoom theatre and recorded video art performance/choreography presented on Youtube, and *Amorphism: Zoom Wedding* and *When the Gods Come*, created and presented as live Zoom theatre. We will explore performance practice methodologies and pedagogies for live Zoom theatre based on these three performances. The pedagogy behind these methods is enabled through a simple technology linked to a computer working with an iPad tablet, smartphone or PC camera and screen. It can be live or video recorded, working on small image-driven scores by recording objects, space, voice, facial expression, or physical body movement. It became clear that we would use live video as a performance outcome in rehearsals.

Zoom performative pedagogies: digital scores for performer, space and audience

The exploration of *telepresence* in theatre provided the necessary context and understanding of what would be essential in recognising the Zoom platform's ability to adapt to the needs of a live performance. A creative methodology was needed as a practice and pedagogy for video communication with the audience that could replicate a stage-auditorium relation and have open access based on the link provided. Teams was closed in 2020 to the University sector, and anyone outside the university could not join. We needed to invite skills in making online productions from the industry sector, which was impossible on Teams. Skype, the long-standing communicational platform, was not developed for group commu-nications and was not adopted by the university. Zoom as a platform was one of the first to become used in 2020 as flexible enough to respond to the needs of theatre performance.[5] The advantage of Zoom in early 2020 was that as an app, it allows access to an individual anywhere in the world to join or form a group, making it easy for group members to communicate regardless of their organisa-tion. Being open also allowed access to an audience that would follow the per-formance live. One needs only an online account and to follow a link to access it, and it can work on any device, being free and having a very affordable professional version. It is simple to use and navigate communication with a larger group of users. It allows recording sharing screens and provides interactivity with the audience. It is very easy for face-to-face communication from home.

Mostafa Karam and Galal Naruib provide a succinct explanation of Zoom video call technology that allows the hosting of live performances. The principle is essential as live Zoom theatre depends on the use of this application for the running of live performance via computer but live for the audiences as it would be in theatre.

> In Zoom, there are two available operating systems – meeting and webinar. In the meeting application, the host, cohost, and participants can mute/unmute their microphones, share their screens, and participate in the show without the control or permission of the host. Its capacity ranges from 100 to 1,000, depending on the plan and licence. Therefore, it is convenient for rehearsals. In the webinar application, in addition to the host and cohost, there are two types of participants: panellists and attendees. Panellists can be seen and heard, giving this option to performers. Attendees can join the event and watch what is going on, but their microphones are muted, and they cannot unmute them alone. Their videos are permanently off. They cannot share their screen. This option, then, is convenient for the role and requirements of audiences. Only the host can enable or turn on the attendees' microphone to allow their reactions and responses to be heard by the actors. Then, each attendee can click the mic button to choose whether to mute or unmute.[6]

With all these qualities, it was clear that digital space in the live Zoom theatre screen can provide an-Other physical theatre space, live and virtually real.

In Zoom theatre, interaction is established between the performer and the audience over the video communicational platform. That allows the performer to access the audience's area on the screen, even if it is just through the camera. In Zoom theatre, we explored with the audience visible to the performers. Either with actors at the beginning addressing the audience directly, acknowledging their presence or while entering the Zoom room and being visible. This approach to performing and the relationship with the audience would impact actors and how they perform. This would be an example of hybrid acting that combines theatre with the screen. The initial moment of encounter, when the performer sees the audience (everyone on camera – gallery view), is essential to create the sense of collectiveness that emulates the encounters in physical theatre. One of the critical things in explorations with students was to work with the mixing of digital and physical space. Transtopia in Zoom performance was created between physical and digital space as part of highly integrated multimedia locations as a telepresence system. The performer is in their physical place that is teleported as a life-like video image into digital space on the screen while the audience is in their location watching.

Live Zoom theatre is a different experience from a live stream or presenting a high definition recorded theatre production. An approach to digital multimedia acting in interdisciplinary performative pedagogies requires a performer to simultaneously interact with other actors on camera and digital technology in different locations, either in a private place, on stage or in a media recording studio. The acting method in Zoom live theatre requires simultaneous use of cinema and theatre directly connecting with the live viewers. In live Zoom, theatre performance happens simultaneously in a personal space and on-screen in real-time. As in a theatre, it engages the audience in live performances, and as in film, it uses a camera to communicate actions and emotions on screen. The representation and intimacy of facial expressions and gestures in Live Zoom theatre would be the same as in film acting. The physical closeness or distance of the audience to the theatre stage determines how the actor will perform and use the full expression of the body in space. Likewise, as in television or film, facial expression to the camera requires training and an approach to rehearsals that is different from theatre. Both approaches to acting and therefore directing are blurred in live Zoom theatre. It also involves changing the actors' perspective by creating a multimedia performance maker, simultaneously performing for the camera and communicating with other actors on screen, manipulating digital images, interacting with their own physical space, recording and live to stream.

The creative participatory practice of the RSVP Cycles or Scores became one of the critical pedagogical approaches and methods of making performance in live Zoom theatre. The pedagogy relies on what comes out of the starting point in devising/adapting material. Resources, such as the performer's body (physically and as a location for emotion); how we feel and relate to others and relationships we establish, and the objects and environment we are in, can be used to improvise at the moment and lead to the exploration of material in Scores.[7] The use of the Scores in performance is a notation of human action, a symbolisation of processes through action in space over time.[8] Scores can be personal or group and are relevant to various human creative methods; in music and dance, scores encompass action and activities happening in space over time. The score can be open or closed. Open – no leader or awareness of identity are required. The group has to find an identity as the RSVP Cycle is about transformation and can be thematically explored through environmental approaches to personal actions.

> My environment can impact my movement, emotions, and how I relate to others. By highlighting these different resources, we create options that give us a sense of agency. If I move differently, how will that impact my emotions? How will this have a change state impact on my relationships? And how, in turn, might *this* impact my environment. Through scores, Anna offers people a chance to play out these different dialogues through a process she calls the life/art dialogue.[9]

Scores relate to time-defined activities in theatre, performance arts, happenings like interventions, multimedia events, installations, physical expression, and participatory environmental space (equally shared by actors and audience), to name a few.

The scenes and segments are not connected in a cause–effect progression, it is not realistic in the treatment of time and space, but scores are independent and lead to each other as a dream-like journey. Similarly, resources used are improvised with materials that lead to an online Zoom performance in the same way as they would in a live performance. The Scores, as independent events, allow actors to put them in an order depending on what is coming out of the performance practice. In addition, the subjective position of the actor-author in devising/adapting material is pertinent to the collaboration and solo performance process in producing and performing for an audience. This is the most critical aspect of scores that comes from the methodology of RSVP cycles; they are process-oriented rather than results-oriented, making them respond well to a plurality of media and interdisciplinarity. As Scores show a change in the content through the process, they point to patterns in motion (choreography), the relationship between body and space: performer's physical presence in any room in front of the camera (computer, laptop, tablet and smartphone) connected to other performers in their performance space, linked through mutual coexistence in cyberspace.

Case Study One*: We'll Meet agian at Ricks* – Video art performance/choreography (YouTube June 2020)

Context

The first case study – video art performance/choreography, *We'll Meet again at Ricks*, was a hybrid performance using the Zoom platform and WhatsApp video

FIGURE 8.1 *We'll Meet again at Ricks* 26th June 2020. Premiere on YouTube.

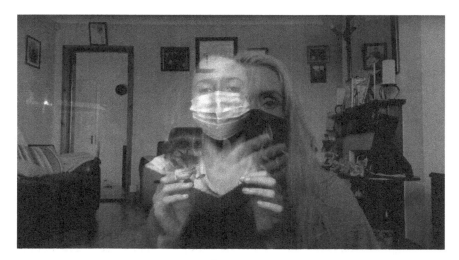

FIGURE 8.2 *We'll Meet again at Ricks* 26th June 2020. Premiere on YouTube.

sharing during the rehearsal process combining recorded and edited video with live performance that was played on YouTube as a production.[10] Rehearsal used as creative methods a combination of Zoom video conference explored as a live theatre medium, filmed on computer camera and smartphones, editing with In Shot or similar simple app and using WhatsApp for communication and passage of the video material to the group, and finally, use of a professional editor to compose the final work as a video film. From the beginning, we wanted to explore the making of Zoom theatre, but the problem was that we did not know how to make Zoom live performance. The opening was announced as a video performance with a set time for the audience to watch live on YouTube. It was collaboratively created by the second-year BA acting students at Royal Birmingham Conservatoire. The process started on May 20 and opened on June 26, 2020, as a live YouTube online video performance, leaving the recording open for viewing. *Ricks* was supposed to be a live devised performance as specified in the acting curriculum for the second year end project. As a group creating in physical space could not take place, we tried to follow the pedagogy and creative methodology of theatre devising. Still, we had to now adapt to working via video communication platforms, a more familiar visual art form, video art, employing digital media under the newly changed circumstances.

The rehearsal process was organised around a weekly review of the whole group devising material; usually, we presented short performances on Friday and then reviewed them, selecting what was good with the input from the entire group. Rehearsals took place online twice a day – morning and late afternoon, but students' work continued as they were working from home. At the end of the workweek review, the performance material would be developed as a resource for the next cycle in the following week. We first started with exploring lighting and sound in space, what is visible and invisible. What is suggested on a screen to the audience, and what do they know is there? We used a camera from a phone or laptop to transmit personal space in a house, an atmosphere of a bedroom or bathroom, and an intimate environment.

The process started with an adaptation of the classic film *Casablanca* (1942), directed by Michael Curtiz, which was initially an unproduced American theatre play *Everybody Comes to Rick's* (1940) and developed into a film script for *Casablanca*. In the beginning, we were unsure if we would make a close adaptation of *Casablanca* into theatre/video performance and how subjective the approach by different members would relate to the starting reference point in the live group devising process rehearsed live online. The love story is set in 1941 at Rick's American Café in Casablanca, where refugees from war-torn Europe come waiting to get a passage to freedom, to leave. Another reference point was a famous British song from the Second World War, *We'll meet again* (1939), performed by Vera Lynn. It is about people being separated by war, which was noted in the Queen's speech on the hardship of coronavirus on April 5, 2020 "we will be with our friends again; we will be with our families again; we will meet again".[11]

As the rehearsal process started, it was clear that the space as the score could not be used as in live theatre. The actors are in different individual locations. The audience is in a separate personal space from the actors; there is no joint physical but virtual digital space. It must be seen as a space within a film or a video with the difference that it is presented live or recorded live to viewers. Relations between body, objects and space as captured on camera and shown on a screen could be seen simultaneously while performing. The impro material filmed by actors themselves provided resources for further playing and improvisation. This part of the rehearsal process in generating material is not different from live devising in a studio; the only substantial difference is the communication model – using digital video technology. Actors use various resources, cameras, and screens to create their scenes.

The first week of the rehearsal exercise was to develop scores using lighting, as in film lighting, all the aspects of shades and how they reflect on the body and objects. In addition, the students were working on their text by developing themes from the film and song. Working on the text and developing visual scores for the camera took most of the rehearsal time in the second and third weeks. The fourth and fifth week was used to edit and compose the video art devised performance. Different pedagogies worked concurrently in this practice. However, from the beginning, the direct approach was to develop skills for live online production: physical, spatial and camera, and to work on developing textual adaptation. The students were asked to introduce objects and different visual and audio perception levels within the screen frame. Following the resources taken from the film *Casablanca* (with the central location of a famous bar called Rick's), we decided to situate the action around the table in their house or a room where each actor would perform their narrative as part of their ritual of waiting to escape.

The pedagogy for this project was not based on any system; it was non-existent. Before Covid-19, no one wrote or researched through practice live online production such as digital Zoom theatre. Dr Paul Sadot, a researcher into video dance and digital corporality, observes:

> each time I read another book on digital performance written before COVID, I could not find what I was looking for. So, we were making it up as we went along and tried to find terminology. I did not have the term *Digi-corporeality* before working on the pandemic lockdown, and the concept of digital Zoom theatre did not relate to me. I could feel some physical connection with the word *Digi-corporeality*.[12]

Sadot's *digi-corporeality* "is a new and intimate kinaesthetic experience, made possible by a unique encounter between socially and culturally diverse bodies in a DIY digital space."[13] Discussion on the corporal body is one of the central discourses within performance studies and indeed within contemporary culture, which becomes amplified once the virtual body is introduced into discourse of performance practice. A body on screen in live Zoom digital theatre has virtual qualities, it is represented through computer technology. In addition, the cinematic quality that is part of an expression of images in Zoom performance is functioning together with live theatre presence in digital space. Sadot explains the interaction between film and theatre on student-actor actions within a score they were exploring:

> In one of the student scores, telling a story by focusing on objects that can be close-up on the screen, for example, a family photo of grandparents, creates a different intimate connection where we hear the narrator's voice and look at the picture. A close-up is only possible as a projection behind an actor in live theatre in physical space, which would be a different emotional experience from an image on the screen. A further understanding of varying levels of liveness was possible once we had a chance to work with students on live online production and raise that question and make it part of pedagogy by listening to what students are making out of it.[14]

Objective and methodologies

The objective was to devise a version collaboratively in the conditions when students are in lockdown, separated, and living in different locations – cities or even countries. Each student actor had to work from home, from a personal space which became the performance location. They created individually and through group sharing using Zoom as a collaborative rehearsal virtual venue and WhatsApp for sharing of filmed material. The decision to record everything live and use it as a video performance was based on a fear that the Internet in individual houses at that moment when we wanted to have a live online Zoom theatre experience would not be strong enough. It was not only to create a devising performance and provide that experience for the students but to explore the possibility of devising live online production and adopting devising methods for live theatre into workable solutions for creating a Zoom theatre. The focus was on the subjective and familiar themes related to lockdown caused by the pandemic. In this way, film and song provided emotional content from which students could start telling their experiences of separation during coronavirus lockdown. Subjectivising starting point and telling our circumstances of the situation each of us was in – confinement, awaiting, loneliness, uncertainty for future, and separation from loved ones.

We had to modify and even develop our pedagogical method that would relate to students and allow them to engage in the creative performance process. It was essential to separate the rehearsals into the elements of interdisciplinary performative pedagogy: writing text, digital media performance, and performance space/architecture. Some practices and pedagogical methodologies followed each other, and others were happening simultaneously. The pedagogical work units had to relate to actors/students learning to create on live Zoom theatre through performance scoring:

- performance text as solo narratives – performers, are writers of their narrative and events
- events in digital media and video performance – *working* with a camera and creating video choreography
- performative space – creating individual performers' physical environment and digital group space

Another objective was to explore what Sadot refers to as "precarity and turbulence".[15] Working online was an opportunity to encounter things; it was not an obstacle but a chance to test what turbulence as instability and conflict can bring out within this pedagogical approach. He points out that when: "we encounter things that were supposedly mistakes, incoherent (for example in live Zoom digital theatre, internet connection may be different and people connect in various times), immediately I think of turbulence, of course, that's going to happen we are in uncharted territory."[16] The live Zoom theatre experiments reinforce and articulate Auslander's writing about different levels of liveness in digital performance.

Employing the method of exploring starting references points for devising – the film *Casablanca* and doing background research into the period of the Second World War and refugee crisis and people trying to escape the war and Nazis, and listening to and reading the contexts of Vera Lynn's song, *We'll meet again*, students were tasked to find individually their resources about starting references that would relate to their conditions in the pandemic lockdown. The topics linked were awaiting or wanting to escape, being stuck in one place, isolation, separation from their life, and forced confinement.

In the group rehearsals, actors/students were introduced to the writing process of creating their subjective narratives based on starting reference points. They were tasked to produce a short solo narrative (monologue) using a quick free writing technique and free association on a topic which we aggreged at the start – lockdown.

Exercises for scoring performance text as solo narratives – actor-author workshop model, led by Gwydion Colder.[17]

- Write down 4–5 own irritations (conflicts) about your chosen theme related to being in lockdown and awaiting. Each student will have their themes. Disturbances have caused turbulence in what is perceived as the normality of everyday life arising from lockdown conditions. The students were encouraged to focus on minor annoyances and not only on more obvious ones. For example, they are running out of hot water quicker as more people stay inside vs more general ones like not being able to go to the restaurant.
- Free flow writing about one chosen irritation causes turbulence, such as brainstorming through writing without stopping for five minutes. Whatever students write is acceptable; it can be vague, general, opinionated, or inconsequential. Once finished, the material will be reviewed for two minutes, looking at the shifts of thoughts. They are given two minutes to make a quick bullet-point list of objects, people, places, or physical sensations mentioned in free-flow writing.
- After creating a list, students will focus on the writing and give it shape by engaging with immediate space and objects necessary for their story and sentence restructuring to clarify the language.
- The students will repeat this process several times using a different irritations as a starting point.
- In the next session, the students will have five minutes to connect the ideas in different monologue sets with transition sentences. The material may be random, descriptive of feelings, or non-sensical but represents the free flow of thoughts and impressions. The students are to examine these writings by bringing the list and looking for any repetition of ideas, words, persons, places, objects, etc. This should be developed further.
- The students were asked to work on a monologue that would bring together these narratives into productions of a monologue, a solo performance of around 2 minutes. The first round of impro writing (for 12 students) was about 25 minutes.
- After the group presentation, students provide feedback to each other and develop in 2–3 minutes another bullet-point list of objects, people, places, or physical sensations that came from a discussion with a group.
- They will perform the solo narrative live on Zoom or filmed on their phone/laptop and share it with the group on WhatsApp.

Exercises in scoring events in digital media and video performance led by Dr. Paul Sadot.[18]
Sadot explains the focus in practice methodology of video choreography:

> Video choreography is a recording of video dancers' movements. Using live
> online production has a whole different idea for the agency involved. Pre-
> Covid-filming, I'm in a space with them and recording their actions on film.
> I would be there with performers with my camera, coming close to them as
> they move through space. I would be in an intimate space and have the
> camera with them, but we wouldn't notice it. I'd be physically present,
> stepping in and out, recording their expressions. In live online production,
> they must use a total agency to create as an actor. They're not just thinking
> about the physical or corporal; they must think about the camera and how to
> stage their action, lighting, and props; they have to think about proximity
> and perspective.[19]

Video Choreography was the central pedagogical implementation in addition to
devising text, as it focuses on the camera and performer's body. This element
differs from theatre live devising performance since it brings new features into the
process relevant to making online video films, such as screen, camera, and editing.
The style of working was developed as video choreography.[20] It was also adapted
to fit a set of workshops for actors in the video recording of a performance that
could not work live in space but had to use a live online platform for rehearsals
and performances. The student actors are separated from each other physically but
connected in cyberspace. The essential exercises developing the relationship
between medium technology and performers' artistic use outline a pedagogical
approach to creating interactivity between video and physical movement.

- Intimacy with the camera: on the first day of practice with a camera and
  intimacy, students were given to come closer to a camera in live communication with a group in Zoom rehearsals and explore that sense of touch
  and closeness. The camera close-up and medium shot as in film have to be
  explored. These are part of the camera shots for the film, and they present
  closeness that cannot be done in theatre.
- Intimacy with immediate space and exploring the body comes with establishing
  location. Personal is heightened because students bring others into their
  room in Zoom connection. There is an exchange in sharing private spaces
  where students are located.
- Playing with technology: students are instructed to be involved in the technical choreography by exploring different effects and what they can do with
  their PC, iPad, iPhone or any other innovative technology. What apps are
  available for editing? We decided to use WhatsApp and In Shot app for their
  individual work's filming and editing process. The students were given 10
  minutes to find the object, film it on WhatsApp and make these objects

relevant and exciting. Students should consider small gestures and objects in the digital format as they can be very representative, being visible in close-up on the camera.

- Visual image: the students used the solo narrative they created in the actor-author session to work with the camera, objects, and spatial environment. The task was to read the text in front of a camera, look for actions and physical objects, and close in on the physical activities with images for which text may not be necessary. The task is to make the text visually relevant for text and image to come together as different scores complimenting each other. In theatre, a close-up of an object (stone, photo, a vase with flowers) or a long sky shot cannot replace text. It is not visible to the back of the auditorium unless it is part of a visual projection in multimedia performance.
- Digital ensemble: the students are to share their work, establish a digital ensemble and learn from each other. This group sharing and discussion will be repeated after each exercise.
- Establishing relationships with your body on screen: as the group meeting takes place in digital reality, they must extend their physicality beyond the body and connect to the screen. From theatre thinking, there is a shift in thinking about how you communicate with the camera and their presence on screen. It is about embracing technology as a performative tool. The students are to create a variety of scores using their body but visible on the screen – for example – eye, hand, head, upper torso, just facial expression, more significant physical movement in space etc.
- WhatsApp group collaboration: ensemble exchange was an ongoing process 24/7. The online platform was used (Teams) for live group creating a performance to review creative individual and group material (either recorded or presented live) and comment upon developing material for the next round of explorations. WhatsApp was used to share individual material with the group and instructor. As the process was developmental, inventiveness was not controlled by the rehearsal time frame; as students created from their homes, the filmed material exchange would go even throughout the night.

Scoring performance space – creating digital and physical environments

The space in live Zoom theatre is not for a theatrical set or a realistic proscenium setting but rather an image/action-driven area that can show the actual location (indoor – room, kitchen, hallway). Still, it can also include real video/film clips showing different events mixed into live online performances. In *Rick's*, one of the critical things we were working on with the mixing of digital and physical space was that the audience and the actor were not in the same area, which is quite different from the traditional theatre experience. Intermedial spaces were created in the relationship between physical and digital space as part of highly integrated multimedia locations as a telepresence system. The performer is present at the moment in a physical and live-form place that is teleported as a life-like video image.

The first reflection on space and audience was how the performer could impact and control, to some extent, the area where the audience is located. We started talking about sending the audience members a letter or a parcel with objects beforehand. The audience could relate to the performer's space when attending the performance. The idea was to give the audience a set of tasks to be in the same environment as performers as they are also at home, having a table, dim lights, candles, and even something that will produce some smell or atmosphere.

The second exercise that we worked on was the idea of the threshold. This exercise aimed to get the students to explore their environment, rooms, and spaces in their homes, especially the transitions. How do you transition from one room to another, from one floor to another, from the interior to the exterior? That was suggestive because it allowed them to understand the transformation, the movement between one place and another.

The other idea we were working on in terms of the objects is that even though the performance was spatially fragmented – taking place simultaneously in different spaces – there had to be continuity between them. However, they could use objects they all had in their houses to bring them to the digital stage, creating the illusion for the audience members when sharing the same things that there was some connexion amongst those spaces.

Summary of outcomes

Over six weeks, each of these pedagogical methods coming within an interdisciplinary mix of performance devising, actor-author writing, video art, and architecture was applied to students' learning, building on each other's practice and providing tools for creating an online performance. However, this mixed methodology approach was not intended nor planned activity from the outset. The aim was to use online rehearsals, which resulted in a devised performance as output and finding a suitable methodology to enable students to create work remotely and separately (unless they lived together). The pedagogical approach to intermedial performance (in the case of online production – film, visual images, soundscape, and live theatre) provides an experience for students to bring multiple media and diverse ways of creating performance. The rehearsal process used the online platform Teams, and 12 student actors worked collaboratively on a video call. In addition, actors worked individually, recording on the cameras on their phones or computers and editing their work in *In Shot*, sharing it with the whole group on the WhatsApp platform. Through live Zoom theatre, students learned how to devise performances within digital media.

In writing subjective narrative activity, the students were writing as themselves, in their name. They were writing from their own experiences, so they were simply truthful. They could draw on and identify performance environment, space, objects, and people, hyper-focusing on one irritation and creating a list of elements that influenced it. Calder points out that conflict is central to any drama story. Students engage with conflict in discussing "conflict with which they struggle, and can identify ways to cope with, overcome, or fail to overcome it. The discussion of that conflict serves as a foundation for their narrative."[21] Working online was an opportunity to encounter things; it was not an obstacle but a chance to test what turbulence as instability and conflict can bring out within this pedagogical approach.

Live Zoom theatre highlights the need to work across various media and disciplines. This work taught us that the next live digital theatre would engage with the actors' practices and the relationship between body, space, camera, lighting, and sound in live online recorded production. An actor becomes a total author, performing, filming, editing, and simultaneously creative individually and collaboratively. Interdisciplinary performative pedagogies must provide teaching and learning experiences that can support the multiple creative roles of a performer. However, there was no particular pedagogy or established practice to follow at the start of creating a live performance with separated actors and the audience removed. There were three groups of students (between 8–12) with a task to devise performance material. Since the students were in lockdown, each living at home could find communication tools to bring them together. We started working with institutional Teams but soon realised that we could not arrange the level of communication and interactivity needed for a live group performance, so we switched to Zoom. Zoom digital theatre was for live rehearsals with students discussing and presenting their work as an ensemble, and Facilitators (Directors) could examine their practice and what they prepared. WhatsApp was used as a communication between the group to pass the work created and filmed individually. These three groups explored some aspects of cinematics but in confinement– from doing a film heavily edited to the mock documentary-style narrative in speaking directly to the camera to video art/choreography. They were using Zoom theatre and WhatsApp as creative tools. Therefore, Zoom theatre came out of video communication for students to collaborate as a live group. Still, it is also presented as an artistic medium, using new technology to create live art, responding to students' circumstances.

Case Study Two: *Amorphism (Zoom Wedding)* – Live Zoom theatre (February 2021, Zoom Theatre, Zoom Platform)

Context

The second case study – *Amorphism*, was fully realised as a live Zoom theatre. It is a play by young British playwright Gareth Jandrell, whose work was previously done in Pleasence Courtyard, Soho Theatre and Bolton Octagon. The play was commissioned for Royal Birmingham Conservatoire Theatre's third-year acting students. From the start, it was written with students and live online Zoom production (due to restrictions on live encounters) in mind. The *Amorphism* as a dystopian play shows a society in a post-cataclysmic period resulting from years of pandemics and war. It is a story about what if the Gods from the ancient world came back to earth, finding pandemics, climate destruction and wars; how would humanity react and restructure itself afterwards? The play was rehearsed online in February and March 2021 and presented as a Zoom theatre production. The cohort of 28 third-year students was split into three groups, each doing a segment of the play. I had invited Rodolpho Vasquez, a Brazilian director and co-founder of Os Satyros, to work with directors and offer an acting workshop relevant to acting and directing on Zoom theatre.

In *Zoom Wedding*, we used the text as a starting resource and adapted it to circumstances where students found themselves after almost a year of lockdown. We see our protagonist in the Zoom wedding in lockdown. Ten years from now, we are still in lockdown in the future. We have learned to accept it as a norm. Our wedding is on Zoom, where people who met on Zoom, living thousands of miles apart, are now forming a lasting virtual community. However, clouds that cover Earth bring water and rain, something very deadly and destructive – it is not clear, but it could be acid rain that melts everything. And some Gods come to change humanity forever, turning us into machines. Their wedding and lives are interrupted, and towards the end, instead of a marriage, we realise that it is a memory of the only one who survived while all the other characters involved have died.

The process of rehearsing *Amorphism* was dictated by the restrictions and obstacles so that pedagogies and practice had to adapt to directors' and students' working methods under the new circumstances. The playwright was flexible with their approach to text as all parts were rehearsed simultaneously. There was no group rehearsal in the same physical space while developing a new script with actors, directors, and playwrights. Also, actors must rehearse differently; being separated in their location, they must control their creative process more. For Jandrell, keeping an eye on the overall project and maintaining coherence between different parts was essential. "In contrast, each piece was conceptually other and traditional roles in theatre-making were blurred".[22] Typically, playwrights in developing a new script would be part of the rehearsal process and talk to actors and director and bring into the script's development through findings that come out of rehearsal. However, working on Zoom theatre was different as groups worked simultaneously, with each actor in another location in another city or country.

The focus of exploring the performative pedagogy provided students with a learning platform whereby engaging in the creative process of making online production; they were exposed to new acting pedagogy. They became interdisciplinary performers who did acting, filming, writing, and producing their material, similar to the concept of a "total author". The students saw the entire process of making a product, in front of a camera and behind a camera, and editing what was good and could be improved. The overall view on production making of becoming a practitioner is something students can take further as part of their performance training.

Objectives and Methodology

The aim was to develop Zoom theatre with the students and learn how to create performance in that medium. The project was collaborative work on the performance as each group and director developed their interpretation and approach to Zoom theatre as a media for live performance. The groups reworked the text and gave feedback to the playwright so the text could be adapted or re-written through group improvisation. The students worked as multiple practitioners being total creators – directories, writers, and cinematographers (working with the built-in camera), and the text had to involve and change with group practice. However, as the groups worked separately, individual episodes would be separate sequences within one big story. It was like a television series of several parts united through a team in conditions, representing the characters who found themselves in those post-apocalyptic circumstances.

Making a custom-made play with an online production in mind aims to explore the possibilities of new performance media outside of traditional theatre's constraints. Live Zoom theatre has no budget that it depends on; there is no physical theatre space for rehearsal and production. As a playwright, Jandrell developed a play through the screen window of the computer, allowing for a big story to be told (as in Ancient Greek theatre) of significant tragic and violent events going on in the world outside. Using visual images as a background or as filmed content that can be introduced into live online production can allow for inexpensive ways of creating the spatial virtual presence that can be part of the story's telling.

As the text was commissioned for the actors, each part allowed an option to be developed further, customised to the group and director and their approach to realising text within the frame of Zoom theatre practice. Jandrell explains:

> I sent each group their text, and the students and directors had a week to develop it as they wanted and then give feedback to me; I then adapted the script as per their development notes and sent back a final version. Each group ended up with their approach to doing that, whether through the director feeding back the findings and ideas from the room to me or directly rewriting the text themselves...It was a unique process where some of the traditional roles you would get in the theatre were necessarily blurred, as we all discovered how to make it work under the circumstances.[23]

In the part *Zoom Wedding*, which I directed (following directing/devising practice of Resources/Scores), the group worked collaboratively using the first part of *Amorphism* as a starting resource and improvising their parts as scores based on the character they were playing. Their improvisations recorded on cameras and shared via

WhatsApp were dramaturgically developed by one of the actor students, Camille Burnett, who took the role of a co-writer and worked with all groups to grow together with our version of the text upon which the performance would be based. The character work was significant considering the camera's intimacy, and we started exploring the characters' lives in a story one day before the scheduled wedding took place on Zoom. Actors improvised their text and the situation where they used their smartphones or laptops to film themselves and share with the group through WhatsApp. They were presenting these scores also live on Zoom once they captured the basic feeling and the meaning of the scene they were doing.

Another example of an approach to analysing a text was in the work of the second group, who explored the second part of *Amorphism: When the Gods Came*, with director Sean Aita. He had to break the choral speaking without any character indication in the text and adapt it to characters played by the individual actors within Stanislavski's concept of "I" in given circumstances.[24] Breaking the text into different sections and making it a character-driven piece became a concept from appropriating text to Zoom circumstances. For Aita, joint speaking or a group voice was difficult in live Zoom because of timing, a microphone that deals with the closest one, and an internet connection, so the group had to arrange the text to be done as an individual narrative. The group approached textual analysis as any other theatre staging of a dramatic text through given circumstances and interferences on characters and situations.

As part of the pedagogical development with *Amorphism* "staged" as live Zoom digital theatre, we discussed working within the Telepresence and Cyborg theatre concept that Rodolfo Vasquez has been exploring with his theatre company over the last 12 years. To start the pedagogical process on Zoom theatre, it is essential to see the difference between the approach to acting for traditional theatre, film, and television and how it is done for online digital performance. We need to know the difference in acting techniques for each medium. Vasquez points out that:

> Acting in traditional theatre is well-known in pedagogical terms, and everybody knows pedagogies for acting in movies. Discussing the phenomenon of presence on a digital platform, telecommunication, and telepresence in digital theatre is essential. As an actor, you are performing through a screen, and then you have to use some elements from traditional acting, but you also have something from film and TV. And you will have to liberate yourself to be able to combine these different approaches.[25]

Vasquez offers the basic structure for using Zoom theatre that he developed with Teatro Os Satyros, Brazil.

- In live Zoom theatre, the actors' methodology requires actors to be able to control where they go on and off stage – the stage being a screen. Vasquez explains that in Zoom, either on the computer or smartphone: "you can turn the camera on and off. With a particular setting in Zoom, you can create live digital theatre for actors and audience so that audience can see the performance in controlled configuring settings to observe playing out of the commission on this digital stage.[26] Vasquez explains that acting on webcams in digital social networking culture, like YouTube, TikTok and Instagram, already uses the same approach in performing narratives as it would be used in Zoom theatre acting; the audience familiar with social media is used to being directly addressed by the performers.[27]

- The first set of workshops focuses on acting in front of the webcam. The second workshop was on the technical settings in Zoom that students must organise on their computers. This can take some time because not everyone is technologically aware of manipulating Zoom to become a creative platform, which can be difficult. Students need to learn to self-operate production in Zoom theatre and how to use Zoom tools to recreate theatre on a digital stage.

- There are two settings that need to be configured for Zoom theatre: 1) Hide non-video participants, 2) Show view – put it on a gallery view. There is also a video instruction shared with the audience as instruction for participating in the theatre event.

- This technological setting turns Zoom theatre into a digital stage that can also be used in rehearsals. The instructions given to the audience are given in recorded messages before the production on configuring your computer equipment on the Zoom platform to live Zoom theatre setting for a digital stage.

  - Look to the lower left of your screen for those using laptops or desktops. You'll see a button labelled start a video and stop a video. On the side of this button is a small up arrow click on this arrow. Click on video settings. You will be taken to a screen where you can see My video setting with a "hide non-video participants" box. Click on it and make sure there is a checkmark. Exit this screen and go to the second set to set up the show view. A "view" button is on the upper right corner of your Zoom screen. Click on a button that says "view". There will be a few options (typically, they are – speaker, gallery, show non-video participants, and full screen); click on the gallery view option. You are all set to watch the show on your computer with this.

  - For watching on a smart mobile phone, go to the three dots on the right lower corner of your Zoom screen and click on the icon. You will be taken to a screen presenting settings and configuration options. One of them is the "meeting setting"; click on it. There will be a few options on the next screen scroll until you see "show non-video participants"; make sure that this option is not selected, and do not click on it. To watch on a smartphone, you must choose the gallery view by swiping to the left from the active speaker view, set by default on Zoom. You will find several screens of the same size when more than one actor is in a scene.[28]

- With the gallery view to see all the participants on screen as a stage, either on the computer or smartphone, the audience and actors in rehearsal/performance can check out everybody there.

- The audience in live Zoom theatre is off-screen muted, but they can, if needed, fully participate by unmuting their microphone or sending text messages in the chat. The actors must be ready for the possibility of the audience interacting with them as if they are all part of a street theatre performance; there is no fourth wall barrier; it is an open interaction spectacle on a public square. With digital visual communication, information is openly shared with the public.

- The student actors combine theatre acting techniques with lights and different spaces and locations in a cinematic way. Exploring light and play is essential for the digital stage.

- The workshops' creative aspects focus on making the material that students/ actors can present to the whole group. As pointed out before, this innovative practice is not different from group devising that happens in a physical space, just that communication is via Zoom, and the process takes place in a digital area.

- Zoom theatre allows a breakaway room where smaller groups can work on their scenes. As they work individually from home and as a group simultaneously, digital performance space becomes an essential point of contact. When there is a need to develop a score group, they are put into Zoom rooms and work virtually within one room.

- There are several Zoom rooms where students are sent to work, break away from the main room, and work on a scene. The students are put to rehearse in simultaneous breakout rooms, and once done, they return to the main room, and in the main room, they perform their scenes and improvisation.

In the second part, *When the Gods Came*, the director Aita selected digital images (copyright-free) representing destroyed postapocalyptic indoor spaces to go as an individual actor's background imposed on a green screen. However, the group had problems using a green screen and in Zoom theatre, and this group experience pointed out that it was challenging.[29] The light was given to students and adjusted for each actor, but the individual computers would register the lighting and green screen differently. The starting idea was that all images would be up on a green screen, and actors would appear in the space, walking in front of a green screen. However, walking in front of a green screen disrupted the projected image and exposed the green background, as the image flashed when walking in front. This was changed to actors being integrated within the image. The photos of abstract destroyed spaces worked for the post-apocalyptic situation of the play, as they can be symbolic of the characters' conditions. Working with a green screen in Zoom provides an opportunity to input various digitally mastered and enhanced images as the computer-created background making an environment where a performer is projected while the performance is running live. In this case, the director applied theatre thinking in creating visual images in-between stage lights and projected images, with theatre staging of actors' entrances in front of an image. However, live Zoom theatre's mode of delivery is simultaneously theatrical and cinematic, as the main visual focus is on the camera's capture of what is visible on a screen and working with a visual image.

In the first section, *Zoom Wedding*, the space represented the found actor's personal performance space and digitally created space as a background. The initial situation was a wedding over Zoom due to prolonged pandemics, wars and climate catastrophes. Zoom video communication was used within the performance's content. All characters used Zoom for real-life communication, and audiences were part of the performance by observing on the Zoom app as wedding guests. The space had the digital image of prepared kitsch – romantic Caribbean background that collapses as their "real" space breaks through as the outside world starts collapsing, exposing their location (room, kitchen, bathroom).

The world is collapsing around them, breaking their communication into silence. We can say that two spaces in live interaction, the physical performers' are presented on a web camera and the digital image space as a background, are interconnected in mediatised experience. In addition, the audience space is part of this mediatised process being acknowledged as part of the wedding event. Their living area is also exposed to destruction from the outside. Eventually, their communication with Zoom's wedding becomes interrupted. For performers and audiences, space is different on the digital stage from the physical setting, as the phone/computer/TV screen frames the personal experience of mediatised space. The area on the screen may be massive as a virtual digital background. Still, the performer is in a tiny space being created as an effect into something else, creating an illusion on the screen as in the film, making different spaces while living in a physical space, home.

Conclusion

The performers' presence in live Zoom digital theatre is much more controlled than in the physical audience and performers' presence theatre. The actors control the image on the screen and what is being seen. Cormac Power explains that in making theatre independent from literature, we need to use other tools of visual perception – space and light and actors' presence on stage. The model he proposes is "auratic", transcending the fictional and representational. In live digital theatre, the "auratic" is achieved through live/recorded images on a screen where space is defined.[30] As a pedagogical tool, Zoom theatre can be an essential mechanism for student actors to develop their awareness of the body/image and presence they create within the performance on screen. The screen presence could be translated into a giant film screen in a theatre space or a computer screen. Incorporating the controlled self-image into practice and pedagogy for student actors could be explored further. It may be a development of explorations connected to Zoom theatre in lockdown conditions. Investigating the use of line production in the community and applied theatre and how it can transcend global communication and allow international work is an essential aspect of video performance and Zoom theatre practice.

Training the group of actors and students to perform in digital space on a virtual stage in live Zoom theatre in front of an audience takes time and patience. The digital space is different from the traditional theatre space, which is fundamentally a public space. A private space, which is in a student/actor's private house, in a bedroom, kitchen, and own bathroom, is a set design being created. Most of the time, these will be used by students/actors to make this experience of space different from film and traditional theatre. The idea of intimacy of being in one's own space and transforming the privacy of a room into a studio for live video performance has to be discussed with the students' actors who will be trained in live digital theatre. In addition, they have to be filming and creating space and lighting designers in all the locations they use, regulating all the lights in all the rooms of the houses that will take part in the online performance. The actor must prepare the lights in the room (performative space) and work on a costume and the set design before going on the screen to test how this performative area is related through the camera. This way, an actor is involved in a complex performative operation. A total author and pedagogical student needs to engage in interdisciplinary performance, acting skills, and technological skills like digital filming and editing. It is a dual process that the actor has to perform simultaneously and see themself in the camera on the screen. It is part of acting handcraft for live digital theatre that this consciousness is developed.

Notes

1 "How the National Theatre Tackled the COVID-19 Challenge", *World News Story* (March 8, 2021) https://www.gov.uk/government/news/how-the-national-theatre-tackled-the-covid-19-challenge

2 Karam, K. and G. Naguib. "The Potentials and Challenges of Zoom Live Theatre during Coronavirus Lockdown: Pandemic Therapy and Corona Chicken (Part Two)", *NQT*, vol. 38, no. 2 (April 2022), p.153. Published as open access: https://doi.org/10.1017/S0266464X22000057

3 Giannachi, Gabriella. *Virtual Theatres* (Routledge, 2004), p.9.

4 Baudrillard, Jean. "The Process of Simulacra", *Simulacra and Simulation* (Ann Arbor: The University of Michigan Press), p.1.

5 Zoom communication was launched in 2013 by Eric Yuan as a free online and app application. Over time, it offered live connections with original video and audio and instant screen sharing for multiple users.

6 Karam, Mostafa and Galal Naguib. "The Potentials and Challenges of Zoom Live Theatre during Coronavirus Lockdown", *New Theatre Quarterly*, vol. 38, no. 2, May 2022, pp. 151–171, p.154.

7 For more on using RSVP Cycles refer to Chapter 3. Here we use Scores as part of the Cycle for pedagogy and practice process.

8 Halprin, Lawrence. *Creative Processes in Human Environment* (New York: George Braziller, 1969).
9 Galizia, Marguerite. "A Week with Anna Halprin – Scores and Resources", Personal Blog, accessed on the website. https://margueritegalizia.com/2016/06/25/a-week-with-anna-halprin-scores-and-resources/
10 See full performance on the YouTube https://www.youtube.com/watch?v=EnbEmiUyHao
11 For the full text of the speech, see The Queen's Speech on Coronavirus: Full text of Her Majesty's address – LBC
12 Personal Interview, .June September 2022
13 Sadot, Paul. "DIY Digi-corporeality" *The Unsteady State Condition* seen on www.paulsadot.com
14 Sadot, Rehearsal notes, June 2020.
15 Ibid.
16 Ibid.
17 The pedagogical method of writing author narrative in performance was led by Gwydion Calder, a PhD student in Royal Birmingham Conservatoire and professional actor.
18 Notes from Rehearsals June 2020.
19 Sadot, Paul. Personal Interview, June 2022
20 Sadot, Paul. Personal Interview, June 2022.
21 Colder Gwydion. Rehearsal Notes, June 2020.
22 Jandrell, G. Interview, 18 March 2022.
23 Jandrell, Personal Interview.
24 Aita has extensive directing experience with different types of theatre, from education to touring to large-scale commercials. He had almost 40 years as associate touring other European countries and worked as associate director of the Royal Northampton theatre, a repertory theatre. From a personal interview with Sean Aita.
25 Rodolpho Vasquez, Personal Interview.
26 Ibid.
27 YouTubers with a considerable following (the most popular in 2022 is PewDiePie Swedish gamer and influencer who has 110 million followers) regularly perform in front of cameras and transmit live on other social networking platforms such as Facebook, Tik Tok, Instagram and WeChat, to name a few.
28 Voice instruction for the Zoom Theatre production *Art of Facing Fear*, Os Satiros, Sao Paulo.
29 Aita, Personal Interview.
30 Power, Cormac. *Presence in Play* (Rodopi, 2008) p.8.

9
CONCLUSION
Performative Digital Futures

Interdisciplinary Performative Pedagogies

> Deadliness, Brook suggests, is not the result of any particular form, content or genre. Nor is deadliness even particularly the result of something we might term quality. Rather, deadliness is the product of a failed relationship between performance and audience. (…) what is important about liveness—how and why it matters—resides not in some essential or ontological characteristic of the performance itself, but precisely in the relationship between performance and audience.[1]

Storytelling is about life, and good stories have liveness that directly connects and communicates their narrative with the audience. In many ways, this book discusses the relationship between the audience and performance within digital space in a new configured environment that came out of a pandemic lockdown, using simple affordable technological tools and methods on platforms that replaced live theatre with a screen such as Zoom live theatre. As we have seen through the chapters, this book comes as a reflection on the performance of creative work and teaching that has been done out of necessity, learning through the process of finding solutions on the go and learning through trials and errors, successes, and failures. The material responded to our experiments on how live digital theatre can communicate liveness that materialises in the act of performance and not deadliness, in the use of digital media on stage, on screen, or both, involving the audience in an immersive and participatory way. What pedagogies can be used to create and educate students in theatre, dance, and performance art to embody the new understanding of interdisciplinary practices?

The ideas discussed in this book have grown out of a research group initially set up in 2018 in Belgrade at the International Federation of Theatre Research (IFTR) conference. Discussions on acting training within an interdisciplinary

DOI: 10.4324/9781003275893-11

context in an international arena were preoccupations of teaching and learning strategies developed at Royal Birmingham Conservatoire. They explored the Centre for Interdisciplinary Performative Arts. It was essential to look at what other interdisciplinary training programmes were doing. From theatre acting, in discussions with our international collaborators, we progressed to performing (including all aspects of performing arts) and ways performance dramaturgical structure and aesthetics can consist of various arts and media. Theatre is not one thing; in contemporary digital media culture, theatre becomes many different things, a medium that can be a home for a plurality of other mediums. The understanding that the composition of live theatre is now connected to the digital multimedia experience and that interdisciplinary collaboration is at the heart of performative pedagogies became apparent after the 2019 IFTAR in Shanghai, where we explored the augmented and mixed reality cycle in *Macbeth Projeto*. With the Covid-19 pandemic, from 2020, we all migrated into online pedagogy and creative practice, learning how to adapt perceptions of observations and interpretations to the new digital platform for live performance, Zoom live theatre. Continuing the work of our international research group online recon-firmed the importance of interdisciplinary performative pedagogies to explore connections forged within performance, which can use performance to create links where they may not have been before. In 2022, during the conference in Reykjavik, the research group interdisciplinary performative pedagogies became a new working group of IFTR.

The key objective of interdisciplinary performative pedagogies is to branch out and connect different disciplines around performance. The experience with live digital theatre points to interconnections of theatre with computers (digital) and architecture (performance space). The Fun Palace, as a laboratory of fun and a university of streets, reflected the vision of the maker of contemporary British theatre, Joan Littlewood and her Theatre Workshop company, as a flexible pro-gramme-driven space that can transform based on user needs. It showed us the path we could follow, reimagining the interdisciplinary performative interactivity. Involved as critical collaborators are the young visionary architect Cedric Price and the cybernetician inventor Gordon Pask. This mix's genius is bringing different points of view from three disciplines into inventing creative practice around the Fun Palace. The collaborating disciplines do not necessarily need to talk to each other; architecture, cybernetics and theatre as singular disciplines do not have much in common. Nevertheless, once they start collaborating and are put together, they bring their input, which allows for synergies to emerge and shape the creative process that produces something different from what it would be within one singular discipline. However, this relationship was not only about setting up a new way of practice but also about pedagogical innovation, following the concept established by Joan Littlewood in "the university of the streets".

The university of streets was at the heart of the Fun Palace visionary commu-nity arts and education project. The concept was based on creating a people's palace following the Soviet Model of the court for working-class arts and education, bringing community and culture together in participatory performance around issues that matter to the community. Joan Littlewood played a significant role in initiating the Cybernetic Theatre through her workshop approach that emphasises an improvisational development of the parts of the performance. Price's imagining of Fun Palace space was "internally reconfigurable to suit changing and evolving use patterns, essentially like a big box containing an architectural kit of parts".[2]

The university of streets is a philosophy of pedagogy for communities and for ordinary people to learn through engaging in making arts and culture for those who may not have had access to what was the monolithic structure of the universities in the late 1960s, but likewise who are outpriced by the high street commercialisation of higher education which equates learning and teaching to a product. Architecturally, the space of the Fun Palace resembles a computer game where participants interact with different environments. Cybernetics set up the mechanics of the Fun Palace and, in many ways, can be seen as a pre-computer digital engagement with users. Suppose we fast forward to 2020 and the use of Zoom live theatre. In that case, we can recognise the models in which theatre is responding to different connections between space and audience and the new role that the performer has in communicating with live and digital content. Live digital theatre needs to be approached both as a creative practice process and pedagogy where learning how to do something is essential to practice.

Digital Legacy: *Phygital* Hybrid Performance and Metaverse

The design of digital platforms has changed the way performance practice has evolved, and our habits as participants or observers. For Gratch and Gratch, there are two significant anticipated changes in the future of our everyday life digital patterns of behaviour.

> First our offline habits of thoughts which were once developed entirely offline, are now developing in tandem with our habits of thought online.... Second, as augmented and virtual reality become more commonplace, our habits of action will develop alongside these technologies and the social norms that the technologies give rise to.[3]

All theatres are telling stories. For example, storytelling in live digital theatre communicating through digital space is not the same experience as in physical space, where storytelling becomes part of a personal narrative in a corporeal notion of a performer being there as in a traditional face-to-face setting. The growth in live and recorded performances posted on YouTube has become a resource that audiences are used to and accept as a way of presenting and receiving stories. Some sites have a considerable number (a hundred thousand) followers for specific content. Habits and social norms of contemporary audiences are now familiar with this type of storytelling. However, live Zoom theatre combined with live theatre in physical space provides a hybrid performance, "phygital", that bridges the digital and the physical worlds. For the audience and performers this is a unique experience that is very empowering. Phygital performance addresses audience through two narrative systems –physical and digital – that function as a simultaneous experience. Live performance is interconnected with video projections making a hybrid live digital theatre..

In September 2021, as part of the celebration of the First Cedric Price Day at Staffordshire University, we were commissioned to devise the interactive, interdisciplinary performance that had as the main starting point the manifesto of Cybernetic Theatre that Gordon Pask developed as an outcome of his involvement on the project of the Fun Palace.

We had the idea to create a cybernetic cabaret that came from the influences of interactive technology and cybernetic theatre on how Fun Palace was imagined. The performance was interactive, combining live with recorded and digitally mediated elements. The procession took us through various rooms or locations that housed different activities, allowing the audience to interact with the presented content. The activities were performed live as a performance and filmed in a cinema room, using live digital Zoom theatre. The Fun Palace Cybernetic Cabaret performers come from different countries, reflecting present-day Britain's international position. The live and online audiences following Zoom were invited to take action with the performance structure and interact with it. The performance starts with the narrator announcing they will curate the audience throughout the show. Curation takes us through the region's history, beginning from Wedgewood and developing to Fun Palace. What are the consequences of the ideas built within Price's and Littlewood's dream of a new design for a space that interacts and responds to the audience/performers? We invited a video choreographer (Paul Sadot), a community dance group from India (Red Curtain Theatre) to perform live on Zoom theatre, a live dance performance artist creating as things were happening (Maria Nikolou), an Architect/Performance designer (Maria Sanchez) and a solo performer (Stephen Simms).

The starting reference points for the Cybernetic Cabaret were the interactive space of the Fun Palace that would provide different contents in which audiences could participate. According to Littlewood's and Price's vision, the Fun Palace had other spaces where participants could engage with films, theatres, dance, workshops, and any activities they could think of. The performance took place in the drama studio at Staffordshire University, which would develop in four different environments. The central area was for the audience, and performance interactivity was occupied by silver balloons floating in space. This sculptural element allowed the audience physical playfulness with the space. On each of the three walls, there was a site-specific event; Andy Warhol (Stephen Simms) was introduced through the concept of the factory, which was a party venue –

Warhol's famous party venue in the 1960s. With this performance, the focus was on bringing together live Zoom theatre and live physical theatre within one experience, and the audience participated in the performance. At the same time, the whole event was filmed and streamed through Zoom for spectators following it live from other points on the globe.

Andy was on the sofa for the duration of the performance, responding to the events and interacting with the audience in the factory. Simms was focused on the visual images of Andy Warhol, whose body transformed into a mannequin as a pop art icon. On the adjacent wall was a durational projection of 1960s' Britain tracing the timeframe of Joan Littlewood and Cedric Price's concept of the Fun Palace. The projected video collaged with the moving body of a dancer who connected the image with the audience in the space. On the last wall, opposite, there was a red theatre curtain, indicating an event still to take place. Halfway through the performance, the curtain was opened, revealing an actor who started communicating to the audience through live Zoom theatre from India. Up to that point, the content was live, physical and mediated; however, with the introduction of live Zoom, there was a moment of disbelief once the audience realised that it was a live interaction and not another video recording. The second part of the performance integrated phygital components in which live, physical and digital interacted with mediated and recorded digital video material. Overlapping these four realities was possible because dramaturgy of live digital theatre, in its hybrid form, had its score, which is independent of one another in the treatment of space-time, image and audience inclusion.

The rehearsal process combined online and physical presence work in the space. Each segment was developed independently and edited together within the studio theatre a few days before the performance. The main concern was the technical capability; a strong internet connection would allow live Zoom theatre to take place. We included video-recorded versions of Red Curtain Theatre performances from India as a backup. However, in the rehearsal, when we tested both video recording and live Zoom performance, it appeared that the immersion that comes from the liveness of Zoom was more powerful than the recorded one.

The Cybernetic Cabaret was one of the first experiences in the world that can be defined as phygital has emerged as one of the main legacies of live digital theatre once the lockdowns stopped. The pedagogical model that combines phygital hybridity within the rehearsal process and production possibilities was further explored in March and April 2022 in a video solo performance as part of a final third-year show. Due to a few different extenuating circumstances, a student on short notice could not participate in a final group collaborative performance scheduled to take place in a physical theatre space. An acting programme at Royal Birmingham Conservatoire is practice-driven, following creative industry standards, with agents and casting calls attached to the end of students' three-year

FIGURE 9.1 Cybernetic Cabaret (2021) First Cedric Price Day, Staffordshire University, UK. Directed by Prof. Aleksandar Dundjerović.

training. The backup option is to do a solo performance that would be supported, like a group production and be open to the audience in a theatre venue. However, the problem was that theatre venues were unavailable, and the possibilities for staffing the solo performance were limited. All facilities and equipment had been booked for other shows months in advance. Also, the production budget was allocated. The resolution was to do a digital video performance that would use in rehearsal phygital performance, relying on a combination of Zoom live theatre, WhatsApp and live face-to-face rehearsals. *The Last Days of Hamlet* is a short 20 minute film that tells the story of Hamlet in fragments just before he dies. Hamlet remembers his life using disjointed sequences similar to the fragmented 1977 play by German dramatist Hiner Muller *Hamletmachine*, based on Shakespeare's *Hamlet* as a meta text. The final structure of *The Last Days of Hamlet* took place in a digital space on a screen both in a rehearsal process and as a final outcome, a video film. Rehearsals with third year acting student Joel McShane, who also collaborated in the devising, did not take place as face to face rehearsals in a dedicated theatre space but rather as meetings, brainstorming what to do, and took place in a cafe, office space, classroom, basically any available room. The student recorded on a smartphone camera using one of several free video editing apps (InShot, Vimeo, and Adobe Premier, to name a few) to create shorts – segmented filmed events around the selected text from Shakespeare's *Hamlet*. Once the filming of the shorts was completed, the material went to the editing and filming television studio, where some additional scenes were filmed in front of a green screen over two days. As a creative-educational activity, this model of phygital theatre within interdisciplinary performative pedagogy that crosses different forms was much more economical and faster to develop and process than the traditional theatre-based work.

There are still many opportunities to explore within live digital theatre context that will open endless possibilities for interdisciplinary digital performance arts, especially looking at the new developments in digital technologies. Metaverse as a future of digital performing arts and live digital theatre is already here referred to as an augmented and virtual theatre, theatreverse, or mixed reality performance; it is part of a digital media world that is taking place online, immersive worlds on different platforms, inside a video game or virtual performance as in a concert or musical video. Simply put, the metaverse is "the internet, but in 3D".[4] Metaverse has a place in future work and human interactions; it will create new hybrid performance disciplines, providing a unique experience. Musical videos were active with virtual reality videos from 2007; in 2015, singer Björk released a virtual reality app. As metaverse technology becomes more accessible in terms of affordability and simplicity, with ease of applicability to human needs, it takes more social and personal space and dominance over human communication and possibly will lead to new ways of theatre education, production and reception. Two-dimensional Zoom live theatre and practice experiences accumulated around the live digital theatre through its historicity and methodologies are precursors, pre-metaverse performance in the future pedagogies of three-dimensional metaverse theatre.

As VR is becoming commonplace our behaving will change. Storytelling in performance has changed in digital space, moving from a corporal-based narrative to a digital body as an avatar. YouTube and Instagram live video performance have become domesticated with the audience, with the founder of thousands and, in some cases, millions of followers. In providing the advanced technical capability for the future of performance-screen convergence, and bringing together artists and engineers, the facility will address creativity that comes out of new experiences of the future of computer technology with Metaverse and 3D screen immersion. The research on the pedagogy of live digital theatre integrates interdisciplinary live performance and screen practices, transforming them using the advanced technological framework, and creating a new creative methodology. It is about facilitating dialogues between the different stakeholders – studios, creative industry, communities, policymakers, and professionals, and capacity building in supporting small and medium enterprises' innovative organisations. Significant changes are anticipated in the future of our everyday lives under the impact of digital patterns of behaviour. With more sophisticated computer technology, new forms of performance/screen/computer technology convergent media (based on AI, AV, VR, Mix reality) will be developing in the direction of computer gaming, where the existence of Metaverse and 3D experiences will produce not only a technological platform but also a new form of artistic content.

Notes

1 Reason, Matthew and Anja Molle Lindelof (eds.) "Introduction: Experiencing Liveness in Contemporary Performance", *Experiencing Liveness in Contemporary Performance: Interdisciplinary Perspectives* (Routledge, 2020), p. 4.
2 Dundjerović, Aleksandar. "Cybernetic Cabaret – Cedric Price's Fun Palace", *Programme for live Digital Theatre Performance* (University of Staffordshire, 2021).
3 Gratch, Lyndsay M. and Ariel Gratch, *Digital Performance in Everyday Life* (Routledge, 2022) p. 212.
4 "Ed on the Metaverse", blog, *Deloitte*: https://www2.deloitte.com/uk/en/pages/consulting/articles/what-is-the-metaverse.html?gclid=CjwKCAjwm8WZBhBUEiwA178UnCpgYv1k7YUIoy2KOOQFLT_k2uzkHfGlW9NinB8XnaAR7megaIVi7RoCKRIQAvD_BwE

INDEX

Page numbers in italics refer to figures.